ARCHAIC BOOKKEEPING

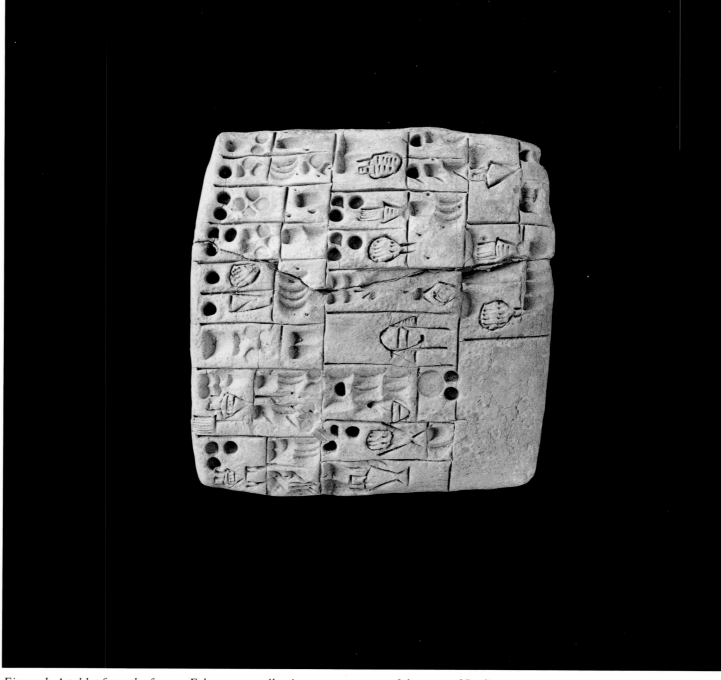

Figure 1. A tablet from the former Erlenmeyer collection, now property of the state of Berlin.

ARCHAIC BOOKKEEPING

**Early Writing and Techniques of Economic Administration
in the Ancient Near East**

Hans J. Nissen
Peter Damerow
Robert K. Englund

Translated by Paul Larsen

**The University of Chicago Press
Chicago and London**

HANS J. NISSEN and ROBERT K. ENGLUND are both at the University of Berlin. Nissen is professor of the archaeology of the ancient Near East, and Englund teaches in the Seminar for the Ancient History of the Near East. PETER DAMEROW is a historian of mathematics at the Max Planck Institute, Berlin. PAUL LARSEN is a doctoral candidate at the University of Berlin.

The University of Chicago Press, Chicago 60637
The University of Chicago Press, Ltd., London
© 1993 by The University of Chicago
All rights reserved. Published 1993
Printed in the United States of America
02 01 00 99 98 97 96 95 94 93   1 2 3 4 5
ISBN: 0-226-58659-6 (cloth)

Library of Congress Cataloging-in-Publication Data

Nissen, Hans Jörg.
    [Frühe Schrift und Techniken der Wirtschaftsverwaltung im alten
    Vorderen Orient.   English]
    Archaic bookkeeping : early writing and techniques of economic
administration in the ancient Near East / Hans J. Nissen, Peter Damerow,
Robert K. Englund ; translated by Paul Larsen.
          p.   cm.
    Originally published as "Frühe Schrift und Techniken der Wirtschafts-
verwaltung im alten Vorderen Orient:
Informationsspeicherung und -verarbeitung vor 5000 Jahren"—CIP
verso t.p.
    Includes bibliographical references and index.
    1. Sumerian language—Texts—Exhibitions. 2. Economic
history—To 500—Exhibitions.   3. Mathematics, Babylonian—Exhibitions.
I. Damerow, Peter.   II. Englund, Robert K.   III. Title.
PJ4075.N5713   1993
499' . 95—dc20   93-909

Originally published as
*Frühe Schrift und Techniken der Wirtschaftsverwaltung im alten Vorderen Orient:
Informationsspeicherung und -verarbeitung vor 5000 Jahren,* © 1990, verlag franzbecker.

Contents

Abbreviations

AfO	*Archiv für Orientforschung* (Vienna)
AO	Musée du Louvre, Paris
AOFU	Altorientalisches Seminar of the Freie Universität Berlin
Ashm.	Ashmolean Museum, Oxford
ASJ	*Acta Sumerologica*, Japan (Hiroshima)
ATU	*Archaische Texte aus Uruk* (Berlin)
ATU 1	A. Falkenstein, *Archaische Texte aus Uruk* (Berlin, 1936)
ATU 2	M. W. Green and H. J. Nissen, *Zeichenliste der Archaischen Texte aus Uruk* (Berlin, 1987)
ATU 3	R. K. Englund and H. J. Nissen, *Die lexikalischen Listen der Archaischen Texte aus Uruk* (Berlin, 1993)
ATU 5	R. K. Englund, *Archaic Administrative Texts from Uruk: The Early Campaigns* (Berlin, forthcoming)
AUWE	*Ausgrabungen in Uruk-Warka. Endberichte* (Berlin)
BagM	*Baghdader Mitteilungen* (Berlin)
BM	British Museum, London
Bodmer	Fondation M. Bodmer, Geneva
CT	*Cuneiform Texts in the British Museum* (London)
DP	M. Allotte de la Fuÿe, *Documents présargoniques* (Paris, 1912)
Erlangen	Institut für Außereuropäische Sprachen und Kulturen of the Universität Erlangen-Nürnberg
Frühe Schrift	H. J. Nissen, P. Damerow and R. K. Englund, *Frühe Schrift und Techniken der Wirtschaftsverwaltung im alten Vorderen Orient* (Berlin, 1990; 2d ed. 1991)
HD	Uruk Collection of the Deutsches Archäologisches Institute Baghdad in the University of Heidelberg
JNES	*Journal of Near Eastern Studies* (Chicago)
LAK	A. Deimel, *Liste der archaischen Keilschriftzeichen* (= *Wissenschaftliche Veröffentlichung der Deutschen Orient-Gesellschaft* 40; Berlin, 1922)
MDOG	*Mitteilungen der Deutschen Orient-Gesellschaft* (Berlin)
MDP	*Mémoires de la Délégation Française en Perse* (Paris)
MKT	O. Neugebauer, *Mathematische Keilschrifttexte* I–III (Berlin, 1935–37)
MMA	Metropolitan Museum of Art, New York
MSVO	*Materialien zu den frühen Schriftzeugnissen des Vorderen Orients* (Berlin)
MSVO 1	R. K. Englund and J.-P. Grégoire, *The Proto-Cuneiform Texts from Jemdet Nasr* (Berlin, 1991)
MSVO 2	R. J. Matthews, *Cities, Seals and Writing: Archaic Seal Impressions from Jemdet Nasr and Ur* (Berlin, 1993)
MSVO 3	P. Damerow and R. K. Englund, *The Proto-Cuneiform Texts from the Erlenmeyer Collection* (Berlin, forthcoming)
NFT	G. Cros, *Nouvelles Fouilles de Tello* (Paris, 1910)
OECT	*Oxford Editions of Cuneiform Texts* (Oxford)
RA	*Revue d'assyriologie et d'archéologie orientale* (Paris)
RTC	F. Thureau-Dangin, *Recueil de tablettes chaldéennes* (Paris, 1903)
SF	A. Deimel, *Schultexte aus Fara* (= *Wissenschaftliche Veröffentlichung der Deutschen Orient-Gesellschaft* 43; Berlin, 1923)
TCL	*Textes cunéiformes du Louvre* (Paris)
UET 2	E. Burrows, *Archaic Texts from Ur, Ur Excavations, Texts*, vol. 2 (London, 1935)
Ur III	Period of the Third Dynasty of Ur
Uruk III	Uruk Archaic level III
Uruk IV	Uruk Archaic level IV
UVB	*Vorläufige Berichte über die . . . Ausgrabungen in Uruk-Warka* (Berlin)
VA	Archaeological collection of the Vorderasiatisches Museum der Staatlichen Museen zu Berlin
VAFU	Seminar für Vorderasiatische Altertumskunde of the Freie Universität Berlin
VAT	Vorderasiatisches Museum der Staatlichen Museen zu Berlin
VDI	*Vestnik Drevnej Istorii* (Moscow)
VS	*Vorderasiatische Schriftdenkmäler* (Berlin)
W	Sigla of excavation finds in Uruk/Warka
WF	A. Deimel, *Wirtschaftstexte aus Fara* (= *Wissenschaftliche Veröffentlichung der Deutschen Orient-Gesellschaft* 45; Berlin, 1924)
ZA	*Zeitschrift für Assyriologie und Vorderasiatische Archäologie* (Berlin and Leipzig)

Introduction

The earliest true script in man's history emerged at the end of the fourth millennium B.C. in ancient Babylonia, the southern part of today's Iraq. The signs of this script were impressed with the aid of a stylus into the still soft surface of clay tablets. Such clay tablets hardened almost immediately in the dry and hot climate of that part of the world. As a result of this hardening, and because such lumps of clay could not be reused, these documents from early Babylonia survived in great numbers. The early script developed into the better-known "cuneiform," the hallmark of Babylonian history and culture; hence the name "proto-cuneiform" for the archaic script, which will be the focus of this book.

Most of the tablets of this early phase were found during the excavations in the ancient city of Uruk in lower Babylonia, conducted by the German Archaeological Institute from 1913 up to the present day and interrupted only by the two world wars and regional conflicts. During the seasons from 1928 until 1976, nearly 5000 such tablets and fragments were unearthed, forming the basic material for a long-term research project dedicated to the decipherment and edition of these texts.

The tablets from Uruk, however, are not the only archaic documents known from this period. Similar tablets have been found in the northern Babylonian site of Jemdet Nasr, and some few originate from the sites of Khafaji and Tell Uqair, likewise situated in the northern part of Babylonia. Although their number is small in comparison to the corpus from Uruk, they share a great advantage for our research efforts. Whereas all of the Uruk tablets, found in dumps where they had been discarded after they were no longer of use, were as a rule in a fragmentary state, the tablets from the other sites were often fully preserved, presenting us with their complete original information. As will be seen in the following discussion, we are faced with the problem of deciphering texts of which both script and language are unknown. Hence most arguments have to be derived from the internal context of the tablets themselves. Textual analysis thus depends on information as complete as possible.

The number of completely preserved tablets available to us has been considerably augmented recently. Toward the end of 1988, a group of 82 archaic tablets, formerly part of the Swiss Erlenmeyer Collection in Basel, was auctioned off in London. Although their existence had been known since their purchase by the Erlenmeyers in the late 1950s, these tablets had not been subjected to detailed study. Through the good offices of the Senate of Berlin, it was possible to purchase most of these tablets for our research. We wish to take this opportunity to again thank the Berlin authorities for this generous support of our work. The authorities of the British Museum (London), the Louvre (Paris) and the Metropolitan Museum (New York) joined us in our efforts to secure most of the archaic tablets of that collection for public institutions, where they remain readily accessible for further studies.

This publication is an edited translation of the catalogue that accompanied an exhibition titled Frühe Schrift und Techniken der Wirtschaftsverwaltung im alten Vorderen Orient [Early writing and techniques of economic administration in the Ancient Near East], held in Berlin's Charlottenburg Palace in the summer of 1990. It was centered around the proto-cuneiform tablets of the former Erlenmeyer collection, however including many more objects dating primarily to the same period as those texts (ca. 3000 B.C.). Beyond offering a list of all objects exhibited and other pertinent information, the catalogue attempted to portray the state of our knowledge of the earliest written records from the Near East. The chapters of the German catalogue containing these still topical discussions are presented here in translation, excluding those parts particularly pertaining to the exhibition.

One aim of the catalogue was to underscore the progress our research had made with the aid of the archaic Erlenmeyer tablets. Because of this aspect, efforts were made to publish in the form of photographs all tablets purchased by Berlin, although for purposes of illustration of the text selected specimens would have sufficed. We have decided to include in the present translation only those tablets of the former Erlenmeyer collection which are referred to in the text. All those who wish to consult the entire collection are referred to the Christie's sale catalogue Ancient Near Eastern Texts from the Erlenmeyer Collection, Tuesday 13 December 1988, to the German catalogue Frühe Schrift, or to the scholarly edition which will be published in our series Materials on the Early Written Documents of the Near East (Materialien zu den frühen Schriftzeugnissen des Vorderen Orients). A short assessment of the archaic Erlenmeyer collection is found in chapter 8 of this book.

The present book is intimately connected with a long-term interdisciplinary research project based at the Free University of Berlin and directed by Hans J. Nissen, a leading specialist in the political and economic history of early Mesopotamia, in whose research Uruk has been particularly important. Since 1982 the Sumerologist Robert K. Englund has served as the project's main investigator, interested primarily in the development of administrative structures and accountancy in the Near East of the third millennium B.C. This project, centered around the study of the so-called Archaic Texts from Uruk found during the excavations at Uruk, commenced in 1964, when Nissen began cataloguing and copying all archaic texts found in Uruk after the publication of a first lot by Adam Falkenstein in 1936. Including all finds of excavation campaigns through 1976, the archaic Uruk text corpus amounts to almost 5000 tablets and fragments. Since 1971, the edition and analysis of these tablets is the major research project of the Seminar of Near Eastern Archaeology of the Free University. From 1976 on, it has been supported by the German Research Association (Deutsche Forschungsgemeinschaft [DFG]) and the Free University of Berlin, for shorter periods by the Volkswagen and Thyssen foundations.

Beginning in 1984, a close cooperation evolved with the Center for Development and Socialization of the Max Planck Institute for Human Development and Education, Berlin. The historian of science Peter Damerow, associate at this institute, has concentrated his efforts on the question of whether the rich material pertaining to the period of early literacy in the ancient Near East may solve problems of cognitive psychology. Damerow has been concerned with the origin of mental structures, in particular the concept of number and the possible influence of culture-specific representations of cognitive systems on the development of such structures.

This cooperation had its impact on procedures and methods of the Uruk Project. As a result of our diverse perspectives in approaching the sources, new methodological concepts have arisen. On the more practical level, this led to the intensification of the use of electronic aids, and in particular to the application of programming methods of artificial intelligence to the analyses of text transliterations and to the text-editing process. Increasingly, the traditional techniques of drawing the individual signs or entire texts were replaced by methods using computer graphics. Owing to the support of the Max Planck Institute and the computer center of the Free University of Berlin, new technological possibilities were put at the disposal of our project, leading, we believe, to new methodological solutions. More important than the technical innovations derived from our interdisciplinary cooperation were the consequences this cooperation had for the study of the contents of the archaic texts, insofar as these combined efforts are targeted to research goals beyond the philological analysis of the written material.

The decipherment of ancient written sources traditionally presents the researcher with one of three goals: the decipherment of a script, the language of which is known; the decipherment of a language when the script is known; and the decipherment in cases where neither script nor language are known but enough textual material is available that an attempt can be launched to decipher one or the other, or both. This classification enjoys only limited application in the case of the earliest form of writing in the Near East, since we know that it did not originate as a means of rendering language but as a monitoring instrument for the purpose of the administration of household economies. It is thus questionable whether or to what extent we can expect to find the traditionally close link between language and archaic script. Obviously, this limits the potential of a traditional philological approach in the form most cogently described by the eminent University of Chicago scholar Ignace Gelb in his *Study of Writing* (Chicago 1952).

We can only speculate to what degree social organization and ways of thinking were influenced by the beginning of literacy. This innovation was quite certainly more than a simple change in the means of storing information, or in the representation of language. Observing that at the end of the third millennium B.C., during the so-called Ur III period, the human labor force was subjected to complete administrative control made possible through the developed techniques of writing (see chap. 11), we must realize that this level of centralization would have been impossible without the methods of information processing developed more than 1000 years earlier. Incidentally, there is more than one comparison with our time—which has witnessed the *second* revolution in data processing—because then as now the development began with arithmetical techniques and not with a need to proliferate knowledge or linguistic communication. Yet, now as then the most dramatic effects of this revolution are felt in the processing of knowledge.

Obviously such concepts involved in the study of the origin of writing are beyond the traditional realm of philology; yet it is equally obvious that any study without a solid philological background would be condemned to failure. The phenomenon of the origin of writing demands an interdisciplinary approach such as we have enjoyed in Berlin; perhaps our approach is not even diversified enough. It derives from our conviction that deciphering the archaic documents does not mean to merely translate them into a modern language, because they were not primarily meant to render language. Decipherment for us rather means the reconstruction of the social context and function of the documents, the study of the dynamics of the development of writing toward a comprehensively applicable instrument of intellectual life, and the examination of the consequences this development had for our way of thinking and our treatment of information. The early documents can thus be freed of some of their ambiguity, but also of their apparent simplicity, and so become early witnesses of the origin and the basic structures of our literate culture.

From the outset, we have paid attention to the fact that the initial publication served both as an exhibition catalogue and as a presentation of the present state of research. Although this book largely retains the initial order of catalogue chapters, there is no danger of its becoming unintelligible without recourse to the exhibited objects, particularly since we had in the original publication taken care to illustrate as much as possible of what we refer to in the text. We have in all figures generally followed Assyriological convention in the depiction of inscribed objects from the third millennium B.C., that is, all tablets are depicted with an orientation which is rotated 90° counter-clockwise to the original orientation of the documents. See the discussion of this convention in chapter 15.

At this point we should like to thank all those who have helped us in various ways in the realization of this book, in particular the various museums as well as Christie's London, who have kindly allowed us to republish the photographs of tablets and objects appearing in this book. Judith Nugée of Christie's was very helpful in our efforts to examine all the archaic Erlenmeyer pieces before, and to contact successful bidders after the auction in December 1988. Irving Finkel of the British Museum played an instrumental role in our preparation for the London auction and our organization of the Charlottenburg exhibition. Jöran Friberg, Göteborg, Jean-Pierre Grégoire, Paris, and Stephan Maul, Berlin, gave us their kind permission to include here tablet autographs which they plan to publish elsewhere (figs. 127, 47, and 58, respectively). Our thanks go also to Paul Larsen, Berlin, for his successful translation of a difficult German manuscript.

The work of the Berlin project continues. Three volumes on the early texts from the Near East have appeared since the exhibition in 1990, and the preparation of more volumes is underway. This work has resulted in new insights. Since the present publication is the report of research in progress, however, we felt compelled to leave most of the original text unaltered. In any case, it will be obvious from reading the book that despite our progress in the past years the understanding of early literate society is only in its infancy.

H.N./P.D./R.E.

1. Environmental Factors

The earliest written evidence from the Ancient Near East, the proto-cuneiform script of southern Mesopotamian and the proto-Elamite script of present-day Khuzestan, dates back to the end of the fourth millennium B.C. Both originated in the great alluvial plains bordering the Euphrates, Tigris, Karun and Kerkha rivers. The reason for their emergence can be partly inferred from the environmental conditions and certain geographic transformations underway during the period.

In its natural state, southern Mesopotamia was a rather inhospitable region, unsuited for intensive human occupation. In order to sustain a sizable population, the environment had to be manipulated so as to meet basic human requirements. There was at all times too little precipitation for rain-fed agriculture, and apart from reeds and clay the region is practically devoid of raw materials. Furthermore, the homogeneous open terrain produced only a restricted variety of naturally occurring foodstuffs. In addition, permanent installations faced the continual threat of extensive seasonal flooding, and so presumably only small population groups could be sustained in favorable locations and only during specific seasons.

The general features of this geographical situation become more apparent if we turn to the past and take into account certain climatological findings based largely on the research of scientists working on the research vessel *Meteor* in the Persian Gulf. The region in question apparently had much water during the fifth millennium B.C., and the sea level was so high that large stretches of the modern shoreline were submerged; further inland, extensive areas of the country suffered fluvial inundations over and over again, turning much of the landscape into perennial swamps and marshlands.

These findings are fully compatible with the archaeological data, which show that permanent settlements had already existed for several millennia in the regions immediately bordering southern Mesopotamia, well before large-scale human occupation of the Babylonian plain can be documented. In fact, indications of the presence of man in this region during these early periods are very scanty. This situation apparently began to alter sometime during the first half of the fourth millennium B.C., when climatic change caused a significant decrease of precipitation within the catchment areas of the great rivers. Consequently, river flow began to wane, floods became less severe, and the sea level of the Persian Gulf relative to the land mass slowly began to drop.

For the second half of the fourth millennium we have to assume that large parts of the Babylonian landscape were draining and that the extent of the terrain not threatened by floods began to increase, giving rise to opportunities to establish permanent settlements amidst open spaces of arable land. Although rainfall continued to decrease, the evidence seems to suggest that during the first period of intensive colonization cultivated land was generally located close enough to either rivers or lakes to permit the diversion of some of their water onto the fields; thus no great effort was needed in the construction of large irrigation canals. The fertility of the alluvial plains and the great abundance of water, as well as the reduced danger of the occurrence of natural disasters, must in fact have created conditions rather like those we might expect to find in the Garden of Eden.

Problems began to appear, however, at the turn of the fourth to the third millennium, when the continued decrease of water began to reduce the supply for irrigation. Although the cultivable area had become larger, irrigation water had to be transported over greater distances to reach the cultivated lands. This was the first time that humans were confronted with the necessity of laying out irrigation canals of some length. which were gradually integrated into entire networks of artificial watercourses. From this time on, larger systems of irrigation canals were characteristic of all periods of Mesopotamian history.

The regions around the Karun and Kerkha rivers, both flowing through lowland Khuzestan, enjoyed environmental conditions in many respects similar to those in Babylonia, although two differences stand out. First of all, the alluvial plain of Khuzestan is substantially smaller than that of Babylonia. Second, parts of this region enjoy a level of precipitation that satisfies the conditions requisite for dry farming. As a result, the history of settlement in Khuzestan proceeded according to laws different from those in Babylonia. Thus although land could be occupied at a much earlier date, the characteristic process of settlement intensification that occurred in southern Mesopotamia during the period marked by the first construction of large irrigation canals is missing.

In the higher regions of the Zagros range to the east of Khuzestan, landscape and environment are completely different. These ranges, which are aligned in a northwest to southeast direction, are cut by narrow valleys. Despite the fact that only restricted patches of land were suitable for human occupation, abundant, regular rainfall and a wide spectrum of naturally occurring foodstuffs within this profuse and verdant region made it possible that small plains—formed by the damming effects of occasional landslides and subsequent silting—provided enough space for the formation of coherent settlement areas.

Looking from east to west, from the ridges of the Zagros Mountains down to the flood plain of lowland Mesopotamia, we

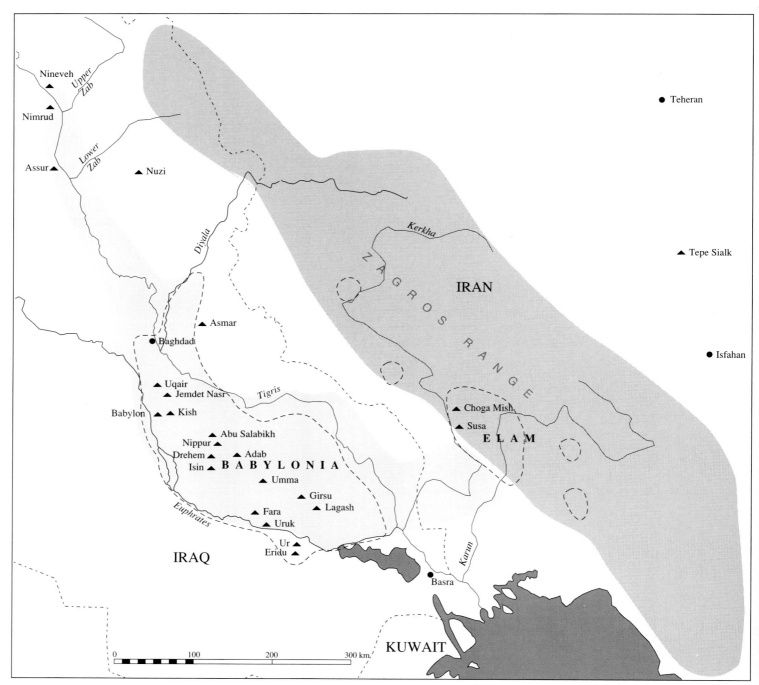

Figure 2. Map of Babylonia and Western Iran showing the regions of rain-fed (light grey) and irrigated agriculture (darker grey), as well as the extension of the settlement areas in question (enclosed in hatched lines).

thus discern several different natural habitats. From small and isolated areas of coherent settlement patterns down to larger areas, from an opulent environment diverse in natural food resources to one of greater restraint further west, from the opportunity of rain-fed farming to the necessity of artificial irrigation, this perspective in fact reflects a probable sequence of land exploitation: on the one hand the possibility of surviving in a region without advanced knowledge of complex techniques of food acquisition, on the other the necessity of having to devise and utilize elaborate methods of food production in order to survive on a permanent basis.

The advent of early civilization in southern Mesopotamia at the end of the fourth millennium B.C. is probably the result of a fortuitous set of circumstances arising with the retreat of threatening flooding in the lowlands and the existence of certain forms of subsistence developed in neighboring regions. Above all, the ready accessibility of irrigation water in conjunction with the presence of fertile soil allowed for the massive land reclamation in Babylonia witnessed during this period. The ensuing population density determined the basis as well as the necessity for the development of complex organizational structures—especially within the field of economic administration.

H.N.

2. The Chronological Framework

Chronology

Our knowledge of the absolute chronology of the early cultural periods of the Ancient Near East—that is, the distance in time between the present and any given moment in the past—is still rather scanty. As a result of the interdisciplinary research of historians who analyze the written evidence, archaeologists who study material links between cultures, some of which have better-known chronologies (e.g., Ancient Egypt), and physicists who establish the amount of the isotope carbon 14 (C_{14}) in, and thus the absolute age of, organic matter found in archaeological levels, it has been widely accepted that the period marked by the first appearance of writing was somewhere between 3500 and 2800 B.C.; the likeliest dating would place this emergence at ca. 3100 B.C. The following considerations are based on this assumption.

We are even less well informed about the absolute chronology of the preceding periods. For them, we must depend exclusively on radiocarbon dates obtained from measurements of organic matter extracted from archaeological deposits. These findings, however, offer no more than a rough framework. The absolute dates given in figure 3, therefore, are merely to be understood as approximations, bearing in mind that the earlier dates are susceptible to considerable fluctuations.

Owing to the uncertainty of exact figures, archaeologists of the Near East have come to terms with the restriction of bringing the various temporal units into a relative sequence in discussing historical processes. Great effort was expended establishing that a given event had taken place before or after another event, or that one king reigned before or after another ruler. These research efforts resulted in an historical framework, the divisions of which are named after ruling dynasties or after important archaeological sites that stand out either because of the exceptional discoveries from a specific period made there or because of the fact that in archaeological research a certain period was first documented at a given site.

Such labels have proven convenient for the terminology of periods with known absolute dates, since they can, on the whole, be referred to in a more precise and at the same time comprehensive manner. Accordingly, some periods are known for ruling dynasties, as is the case of the "age of the First Dynasty of Babylon," the "age of the Third Dynasty of Ur" (shortened to "Ur III"), or the "age of the Dynasty of Akkad," all of which are periods at the end of the third millennium B.C. and at the beginning of the second. The number ascribed to each dynasty is taken from its position in ancient Mesopotamian records that list in chronological order the ruling dynasties for various Babylonian cities.

As we will see in chapter 15, documents dating to the time before the middle of the third millennium B.C. are of very limited historic value. Even when they begin to offer historical information, such documents fail to indicate whether one of the local dynasties held supremacy over the others. This long period, which includes a protracted phase as yet very poorly illuminated by written documents, is therefore referred to simply as the Early Dynastic period. On the basis of archaeological observations made of specific architectural changes through a sequence of layers, the Early Dynastic period has been divided into three subperiods.

Our understanding of the developmental structure of the phases before the Early Dynastic period is entirely dependent on archaeological criteria. Those phases were named after the main archaeological sites Uruk and Jemdet Nasr. Since all of the characteristic features of the following Babylonian cultural history were already present in the latter part of the so-called Uruk period—thus testifying to an already high degree of cultural development at a very early stage—it seems justified to refer to this entire age as a period of early high civilization. Indeed, with the virtually simultaneous appearance of monumental art and architecture as well as writing, developments become perceptible, each of which on its own would be indicative of an advanced stage of cultural development.

The Dates and Circumstances of Discovery of the Archaic Tablets from Uruk

The most prominent archaeological site of the period in question is the ancient city of Uruk, today a vast landscape of ruins in southern Babylonia (fig. 4). Since early in the twentieth century, German archaeologists have been carrying out excavations at regular intervals at the site (with interruptions during the two world wars and regional conflicts), which was continuously occupied from the fifth millennium B.C. until its abandonment in the fifth century A.D.

For the time before 2000 B.C., eighteen archaic layers, counting from top to bottom, were identified within Eanna, the central, sacred precinct of the city. Those layers numbered VIII to IV were ascribed to the Late Uruk period, layer III to the Jemdet Nasr period. Layer I with its subphases dates to the Early Dynastic period (layer II turned out to have been an erroneous designation and has therefore been excluded from current terminology).

The extensive buildings of the Uruk III levels were erected on great terraces after the older buildings had been razed and their grounds leveled. Thus, surface pits and holes were filled with

		Period	Writing Phase	Historical Developments
	3400	Early Uruk		
Beginning of Proto-Cuneiform	3300		Numerical tablets and clay bullae	Beginning of large-scale settlement of Babylonia
	3200	Late Uruk	Archaic texts from Uruk:	First urban centers
Beginning of Proto-Elamite	3100		Writing Phase Uruk IV,	Age of early civilization
	3000	Jemdet Nasr	Writing Phase Uruk III	
Beginning of Hieroglyphics	2900	Early Dynastic I	Archaic texts from Ur	
	2800			
	2700	Early Dynastic II		Formation of large irrigation networks
	2600			
	2500	Early Dynastic III	Texts from Fara	Rival city-states
	2400		Old Sumerian texts	
	2300	Dynasty of Akkad	Old Akkadian texts	First regional state
	2200	Gudea of Lagash		
	2100	Ur III	Neo-Sumerian texts	Centralized state of the 3rd Dynasty of Ur
Indus Script	**2000**	Old Assyrian	Old Assyrian texts	
	1900	Old Babylonian	Old Babylonian texts	
	1800			
	1700			Hammurapi of Babylon
	1600			
	1500			
	1400			
	1300	Middle Assyrian		
	1200	Kassite		Kassite rule
	1100			
	1000			
	900			
	800	Neo-Assyrian	First Aramaic texts	Assyrian empire
	700	Neo-Babylonian		Babylonian empire (Nebuchadnezzar II)
	600			Occupation of Babylon by Cyrus in 539
	500	Achaemenid		
	400	Seleucid	Revival of cuneiform under the Seleucids	
	300			

Figure 3. Chronological chart.

Figure 4. Plan of Uruk with the central district Eanna.

A plan of Eanna (fig. 5) shows the number of tablets found in each excavation square measuring 20 × 20 meters. Judging from the distribution and concentration of tablets in various areas unconnected to major buildings as well as from the random distribution of lexical texts, it seems clear that no contextual relationships existed between certain buildings and groups of texts.

Since the tablets had become irrelevant before they were disposed of in the rubbish dump that was used as a source of fill for surface irregularities of the large terrace below the buildings of Archaic Level III, they were obviously older than the earliest subphase of that layer. Although we are left in the dark as to their exact date or origin, we can assume that they are not older than the buildings of Archaic Level IV, since no tablets were found in the layers below them. Unfortunately, we cannot establish a stratigraphic link between the tablets and any of the three subphases "c," "b," or "a" of Archaic Level IV. In order to get a better grasp of the dates of these texts, we are thus obliged to develop new

cultural waste, consisting of weathered and broken mud-bricks as well as ash, animal remains, pottery sherds, and the like. This debris had apparently been taken from large waste deposits located elsewhere, which seemingly had been left by the great storage facilities from the lower levels whenever they were cleared of refuse. In this manner, large amounts of various kinds of once sealed objects found their way into the debris (see in particular chap. 4). After authorized individuals had broken sealed stoppers or collars in order to gain access to the stored contents of containers, the fragmented sealings may have been kept somewhere for control purposes but then lost their purpose and were consequently disposed of.

Written documents were unquestionably treated in the same way. They served to carry out future checks on, for example, the amounts of barley delivered to a particular granary on a specified day or to keep track of the amounts of barley or beer distributed to named laborers. After a certain time had lapsed, this information was no longer useful. Consequently, the tablets were probably thrown away at regular intervals, thus landing on the refuse heaps.

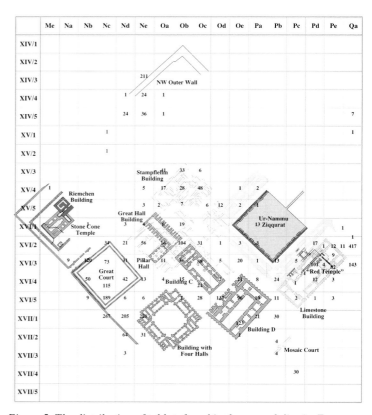

Figure 5. The distribution of tablets found in the central district Eanna.

6

criteria based predominantly on the internal evolution of the script itself (see chaps. 5 and 15).

In short, these findings suggest that there is scarcely enough time between the oldest tablets of script phase IV and the tablets of phase III to support the existence of an intermediate period between the two. The text corpus of script phase IV, moreover, seems itself so homogeneous that one is inclined to date all its tablets to a relatively short period. It therefore seems most likely that the period of the beginning of writing is more or less contemporary with the last of the stratigraphic subphases of archaic building layer IV, that is, with level IVa.

Similar observations apply to another group of tablets from the period of archaic building level III. A considerable number of these texts were found in layers of debris upon which the buildings of layer IIIa were erected. The proposed dating of these tablets to the period of the preceding layer IIIb therefore seems quite plausible.

Despite the relatively safe assignment of these tablet groups to the archaic building layers IVa and IIIb, we have been forced to abandon the habit of referring to them as tablets from the respective levels. In order to stress that the dates of the tablets were *not* established as the result of a direct link between them and their stratigraphic location, we modified the terminology slightly to indicate the paleographic development of the script employed in the texts. Consequently, we date the archaic tablets according to their respective evolutionary phase of script. In reference to the stratigraphic nomenclature, these have been called script phase IV and III.3–1.

Early Scripts outside of Babylonia

Insofar as the dates of the archaic texts found in regions outside Babylonia are concerned, we have again no choice but to operate in terms of relative chronology. By means of comparison of archaeological artifacts from different regions, a number of chronological horizons are identified for each region, of which some were, others were not from the same period.

In this way it has been established, for example, that the period characterized by the emergence of the earliest written evidence in Mesopotamia (in archaeological terminology, the Late Uruk period) is older than that of the oldest texts from Egypt, since the Late Uruk period in Mesopotamia roughly coincides with the period of Negade II in Egypt, a time when inhabitants of the Nile Valley still had no script in the strict sense of the word.

Accordingly, the assumption that the proto-Elamite script of southwest Iran appears somewhat later than the archaic script in Mesopotamia is based on the observation that the so-called proto-Elamite period is contemporary with the Jemdet Nasr period in lower Mesopotamia, which itself is attested to by the archaic layer III in Uruk immediately following the Late Uruk period.

In the case of the Indus Valley script, again primarily archaeological evidence has assigned the date of its appearance to a relatively late period. In the course of far-flung trade relations between the centers of the Indus Valley and Mesopotamia, seals containing inscribed Indus characters had found their way to Babylonia. Archaeological investigations led to their discovery in architectural layers which in accordance with internal Mesopotamian chronology date to a period around 2000 B.C.

The tablets containing proto-cuneiform writing from lower Mesopotamia, therefore, represent to the best of our knowledge the most ancient evidence for a phenomenon we today call literacy, notwithstanding all the reservations this term evokes. However, while it may be argued on the grounds of similarity in both material and writing technique that the proto-cuneiform script in Babylonia was the forerunner of the proto-Elamite script further to the east, there is no evidence indicating a link with the earliest script in Egypt, apart from the basic concept of writing itself, which may be seen as a possible connection. In fact, we are well enough informed about the relations between the regions to postulate that the early Egyptians were quite aware of the Mesopotamian practice of writing.

As for the Indus script, it is also improbable that the inhabitants of that river basin had no knowledge of the practice of writing in Babylonia, since the two regions enjoyed intensive trade relations. On the other hand, the completely different nature of the Indus signs makes unlikely any direct influence from Mesopotamia in this respect.

H.N.

3. The Early History of Babylonia

The Ancient Near East is justly regarded as one of the regions, if not *the* region, in which man for the first time successfully developed the means of survival that eventually were to lead him toward almost complete independence from the vicissitudes of nature. Having commenced on this path, he not only assured his own survival, but above all was able to increase his food production with such efficiency that over time the labor required to produce a certain amount of food decreased considerably. The resultant food surplus served to support a developing process in the proliferation of various activities no longer primarily centered around food production.

In contrast to earlier forms of primary subsistence such as hunting, fishing, or gathering, the beginning and the subsequent intensification of food production was aided by the fact that many areas throughout the Near East were rich in wild plants and animals that responded positively to human efforts to gain influence over their reproduction. The result was an increase in the yields of such cereals as barley and wheat as well as of now domesticated animals, mainly sheep, goats, and cattle.

Consequently, a segment of the population was now no longer required in the production of food and was thus freed for other activities. This process not only stimulated the division of labor, for instance in the crafts, but it also accounts for the emergence of a new group of people best described as official coordinators or administrators. This new development was to become one of the determining factors of the following course of history of the Near East.

The favorable environmental conditions in parts of the region as well as the potential for differentiation within the society acted as catalysts on the growth and spread of those organizational structures which during the fifth and fourth millennia B.C. had optimized land use to such an extent that the colonization of the alluvial plains such as that of Babylonia became a feasible venture. Without this amount of experience in agriculture and animal husbandry or the ability to master certain organizational challenges, the massive exploitation of the Babylonian lowland would have been inconceivable.

By the middle of the fourth millennium B.C., slight climatic changes had helped to drain the Babylonian alluvial plain formed by the lower courses of the Tigris and Euphrates rivers. For the first time, this area was opened to large-scale human occupation. Incidentally, organizational experience was imported with colonization, so that the agricultural exploitation even of this so undif- ferentiated landscape was possible. Yet, the new challenges were different, so that application and adjustment of these experiences to the new requirements led to new developments.

Our limited detailed knowledge of the circumstances and structures that prevailed during the periods before the intensive colonization of Babylonia in fact reflects our poor ability to trace them. What we see is only the immediate result, that soon after colonization a large number of new structures developed. On the one hand, these structures were apparently the result of adjustment to a new environment; on the other, they also held the seeds for the formation of completely new social structures—indeed they may have required them. Although new structures become tangible in the scope of social differentiation (as demonstrated in chap. 14), they become clearly visible only in the area of economic administration. In the next chapter we will demonstrate how, through processes we are yet unable to grasp, economic units had apparently grown to such an extent and become so complex that in order to maintain a certain degree of efficiency they became increasingly dependent on controlling mechanisms, of which the most developed form was writing.

The degree of complexity of a human sedentary society is to some extent reflected in the appearance of its settlements. As a beginning, we can reconstruct this complexity by distinguishing between different settlement sizes, which often can be calculated from the extent of the ruins of ancient sites. This procedure is based on the assumption that larger settlements indicate a higher degree of social and organizational complexity than smaller ones.

One of the basic principles is that the administration of a small settlement ("village" or "hamlet") requires less administrative expenditure than a larger one ("town"). This, in return, implies that a town cannot exist without a minimum of complex admini- strative components.

The second assumption relates to the observation that if, dur- ing land reclamation in a given territory, the potential settlement area of that territory turns out to be larger than the area one settlement needs for its food supply, several new settlements will soon emerge and develop within the same territory. A settlement area is defined as a territory that offers uniform environmental preconditions for the founding of settlements, as well as easy communication between such sites. The underlying reasoning is that there is a threshold value for the size of administrative units, beyond which administration becomes problematic. Rather than allowing one unit to proliferate into an unwieldy size, a series of smaller settlements will emerge which are themselves admini- stered from a higher organizational level.

In our description of the environmental features of the Near East, we saw that the size of settlement areas gradually increases from east to west within the region from the Zagros Mountains to the Babylonian lowlands. We observed a sequence of mountain valleys and small plains in the Zagros, and the wider plains in the western margins which eventually opened into a coherent flood plain in the region of Khuzestan. The open and uniform habitat in the river basin along the lower stretches of the Euphrates and Tigris rivers, finally, formed the last phase in that sequence.

In light of both basic assumptions pertaining to the complexity of settlement systems, it is therefore hardly surprising that within the latter settlement area we indeed witness the emergence of a considerable number of settlements of varying sizes dating back to the time when geoclimatic transformation first began to open the wide terrain of Babylonia to large-scale human occupation. Looking at the distribution of these settlements, we notice moreover a small number of exceptionally large sites surrounded by several smaller ones which, according to principles of settlement geography, seem to indicate the presence of former centers and their respective dependencies. As already mentioned, centers are not only characterized by their expanse but also by the complexity of their organization. The degree of organizational complexity within a settlement varies considerably according to its position within the organizational settlement hierarchy as a whole. A given settlement may assume centrality for a series of subordinate settlements on a lower level, and these subordinate settlements may themselves form centers for more settlements on an even lower scale. Here, one would speak of a three-tiered settlement system.

An analysis of the settlement patterns in the countryside around the ancient city of Uruk disclosed that during the Late Uruk period that city formed the uppermost level of a *four*-tiered hierarchical settlement pattern. Although archaeological criteria can scarcely furnish sufficient evidence to explain in a satisfactory way the true nature of this centrality or its effects upon neighboring sites, evidence clearly demonstrates that the organizational difference between Uruk itself and the villages within its range of influence was certainly tremendous. Since textual evidence presented in the following chapters will demonstrate how complex administration really was at that urban site during this period, we may keep in mind these deliberations in order to find plausible explanations for the observed phenomena.

One of the findings from an analysis of the settlement patterns in the area around the city of Uruk was that the large-scale occupation of the territory must have taken place within a relatively short period of time. Whereas more than a hundred sites were assigned to Late Uruk, only eleven were safely dated to the preceding period. This implies that people had settled the area earlier. Moreover, it suggests that a massive population increase in Babylonia must have taken place within a period too short to be accounted for by domestic population growth, since the observations demonstrate that the number of sites multiplied by at least a factor of ten within a period of two hundred years at most.

Since the beginning of research in the early history of Babylonia, questions have consistently been articulated pertaining to the ethnic origin of the people responsible for the advent of early civilization in the region. The problem was partly solved with the realization that the earliest more or less comprehensible texts relating to historical events dating to the Early Dynastic III period were written in a language identified as Sumerian. The question was thus whether the same linguistic affiliation applied to the oldest tablets, that is, to the archaic texts dating to a time 500–600 years earlier. Since it was generally assumed that these earlier documents were also of Sumerian origin, the question was raised whether the Sumerians were the indigenous inhabitants of southern Babylonia or whether they had migrated into this region from somewhere else. Neither question can as yet be fully answered.

We shall return to the scant evidence suggesting that Sumerian was an element of the spoken language during the archaic writing phase Uruk III, also known as the Jemdet Nasr period (see chap. 15). Because of the continuous tradition between the writing phases IV and III, it might be adduced that the same applies to the earliest phase as well. Apparently, however, the later Sumerian language yields a number of non-Sumerian words whose symbolic designations are also attested in the oldest writing phases. Although we are yet unable to identify foreign elements, the theory has been proposed that the words might represent linguistic survivals of the original language of the region. Consequently, the Sumerians may be considered foreigners.

For the moment, however, these questions cannot be fully answered one way or the other. Proponents of the immigration theory might find it plausible to ascribe the age of massive population growth at the beginning of the late Uruk period to a Sumerian influx. As far as the origin of the Sumerians is concerned, evidence is even scantier, partly because every attempt to affiliate their language to any known tongue remains unsuccessful, although none of the languages of comparable basic structure, such as Turkish, Hungarian, Basque or even Dravidian, have been left out of these attempts.

Quite aside from the origin of single linguistic elements, we are in a position to assume with some degree of confidence that the population of Babylonia during the period in question consisted of a mixture of several ethnic groups. Even if we tend, on the basis of later evidence, to agree that the Sumerian factor was dominant during the archaic periods, this assumption remains open to further discussion.

The mentioned organizational challenges relating to administration and maintenance of such large settlements as those that occurred in Babylonia were not the only ones facing early inhabitants. Since the continuing decrease in water supply, which in the beginning had facilitated land reclamation in Babylonia, was gradually creating water shortages, measures had to be taken to assure the continuous flow of irrigation water onto the fields. Earlier, water supply had never presented any problems. Any increasing need to expand the irrigation networks could be met by the existing organizational structures of the time; the scale of such communal undertakings, however, required the further extension of the existing organizational structures.

Water retreated into the main channels of the Babylonian rivers. Thus, arable land needed for the sustenance of settlements tended to be restricted to the territory adjacent to these watercourses, causing a drastic decline in the number of settlements. At the same time, the remaining settlements can be shown to have grown considerably in size, possibly as a result of a natural increase of the local population, but equally possibly as a result of immigration from the abandoned settlements.

In this context, we are again unable to describe the exact processes involved in the adjustment of the inhabitants to the new situations, since these changes took place during periods preceding the appearance of understandable and historically significant texts. Again, we can only speculate about these developments based on inferences drawn from the earliest historical documents dating to the Early Dynastic III period. Territorial disputes concerning dominion over land and water and consequent attempts to solve such disputes by imposing structures of higher authority constitute the beginning of an ever-growing potential for conflicts between power centers. These conflicts eventually led to the formation of the first authentic regional state on Babylonian soil, the state of the Dynasty of Akkad (ca. 2350–2200 B.C.). Considering that at this stage the largest part of the population lived in urban centers numbering in excess of forty to fifty thousand inhabitants, we can sense the scale of social conflict within those urban communities, which probably led to the first compilation of legal codes and judicial ordinance.

On the political and administrative level, the use of mediators to settle disputes, the institutionalization of instances of imposed decision-making, the tightening of authoritarian control through strict application of theocratic ideology as well as the implementation of a thoroughly organized centralistic state under the Third Dynasty of Ur (ca. 2100–2000 B.C.) should in fact be seen as nothing less than the consequent efforts to come to terms with the surging conflicts mentioned above.

It would be surprising if the administrative system of the economy had remained unaffected by these continuing transformations. The clear impression that the administrative system of the Ur III state was more complex than that deduced from the archaic texts from Uruk cannot be explained away by underscoring the paucity of early data or our rudimentary knowledge about the period of the early documents. The relatively high degree of similarity between the basic structures of the economic administrative systems in Mesopotamia over a time span of more than 3000 years remains, on the other hand, intriguing. In the following chapters we shall therefore have cause to return to these similarities.

H.N.

4. Prehistoric Means of Administration

In explaining the administrative processes and techniques apparent after close scrutiny of the early written records, it is evident not only that from the beginning a system of complex bookkeeping evolved but also that the same was true for the economic activities themselves. By the time of the first written records, these activities as well as their monitoring had obviously acquired such strict rules that one is tempted to suggest the presence of a longer development prior to the period marked by the first texts. This can only mean that more or less similar structures existed before writing came into being, but since the nature of the earlier transactions is not recorded, it seems impossible to make any headway on this subject. However, in examining the archaeological evidence from the period immediately preceding that of incipient literacy, many features appear which are related to the idea of and which should therefore be viewed as the immediate precursors of writing.

Aside from the exact contexts of the preliterate accounting mechanisms, whether they are recording stock inventories, registering deliveries to and from central storage facilities, or noting quantitative fluctuations of domestic livestock, all have in common that they are complex operations, each utilizing different types of information. On a more basic level, the procedure of recording such information may be reduced to stating the type and number of the treated product, its location and date of entry, and sometimes even the names of the individuals involved in the transaction. Should it have been considered necessary to reconstruct these events, to check on the final balancing of accounts, or to resolve any inaccuracies, review of this information would have been necessary.

Great memory capacity such as that known from preliterate societies most probably enabled the ancient Babylonians to control such data without recourse to written records. In this manner, the development within an economic unit could thus be monitored even over longer periods of time. For the early phases, it is also assumed that in relatively small communities social control was so well developed that surveillance by sanction had not yet become necessary.

By the time of the emergence of the first written documents, however, this developmental stage had long since passed. Social control had now been replaced by an elaborate system of surveillance and administration. Not only the quantity of transferred goods but also the complexity of the respective transactions had extended beyond the capacity of human memory. Ways had to be found by which "objective" control was guaranteed. The course that was taken in early Babylonia to achieve that type of control was an impersonal system of recording information.

The earliest records known to us are mostly concerned with quantities of goods as well as with the identification of certain individuals. More information about type and location of goods was probably connected with the methods by which and the place where the goods were stored. Since all the archaic documents from Uruk were found in rubbish layers, they were in every respect devoid of any wider functional context. Indications of locality, date, and the other necessary information concerning the types of the products dealt with could, on the other hand, only be included after the invention of writing, provided that the products were not better defined by means of intricately shaped or decorated counting symbols.

Numbers

The most ancient counting symbols are the so-called tokens, each token representing a counted unit. A small heap of tokens would thus represent the sum of the counted units. A unit could either be a discrete entity, like a sheep from a flock, or a specified measure of a certain product, such as grain. In this manner, the total number of animals in a herd or the capacity units in a granary could be established and monitored. From the neolithic age (seventh millennium B.C.) on, stone tokens were gradually replaced by tokens made of baked clay, the latter having the advantage that they could be formed into any desired shape. Clay tokens were particularly popular in stoneless Babylonia.

Whereas in the beginning each token would have represented a counted unit, from very early times onward a particular number of units of the same value could be replaced by a specific symbol standing for this number of units. By combining various symbols, relatively high numerical values could be obtained. The large quantities of clay tokens found in various simple geometric shapes such as spheres, rhombuses, discs, and tetrahedrons, may therefore each be thought of as the representations of different specific numerical values (fig. 6).

For the following operational step, one has to imagine that such totals, each formed by a combination of different-shaped tokens, were then put away in a safe place with restricted access, since only in this way could the size of the number be retained over a long period. When the tokens were extracted from their container some time later, their represented value could be compared with the counted amount of the same product. Although we know little about the type of container the tokens were stored in, it seems very likely that they were kept in small bags of perishable material such as cloth or leather.

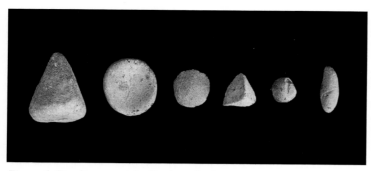

Figure 6. Simple, geometrically shaped tokens.

Sealed Bullae

At some point shortly before the first texts were written, the necessity had arisen to provide a more efficient guarantee of the authenticity and accuracy of the stored tokens. This need is reflected by the evidence that tokens were enveloped in a round lump of wet clay, "bulla," whose entire surface was subsequently sealed with cylinder seals (fig. 7). The contents were thus secured from unauthorized access. The authenticity of the information contained inside was therefore protected until the moment the bulla was broken (see chap. 16). Occasionally, impressed signs on the outer surface of the clay balls referred to the tokens stored inside them (see fig. 8; see also *MDP* 43, no. 582).

Compared to the masses of excavated scattered tokens that were originally part of such interrelated groups, the number of those still preserved inside the original clay balls is extremely small. Therefore, museum authorities have refrained from opening the bullae, believing this would inflict irreparable damage to the sealed surface. Modern scientific methods of scanning the bullae contents employing X rays have not proven successful in all instances (see fig. 111). Two problems therefore remain unsolved. The first is, how are we to determine the true numerical values of the tokens in order to know how many tokens of one shape were replaced by one token of another shape? (Such bundling rules have been identified from the time of the first written records; see chaps. 6 and 16.) The second question is, did these tokens already contain information about the type of the counted product, or did this information have to be added? The latter assumption may be supported by the evidence of a large number of scattered clay objects with incised patterns on their surface. Some of these clay objects were even formed into shapes that closely resemble later written signs. In such instances, these clay objects may be assumed to identify the counted object (fig. 9).

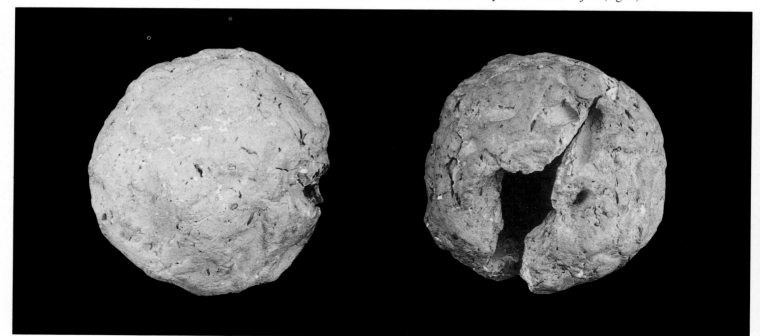

Figure 7. An intact (left) as well as an opened sealed clay bulla (right) from Uruk.

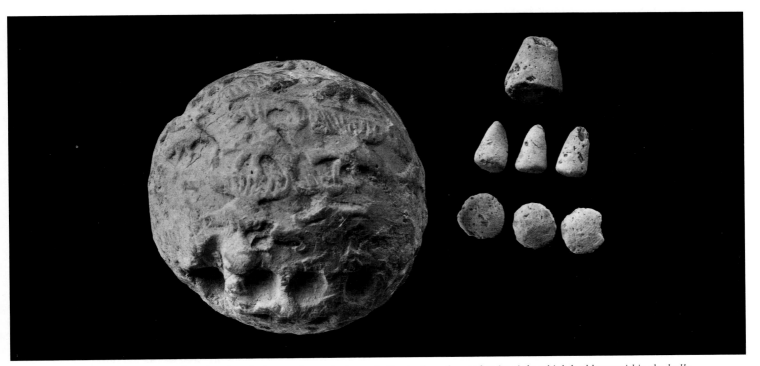

Figure 8. A sealed clay bulla from Susa bearing the impressions of tokens similar to those located to its right which had been within the bulla.

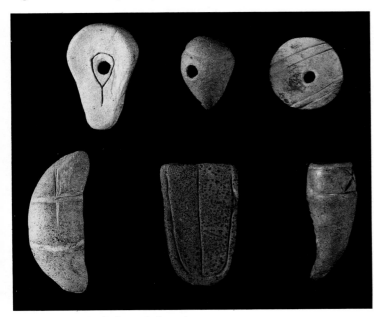

Figure 9. Peculiarly formed clay tokens.

Numerical Tablets

From the time immediately before the emergence of writing we may observe yet another method of recording numerical values. The system consisted of making round or oblong depressions along the edges of flattened, approximately rectangular clay objects. Still of unknown function is a group of tablets made of gypsum, each containing only a few round impressions which, however, seem to represent numerical values (see fig. 110). Even when tablets were intact and their information thus fully preserved, we are still not in a position to decipher the actual system of value replacement used (see fig. 113a). Unfortunately, these rules of value replacement cannot be proven to correspond to any of the applied systems identified in the earliest texts. As in the case of the clay bullae, numerical tablets could be sealed by an individual present at or monitoring the transaction.

In addition to these tablets, which most certainly are older than the proto-cuneiform script, there is a considerable number of numerical tablets that resemble those with genuine script not only according to their shape but also by the way in which the numbers were "written," as well as by the sequence of the numerical entries (fig. 10; see as well the tablets W 11040 and 20239, published in

Figure 10. A sealed numerical tablet.

ATU 2, pl. 17, and in *Spektrum der Wissenschaft*, Feb. 1988, p. 85, respectively). They often bear sealings as well. Unfortunately, neither typological nor stratigraphic features reveal any information as to their date relative to the first proto-cuneiform tablets.

Metrological Systems

An important step in the progress of control over economic activities was the introduction of standardized measurements allowing for comparability and accountability in recordkeeping. Registering and counting procedures only make sense if the counted units are in some way or another interchangeable. Whereas discrete units are freely exchangeable, as in the case of animals (each animal represents one unit), other products require explicit definitions concerning the measuring system to which the counted units conform. From the earliest texts we know that area as well as capacity units already existed.

For the preliterate period, on the other hand, we can only assume the existence of defined measures for most products. In the case of capacity measures, though, we have solid evidence of a measuring system in the form of a group of open bowls quite characteristic for the Late Uruk and the Jemdet Nasr periods. Archaeological findings suggest that these bowls were in fact units for capacity measurements (fig. 11).

It is indeed intriguing that such mass-produced bowls, the so-called beveled-rim bowls for the Uruk period and the conical cups for the ensuing Jemdet Nasr period, constitute up to 80 percent of the total pottery assemblage and that the majority of these vessels had the same approximate volume capacity. That volume represents approximately half of what, according to later texts, was distributed as daily barley rations to the employees of large households. It therefore seems very likely that the capacity of the vessels is consistent with a unit used in measuring volumes. Although the interpretation that the bowls represent ration units is still subject to controversy, the fact that their pictographic representation occurs in a compound ideogram normally translated with "(rationing) disbursement" actually gives credence to this interpretation (fig. 12).

Figure 11. A so-called beveled-rim bowl (left) and a conical cup (right; reduced by 50%).

Individuals

A discussion of the people involved in the transactions is conditioned above all by the seals they used. When rolled over a soft surface such as moist clay, a cylinder seal leaves behind the negative impression of the image engraved in its jacket (fig. 13). Not only does the seal impression secure the integrity of the surface of a clay document, but the individual who impressed his seal is also identified as the guarantor of the transaction involved. Apparently, it was the latter aspect, the action of guaranteeing, that played the most important role, since this action is most consistent with the series of attempts to store information on economic activities, as we have seen earlier. A sealing hence recorded who was present at the moment of the transaction and determined who was responsible for that transaction. Furthermore, it disclosed under whose authority the guarantee was given. Thus, in the case of a later check on the circumstances of the transaction, the sealing was, next to number and measure, another piece of information conveyed by the procedure.

This aspect made special demands on the manufacture of the seal. Anyone charged for any reason whatsoever with the surveillance of transactions needed to have a seal that made possible an irrefutable identification of his person. This fact explains the great variety of figurative seals appearing in the Late Uruk period and gives the impression that the number of people involved in such transactions was at this time quite large.

Scenes best interpreted as cultic, for example, processions of human beings approaching a building, carrying objects on their

SAG   NINDA   GU₇
head   rationing vessel disbursement

Figure 12. The composite sign consisting of SAG, "head," and NINDA, "rationing vessel," with the meaning "disbursement."

shoulders or in their hands—probably offerings, insignia or the like—are relatively common (figs. 13–14).

A good example of the variability within a single glyptic theme category is presented by the so-called prisoners scene (fig. 15). Three different types of figures are distinguished in this frieze. The first one is a man in a static pose. His beard and the long spear he is holding as an apparent attribution of power signify that he was an important person. He apparently had a higher social rank than all the other figures represented in the scene.

The rest of the scene is filled with a confusion of naked individuals which clearly form two separate groups. The first are figures standing in upright position, holding sticks or batons in their hands, some in a position as if prepared to strike. The others are cowering and scattered over the ground, their legs bent up to their stomachs, their arms tied together behind their backs. Only in a few instances do we find a standing figure that does not seem

Figure 13. A seal from Uruk and its modern impression (actual size).

to be holding a weapon, who thus, judging from his cowering posture and the shackles around his wrists, apparently belonged to the latter group. The context is quite clearly one of a victorious group celebrating its conquest of an enemy, the bearded figure manifestly representing the leader of the triumphant party.

This scene can be rendered in different manners by changing the number or position of the different members of each group, without being compelled to alter its basic statement. In one case, the main figure was even left out, which nonetheless does not keep us from ascribing the represented figures to one or the other group just described. It is striking that such variations are generally very slight, suggesting that the number of allowed variabilities indeed had been utilized.

In other cases, the variations within one and the same motif are so minute as to be scarcely noticeable, although this is to some extent to be explained by the randomness of the excavated material at our disposal. Nevertheless, noteworthy is the great range of variability among the main motifs, to which we must also reckon the various possibilities of rendering animal depictions (fig. 16). Rows of identical or different animals are thus to be included in this range, as well as contest scenes between predatory and prey

Figure 15. Two versions of the so-called prisoner scene.

animals and other scenes consisting of animals in front of architectural façades, but also themes in which animals are shown one against the other in heraldic pose, sometimes interwoven with grotesquely elongated necks.

This wealth of diversity allows a maximum number of individuals to possess their own specific seal. Innumerable administrative activities as well as a whole range of relevant clay objects required the use of this personal signature. Most prominent are the various types of stoppers of moist clay that were plugged into the openings of pottery vessels, or the simple clay lumps that were kneaded around the string knots on bags, boxes, and even door locks. Many of the fastenings still have the impressions of those strings on their inner surface. The contents of the container or the room in question are thereby certified as being under the responsibility of the person or the authority who had left his seal on the fastening.

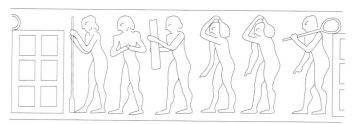

Figure 14. Fragment of a jar collar containing parts of a sealing representing a procession going toward a building.

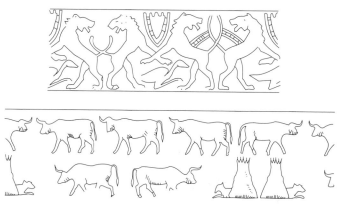

Figure 16. Seal images representing animals.

Figure 17. Seal impression on a tablet from the former Erlenmeyer collection.

The Metropolitan Museum of Art, Purchase, Raymond and Beverly Sackler Gift, 1988. (1988.433.1)

Moreover, in order to further assure later identification, the event during which a vessel or room was sealed could be attended by several persons who, in case of need, could be called upon to act as witnesses. This was probably also why documents were still being sealed long after the invention of writing had made it possible to simply record the names of the witnesses. A good example is the only sealed archaic tablet of the former Erlenmeyer collection, now in the collection of the Metropolitan Museum of Art, New York (fig. 17).

A unique seal from the former Erlenmeyer collection (fig. 18) carries, in addition to a standing bull in the same style as those under discussion, five signs which are undoubtedly renderings of ideograms. The reed-bundle, symbol of the goddess Inanna of Uruk, is combined with the sign EZEN ("festival") and signs representing a star, the rising and the setting star. This notation may be translated "The festival of the evening/morning Inanna (= Venus)." Although further interpretation is difficult, it is very improbable that this should be understood as a personal name—personal names as a means of identifying the seal owner

are in fact first attested in the latter part of the Early Dynastic (Fara) period.

Beyond being able to transmit isolated information, seal impressions could, as we have seen, be left on objects yielding additional information, such as in the examples of the bullae and the numerical tablets. Thus, a substantial contribution to the improvement of the quality of the stored information as a whole was made. Being sealed, these documents no longer gave information concerning merely quantities of goods, but also concerning the persons who were responsible. Many more comparable attempts to expand on the kind of information in this way probably existed, none of which have been preserved. However, the room for improvement must have been rather restricted, since the expansion of information storage would no doubt have to be paid for by rendering the accounting mechanisms even more elaborate.

The preceding observations relate only to the numerous sealings which yielded a great variety of figurative motifs. Unfortunately, the number of original seals of this type is very

Figure 18. Impression of a seal from the former Erlenmeyer collection with incised ideograms.

small, although the evidence from thousands of sealings suggests that this seal type was generally quite common.

This category differs in nearly every respect from a second category of seals. Most of these smaller seals either bear abstract, practically geometrical motifs or are so abstracted from figurative designs of the first category as to appear geometric. Next to these seals, another group bears likewise abstracted motifs which, however, are more reminiscent of the figurative repertoire of the first seal group (fig. 19). Even though the range of iconographic variation of these seals is fairly broad, it is nevertheless manifestly narrower than that of the first group, and much less suited for elaborate internal differentiation.

In addition to their relative uniformity, many of the seal designs of the second group were engraved by means of mechanical tools, restricting the possibility of variation of the incisions carved on the seal jackets. While the drill could be used only to produce hemispherical cavities of different sizes, the cutting wheel could only incise straight lines, since even the slightest curvature would provoke a widening of the line at the vertex of the curve. In some seals, however, that effect was purposely incorporated into the motif. A final difference between this and the figurative group is that the abstract group is represented by a great number of original seals, whereas the evidence of their sealings is rather scanty.

From all these contrasts, one is tempted to infer that this second seal group had a different *Sitz im Leben,* as supported by the archaeological evidence that these seals were not used at those locations where economic administration is attested by inscribed clay tablets and various sorts of sealed locks. It is in fact striking that no cylinder seal of the second group was extracted from the extended debris layers in Uruk yielding approximately 5000 clay tablets and sealed fragments.

Similar conclusions can be drawn with regard to the internal compositions of the seal designs. While the first seal group is partly defined on the basis of its great range of internal differentiation, thus assuring that a maximum number of individuals had their own personal seal design, this is not the case for the second seal group. Indeed, this latter group is not only characterized by the restricted number of motifs, but also by the reduced possibilities of internal differentiation. It has therefore been suggested that these seals ought not to be viewed as personal signs of individuals but rather as seals of specific corporate institutions. Although this proposition still requires better justification, no other plausible suggestion as to the function of these seals has as yet been made. Intriguing, although not very helpful in this context, is the phenomenon that, in contrast to the seals of the figurative group, seals of the second group have been found in scattered regions covering the entire Near East, for example, beyond Babylonia in Syria, Anatolia, and Egypt. This phenomenon can only be explained as the result of the extended trade relations Babylonia already enjoyed with these regions at the end of the fourth millennium B.C.

With the exception of the second seal group, which for the moment cannot be placed within a closer functional context, all the artifacts discussed in this chapter not only demonstrate their respective role in the economic life of the period, but also show to what extent they are to be regarded as indicators of early preliterate information storage. They may thus be placed in context with other precursors of writing, which itself was without doubt the most successful and portentous solution to the problem of adapting the possibilities of information storage to the growing demands of archaic society.

H.N.

Figure 19. Seal of the abstract group.

5. The Emergence of Writing

In chapter 2, the dates and circumstances of the discovery of the archaic tablets from Uruk were discussed. It was seen that writing appeared for the first time toward the end of the Late Uruk period, most probably during the period defined by the archaic building layer IVa in Eanna.

Through paleographic comparisons between the texts of script phases Uruk IV and III, Assyriological research established early on that the differences between the two phases are easily detectable insofar as the changes in the techniques of writing had significantly altered the shapes of the respective signs (see the more detailed discussion of this phenomenon in chap. 15). The dating of the texts is thus connected less to stratigraphy than to paleography.

From the time of the first discovery of the texts, it was more or less obvious that within each of the identified script phases there were hardly any notable differences in the execution of the signs. In fact, the script of the earliest tablets revealed such a relatively great conformity that doubts were raised that they indeed represented the earliest form of literacy. It was repeatedly suggested that as yet unknown and less conventionalized precursors must have preceded these tablets. The fact that the alleged precursors remained undiscovered was dismissed with the theory that they had been written on perishable material such as wood or bark which, of course, would hardly have survived the aggressive climatic conditions of Babylonia.

In the previous chapter, it was demonstrated that a whole series of precursors did in fact exist, although not in the form of the presumed written documents containing more primitive symbols, but evidently more in the sense of primitive ways of mastering problems of information storage, to which script presented the ideal solution. To judge from the variety of the attempts to achieve an effective recording system, it seems reasonable to assume that the problems were regarded as imminent.

Under such conditions, it should not be surprising that, first, after having developed a system for recording quantities as well as, possibly, one for denoting goods and containers by means of experimenting with small clay models, the next developmental stage in the process no longer appears to be of considerable length. It consisted simply of drawing defined symbols onto the surface of the well-known information carrier clay. So, if the invention of writing is merely to be conceived of as the result of a sequence of developments, this step nevertheless remains the most decisive one on the way to an entirely new—if not revolutionary—information technology.

Second, in looking at the "prehistory" of this development, it becomes apparent that anyone dealing with the problem of recording information must have recognized writing, once it had been developed, as the most efficient and comprehensive solution to the matter. It is therefore conceivable that the development of this idea into a universally applicable system with compelling strong conventions could only have taken place within a very short time—in fact so short that with our present methods we are no longer in a position to distinguish more clearly between the various phases within this preliterate period. Although uncertainties relating to both practicability and connected organizational procedures must have characterized the beginning phase of writing, we have no means to isolate such a formative phase in the script. The appearance of writing as a fully developed system receives herein a plausible explanation.

From the point of view of society in general, we should rid ourselves of the notion that the emergence of writing marked the beginning of an entirely new era. The preliterate means of administration, discussed variously above, demonstrate that society had not only come to master similar administrative problems during previous periods; they also demonstrate that organizational structures were more or less the same in earlier periods. In chapter 14, an additional source shall be quoted through which these structures can be traced. That chapter is largely centered around a so-called lexical list (see below for further discussion) enumerating archaic titles and professions. The arrangement of the entries in this list according to rank most likely reflects the hierarchy of the upper social classes at a certain time. Since the earliest copy of this list dates back to script phase IV, parts of the social structure from that early period are illuminated, and since it is highly unlikely that such a strict hierarchical stratification should have developed within a relatively short period, we seem in this list confronted with a manifestation of the social structures from the time *before* the invention of writing.

Hence, it can be adduced with some degree of confidence that the organizational structures of society and economy were already well established when literacy came into being, shedding direct light on parts of a well-developed economy of the time. The distribution of economic and social responsibilities had apparently already been accomplished or, if not, was at least fixed to such an extent that the following centuries only witnessed minor corrections in this stratification.

Another observation finds herein an explanation. From the very beginning of writing, we have a very diversified typology of written documents. A first text category consists of so-called tags

Figure 20. Pendant etiquettes from Uruk dating to script phase Uruk IV.

consisting of small, transversely perforated tablets, usually containing but few ideographic signs and no numerical notations (fig. 20). These signs do not belong to the well-known repertoire of symbols representing goods such as plants, animals, textiles, and metals. The tags therefore may carry personal names and were probably attached with a string to containers or other items, stating the proprietor or receiver of such goods.

The second text category is characterized by a slightly larger tablet type containing only one unit of information, consisting of a numerical notation accompanied by a small number of ideographic signs (fig. 21). In contrast to the following category, the surface of these tablets is not partitioned into columns and cases.

Figure 21. Administrative text from Uruk containing just one unit of information, dating to script phase Uruk IV.

Difficulties remain concerning the meaning of their contents, but it is evident that these texts are to be placed within a wider administrative context. The numerical notation probably states a quantity of a certain product, whereas the ideographic signs probably again depict the product itself and a personal name.

The third tablet category is the largest in number. It is characterized by the division of the surface of the tablet into columns and cases, each case containing one unit of information. There are enough reasons to believe that these entries in some way or another relate to each other, although this has only been proven in a few instances.

In such cases, the sum of the numerical notations in the cases on the obverse is entered on the reverse of the tablets (fig. 22).

Unfortunately, on most of the archaic tablets, in particular on those from script phase Uruk IV, the information given is kept as concise as possible. Everything expected to be known by the reader was omitted by the scribe. Thus there was obviously no need to elaborate on syntactic relationships, for example, to include extra information about the sender or the receiver of goods involved. It apparently sufficed to report the quantities of the goods in question. The nature of these products was often

Figure 22. Administrative text from Uruk in which the entries on the obverse (upper) were totaled on the reverse (lower); from script phase Uruk IV.

obvious from the type of numerical signs employed (see the next chapter). At the end of the text, the name of the responsible person or institution was added (fig. 23). We are thus merely able to detect a relationship between the entries, but not the nature of this relationship.

Furthermore, there are tablets which, although they contain numerous entries, do not give the sum of the numerical notations on the reverse. In these cases the checking procedures apparently only concerned the number of individual transactions, but not the total amount of the enumerated products.

So, without being able to pinpoint the particular procedures related in the texts themselves, it nevertheless remains possible on the basis of formal observations to appreciate the fact that different types of procedures required different methods of recording, in other words, that certain prescribed rules were to be respected, according to which certain matters were recorded.

The group of tablets from the second earliest writing phase, Uruk III.3, is quite small. Its members still bear some graphic elements of script phase IV, but also some that only become current in script phase III.2 (fig. 24).

By far greatest in number are the tablets preserved from script phase III.2. The writing itself demonstrates extreme conformity, not only in the tablets from Uruk (fig. 25), but also in those excavated at the site of Jemdet Nasr, the ductus of which is practically identical to that of script phase Uruk III (see the text copies in fig. 62 below). This was, incidentally, why the layer Archaic III in Uruk was correlated with the period named after Jemdet Nasr. Because of this fixed appearance of the signs of script phase III, the archaic texts from the Erlenmeyer collection as well as nearly all other known tablets acquired through the antiquities market can also be safely assigned to that period.

Tags are scarcely attested from this period on, much the same as the category of tablets that only contain one unit of information. Most of the tablets now belong to the category containing lists with series of information units being summarized in different manners. Additional notes, such as extra administrative terms, become more frequent (fig. 25). On the whole, the ways in which data are stored and processed increase in complexity, although it remains questionable whether this constitutes progress in the actual methods themselves. A fuller discussion of the complexity of recorded administrative methods may be found in chapters 7–9 below.

The supposition that the appearance of writing is to be viewed merely as an additional, albeit crucial step in a sequence of experiments in implementing effective control mechanisms in the economy is enhanced by the fact that the great majority of the 5000 or so written documents from script phases IV and III deal exclusively with administrative procedures. Bearing in mind the large number of texts, it is certainly no coincidence that not one of them is clearly related to religious, narrative, or historical topics (for a possible exception, see now R. K. Englund and H. J. Nissen, *Die lexikalischen Listen aus Uruk* [=*ATU* 3, 1993], pp. 25–29, to the so-called tribute list). This fact strongly implies that such text genres were simply not written down and is a clear refutation of the hypothesis that writing was invented as a response to the urge to record accounts of religious or narrative character.

One text category does, however, differ from the administrative texts. This category is already characterized by the formal aspect that the individual cases on the tablets, which as administrative texts usually contained numerical notations of varying values, here bear a stereotypically repeated sign at the beginning of each entry which is normally used to denote the unit "one" in

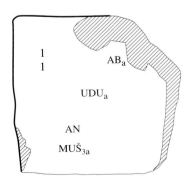
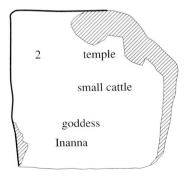

Figure 23. Copy of a tablet fragment from script phase Uruk III with transliteration and translation.

Figure 24. Administrative text from Uruk dating to script phase Uruk III.3, containing an account concerning metal objects.

the sexagesimal system, but which in this case is probably to be seen as a sign signifying the introduction of each new entry.

Some of these tablets reveal more about the contextual nature of their category, since the similarities between the sequentially occurring ideographic signs as well as the repetition of the numerical sign just mentioned clearly stand in some relation to the connotational meanings of the entries. In some cases, the sequentially occurring signs are rendered in such a naturalistic manner that various animals like birds, fish, and domesticated animals are easily recognized as being the common denominator of a list (fig. 26). In figure 86, a fragmentary text is shown which enumerates

types of textiles as well as vessels of various contents. Another such text can be identified as a list of trees and wooden objects, since each of its entries is preceded by a sign denoting wood. Other compilations can only be identified as lists by their format; in some cases, analysis reveals a common theme of their contents. The best example for such a list is the titles and professions list discussed in chapter 14.

Lists will also be discussed in connection with the scribe and his education, since they probably played an essential role in the transmission of the art of writing, that is, in the education of a scribe. In the present context, it should be underscored that this

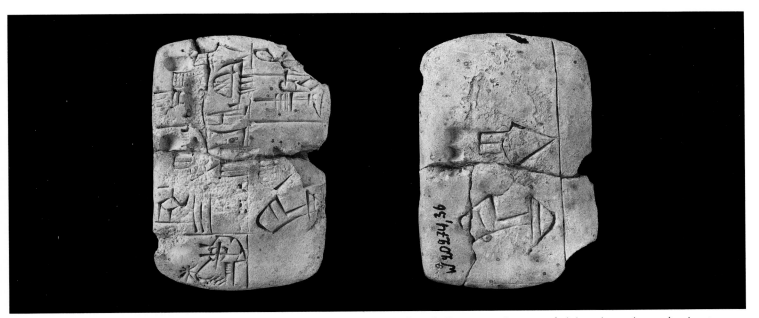

Figure 25. Complex administrative text from Uruk dating to script phase Uruk III.2, including summations, an administrative notice, and a signature.

Figure 26. Complete pig list from Uruk dating to script phase Uruk III, with addition of the entries on the left margin of the obverse.

text category is already attested among the oldest written documents, although in very small numbers. Nevertheless, because of the circumstance that such lists have been transmitted, preserved in the form of copies from the following script phase Uruk III, we must conclude that some may have been copied from now lost forerunners which already existed in phase IV.

It is possible that these lists bear a close contextual relationship to the establishment of the proto-cuneiform writing system, since one could imagine that the invention and definition of its signs automatically required such compilations of theme-related sign groups. On the other hand, it seems just as probable that they represent written conventions of already thematically sorted compilations which were destined to bring order into the growing world of written symbols. It is conceivable that the titles and professions list mentioned above served in part to document the social hierarchy as transmitted from the preliterate period. It is, however, inconceivable that the need to put such lists on record acted as the *stimulator* of the development of a writing system.

H.N.

6. Archaic Numerical Sign Systems

Approximately 1200 different signs and sign variants have been isolated in the archaic texts. Some 60 of them (see fig. 27) have been identified as numerical signs. These signs are conspicuous because of their peculiar graphic forms: in contrast to the great majority of the ideograms, they were as a rule not incised in the moist surface of a clay tablet, but were rather impressed with a round stylus held either in a vertical or in a oblique position in relation to the writing surface. In some cases, additional marks were incised with the sharp end of a pointed stylus.

Since all administrative texts contain numerical signs, some of them are far and away the most often attested signs in the archaic text corpus. Because of the nature of the texts, numerical notations are at the same time key information carriers. Accordingly, they deserve special attention.

In contrast to the other ideographic signs, some of the numerical signs, especially the most frequently attested ones, retained their original graphic form over the course of many centuries. They even occur in relatively late, and virtually entirely comprehensible text groups of the Ur III period a thousand years later, during which time these curvilinear signs were gradually replaced by their cuneiform correspondences.

For this reason the well-known sexagesimal number signs for 1, 10, 60, and 600 were easily recognized in the archaic texts and deciphered without apparent difficulties. For many years, scholars had therefore considered the decipherment of the archaic numerical signs as relatively secure and so effectively repressed the fact that the allegedly certain decipherment was only valid for very few of the 60 known numerical signs. Moreover, whenever assumed arithmetical values of the signs disagreed with the calculations given in the tablets, scholars reverted to the belief that such contradictions occurred as a result of calculation mistakes on the part of the ancient scribes rather than to question the infallibility of modern interpretation.

Many peculiarities of the archaic numerical signs were simply disregarded. For example, the phenomenon that in context with cereals, the sign ▶, which usually stands for 60, seemed to adopt the value 300 (correct is 180) and that in context with surface measurements the sign •, normally meaning 10, received the value 18, was rather indifferently considered a matter of exceptions to otherwise obvious rules. No one had formerly suspected what today is known to be the case—that in the archaic texts, more than in any other text corpus, the arithmetic values of the numerical

signs were subjected to change depending on the context involved.

In 1936, the German Sumerologist Adam Falkenstein gave the first comprehensive account of the archaic texts which had been found during the early excavation campaigns at Uruk. In his attempt at mastering the prodigious bulk of peculiar signs, he differentiated between three different categories of numerical signs. The first group was considered to represent the sexagesimal system, the second a competing decimal system, and the third group a system of fractions.

In the assumption that graphic differences represented merely irrelevant variations of identical values, Falkenstein was nevertheless confronted with the problem that in the end he was left with too many signs denoting too few numbers. In spite of these obvious deficiencies, Falkenstein's compendium of the archaic numerical signs was to remain the most authoritative source concerning the history of archaic numeration for the 40 years to come.

It was only in the middle to late seventies that the problem of ordering and interpreting the numerical signs in the published archaic texts was subjected to renewed scrutiny by the Soviet Sumerologist Aisik Vaiman and the Swedish mathematician Jöran Friberg. Even though they came to partially diverging results, both made some important discoveries.

Vaiman demonstrated that the numerical signs of the archaic texts belonged to a larger variety of systems than postulated by Falkenstein. Friberg, on the other hand, proved that the theory of a competing decimal system was based on a logical error going back to the publication of the earliest proto-Elamite texts by Vincent Scheil in 1905 (for the correct structure of this system see the ŠE system in fig. 28). The underlying mistake was that the sign •, except in its usage as a measure for field surfaces, had a fixed value, namely that of "10." Repeated and indiscriminate adoption of this notion lead to the belief that this was an established fact, although a more careful analysis of the calculations contained in the texts would soon have led to other results.

This was, broadly speaking, the situation in 1983 when we as members of the Berlin research project Archaische Texte aus Uruk decided to reanalyze the archaic numerical signs on the basis of all excavated tablets known to that date. A new approach for this analysis was chosen. The method usually employed to analyze archaic numerical sign systems before we started consisted of the extraction of a maximum of information from a small number of preserved calculations, after which these determined values were ascribed in other texts to graphically corresponding signs whose numerical values were not otherwise obvious. Instead of trying to establish the numerical values directly, we commenced with an attempt to uncover as much as possible about the rules according

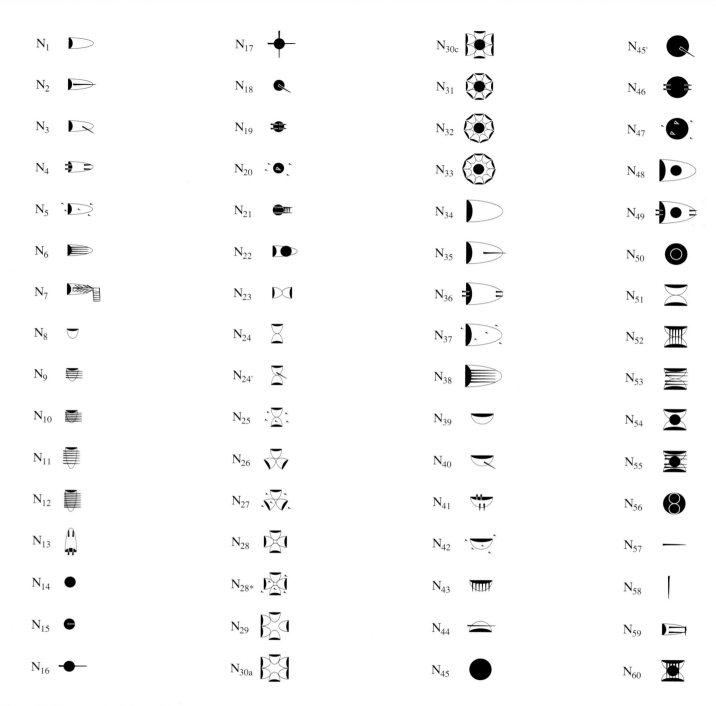

Figure 27. The numerical signs of the proto-cuneiform texts from Uruk.

to which the signs were employed. Hundreds of isolated fragments devoid of any apparent context, which until then had played virtually no role in the identification of numerical sign systems, suddenly became crucial sources of information. In a computerized jigsaw puzzle, assumed rules were tracked down and once found immediately exposed to testing on the entire text corpus.

It happened that the ascertained rules were often incompatible with the generally accepted interpretations of the signs as representing "numbers." For example, the three signs ▷, ⧖, and ▶ represented, according to traditional interpretations, the numbers 60, 120, and 600, respectively. We made the peculiar discovery that the signs for 120 and 600 never occurred together in a single notation. When necessary, the sign for 120 was impressed five and more times, instead of using the sign for 600. On the other hand, in notations bearing the sign for 600, the sign denoting the value 120 never replaced a value equal to twice the sign for 60.

Our analyses of these and similar peculiarities concerning the usage of the signs produced a simple and plausible explanation. In fact, almost all of the 6500 notations then stored in electronic files could be assigned to a restricted number of different numerical systems (see fig. 28). Each of these systems possesses a well-defined range of applicability. In this respect, the signs for 120 and 600 never occur together in one notation because each belonged to a different numerical system which did not apply to identical products.

The most unusual characteristic of the archaic numerical signs is their arithmetical ambiguity already described above. This phenomenon is explained by the fact that identical signs can occur in different systems and consequently inherit different numerical connotations.

Most notations are assignable to one of the following five systems: the sexagesimal or the bisexagesimal system, the ŠE system, the GAN$_2$ system or the EN system (ŠE, GAN$_2$ and EN are signs that stand in relationship with each of the respective systems). In addition to the basic systems, several derived systems were isolated with identical arithmetical structures, but diverging graphic representations as well as applicability. Finally, there are some other numerical sign systems, for example the U$_4$ system used in timekeeping notations, combining both numerical and ideographic signs and thus emphasizing special metrological connotations

The fields of applicability of the systems seemed to follow no intelligible rules. The sexagesimal and bisexagesimal systems as well as their derivatives were used for discrete, that is, countable objects. While the functional ranges of the basic systems were relatively very broad, the derived systems were only used for quite specific contexts. Accordingly, the S' system as a derivative of the sexagesimal system was apparently used exclusively either for the recording of slaughtered or perished cattle of the current accounting year or for denoting a specific type of produced or distributed beer. The ŠE system and its various derivatives qualified exclusively capacity measures of cereals, whereby each system most probably was used in connection with a specific type of grain. The GAN$_2$ system was used to record field measures, whereas the function of the EN system remains unknown.

There is clear evidence for the existence of additional numerical sign systems. Alone the fact that 25 of the total of 26 texts giving testimony to the EN system were excavated at a single locus cautions reserve in the assessment of our knowledge of archaic numeration and metrology. Had it not been for this fortuitous discovery, we would be virtually unaware of its existence today. Ten of the sixty numerical signs contained in the list in figure 27, moreover, do not belong to any of the identified systems. Three of them were apparently scribbled by an awkward pupil. As to four of those remaining, we are not sure whether they constitute derivations of other, as yet unknown numerical signs or whether they are in fact numerical signs at all. For at least two of the ten signs, ⋈ and ▬, we can affirm that each formed part of two additional systems, about which we know nothing due to the fact that no informative texts have been unearthed with notations in these systems.

P.D./R.E.

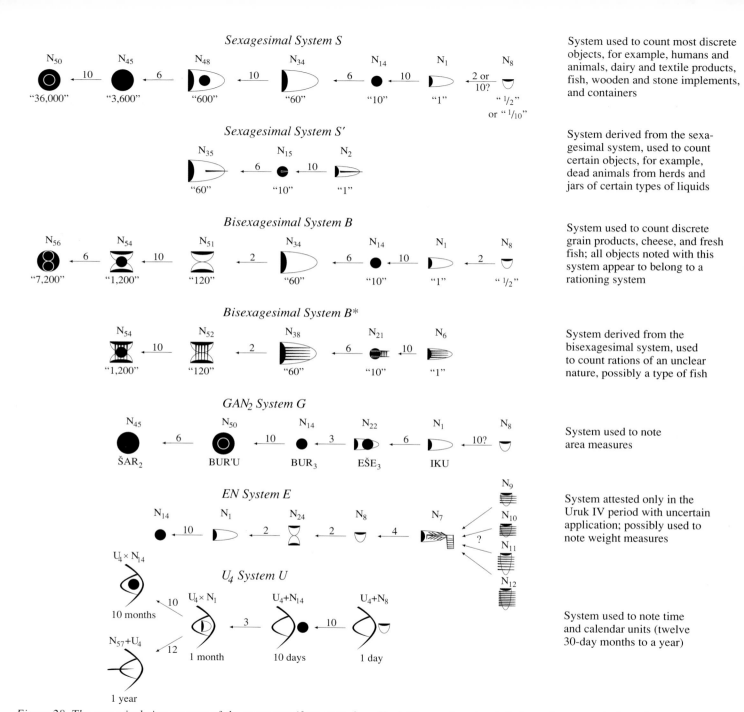

Figure 28. The numerical sign systems of the proto-cuneiform texts from Uruk (the numbers located above the arrows indicate how many respective units were substituted by the next higher unit).

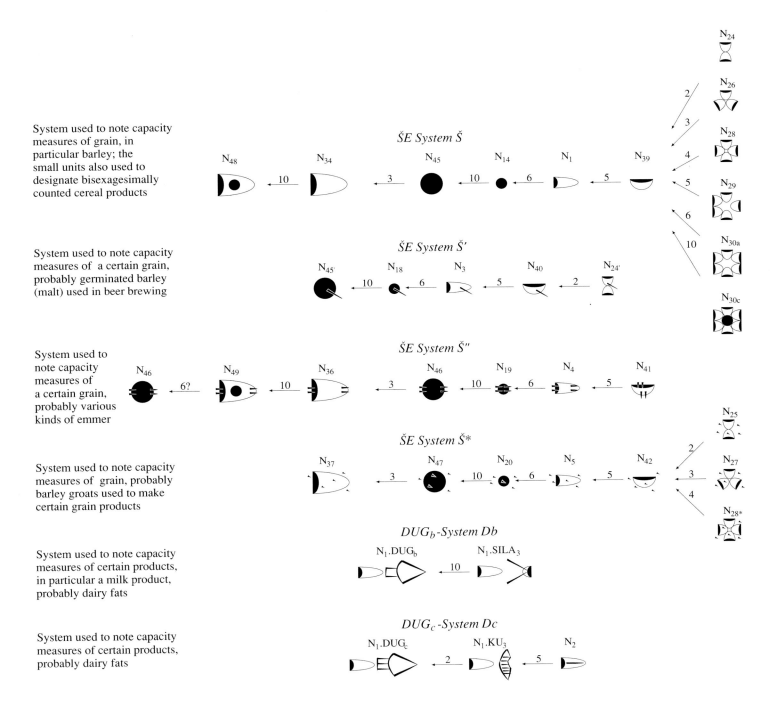

System used to note capacity measures of grain, in particular barley; the small units also used to designate bisexagesimally counted cereal products

ŠE System Š

System used to note capacity measures of a certain grain, probably germinated barley (malt) used in beer brewing

ŠE System Š′

System used to note capacity measures of a certain grain, probably various kinds of emmer

ŠE System Š″

System used to note capacity measures of grain, probably barley groats used to make certain grain products

ŠE System Š*

System used to note capacity measures of certain products, in particular a milk product, probably dairy fats

DUGb-System Db

System used to note capacity measures of certain products, probably dairy fats

DUGc-System Dc

7. The Archaic Bookkeeping System

In chapters 4 through 6, the emergence of writing as an instrument in the management of economic transactions was discussed. Only in the course of the third millennium B.C., however, did writing achieve that degree of complexity requisite to becoming a universal means of communication, thus establishing its position as a tool for the representation of spoken language which we today take for granted. Originally, however, the proto-cuneiform script was almost exclusively restricted to bookkeeping; it was an "accountant's script." With the exception of the preserved texts of the archaic period which served as "copy books" for the education of future scribes (see chaps. 13 and 14), these documents are entirely of administrative character.

In the course of its evolution, writing assumed new functions without losing older ones. In the periods of the third millennium following the archaic age, administrative documents still continued to form the great bulk of the complete text corpora, and even in later periods they constituted a substantial percentage of all written material. In this respect, the archaic tablets assume a point of departure for two completely different and increasingly independent developments. On one level, the archaic accounting script later developed into language-functional cuneiform, while on a second the system of accounting itself became more and more effective, eventually turning into a powerful instrument of formalized control of economic procedures, employing sign systems and document forms. In this chapter, we shall have a look at the general features of this second line of development; in the following chapters, a series of concrete examples shall serve as illustrations of this development.

Several text categories demonstrate progress in the techniques of bookkeeping. The following discussion will concentrate on the category connected to the management of cereal products, partly because these texts seem the most suitable for an accessible understanding of the essence of ancient accounting and partly because they constitute the largest homogeneous text group within the Erlenmeyer collection discussed previously. Moreover, texts concerning cereal administration are broadly representative of the economic administration of the third millennium, since cereal production was the major economic factor contributing to the wealth of urban centers in Mesopotamia, so that its administration was understandably the central concern of bookkeeping, leading to a high degree of complexity in its use at a very early stage.

The fact that in the beginning writing evolved more or less exclusively within the limits of bookkeeping not only determined the general format of the early tablets, but moreover influenced the internal structure of the script itself. Three main features fundamentally distinguish early script from later writing systems. These features qualify the earliest script as the beginning of a new and relatively independent development of bookkeeping techniques:

1. The meanings of the script symbols and signs were determined by processes in production, distribution, and administration and therefore cannot be considered to be identical with their corresponding linguistic concepts.
2. The position of the signs within the texts was determined to a lesser extent by criteria relating to language syntax than by the "tablet format." This layout was specific to particular economic transactions; it determined how and where a given bit of information was to be displayed.
3. The tablets were seldom isolated information transmitters; rather, they almost without exception represent a part of running bookkeeping procedures in which pieces of information from one tablet were transposed to another.

The various tablets from the earliest phases of writing therefore bear closer resemblance to such modern documents as punched cards, dockets, clearing checks, balance sheets or many other formalized data carriers than to independently and freely composed manuscripts in the modern sense.

But on the grounds of that very fact, the modern reader is confronted with almost insurmountable difficulties in his attempts to grasp the functional context of archaic documents. Since the information conveyed by the texts is kept at an extremely rudimentary level, we are left with the impression that the texts themselves are incomplete. Although we are able to establish without major effort what and how much was transacted and who the people involved in the transactions were, all of which is represented by the inscribed signs themselves, we are yet unable to clearly delineate the meaning of the tablet as a document of a particular, yet implicit transaction within a larger context of economic units. Thus, in the same way as we are told by a receipt that something has been received and receipted, while nothing is said about what a receipt actually is, the archaic tablets remain silent about the nature of the transactions they refer to. Only in those rare cases where we have a chain of documents, each relating to but one step within an entire sequence of interlocking transactions, can we reconstruct that sequence and thus stand a chance, however slim, of tracing the true purpose of each tablet against the background of the underlying economic transaction.

The reconstruction of such processes can best be illustrated using the least complex documents preserved. Figure 29 exhibits

Text a

Tablet with only one entry: 196 units of a grain product in a bisexagesimal notation

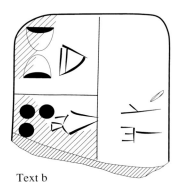

Text b

Tablet with two entries (first column) and a signature (second column): 120 grain rations and 30 jars of beer

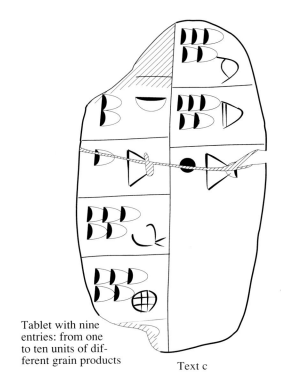

Tablet with nine entries: from one to ten units of different grain products

Text c

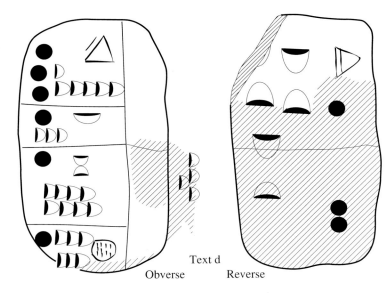

Text d

Obverse   Reverse

Tablet with four entries on the obverse, a notation on the edge and possibly a summation (?) on the reverse (damaged): The obverse contains entries concerning various grain products. The entries on the reverse are collectively designated ▷ (NINDA), i.e., "grain rations." Possible reconstruction of the total:

$$5 \times (35 + 13 + 18 + 16) = 410 \ (\text{i.e.}, \ 3 \times 120 + 5 \times 10)$$

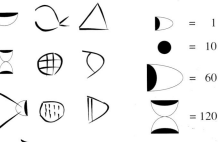

signs for grain products:

numerical signs of the bisexagesimal system:

= 1
= 10
= 60
= 120

beer

Figure 29. Simple tablet formats of archaic administrative documents.

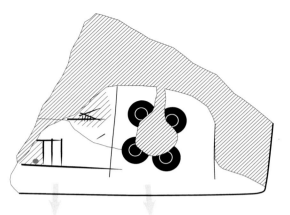

Field surface

4 bur'u (about 640 acres)
According to yields known from later
texts, the harvest from this preserved field
surface would be about 220 tons of grain.

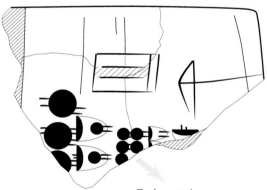

Grain notation
The preserved part of the
notation corresponds to an amount
of about 550 tons of emmer.

*Figure 30. An archaic account, probably the final account of a year's
harvest.*

some examples of that text type of low informational value. All of
the texts relate exclusively to cereal products discussed exten-
sively below in connection with the activities of Kushim (see the
next chapter, especially the calculations of grain measures contained in the tablet *MSVO* 3, 2, in fig. 38 below). Such texts
document the most rudimentary level of accounting operations in

early redistributive city-states, namely, the bookkeeping control of
the receipts and expenditures of storage facilities and stocks
belonging to the palace and temple households.

Text 29a is the most basic of this tablet category. It has just one
numerical notation, but possibly contained another sign in the broken corner referring to the type of the product recorded. Since the
numerical signs disclose that the bisexagesimal system was being
applied (chap. 6), the document will have dealt with cereals, so
that the lost sign was probably 𝅘 (NINDA), "grain ration." No
additional information about the origin or destination of the
quantity of grain products recorded on the tablet or about the
tablet's function can be extracted from the document.

Text 29b is somewhat more explicit. In its first column it has
an entry including the sign 𝅘 (NINDA), again designating cereal
rations, plus a second entry, this time with the sign ⬭▷ (DUG_a)
pertaining to beer rations. In the second column an individual is
named. Once more, we are informed neither about the function of
the tablet nor about the role of the mentioned person. The context
nonetheless suggests that the text records a distribution of rations,
with the person being either a receiving supervisor or else an
official responsible for the delivery.

The third text (29c) contains nine different entries, each
consisting of only one numerical notation and one sign denoting a
cereal product. Here as well, additional information relating to the
function of the tablet can only be inferred from its contextual
relationship to other, more informative tablets, to tablets that
directly refer to the information stored on the tablet in question, or
possibly even from an archaeological find producing archival
evidence. Although such tablets are not preserved, similarities in
the order of entries in this text with other tablets such as the
example from the Erlenmeyer collection yielding cereal calculations (fig. 38) may just the same be informative about its contents.

The most complex of these four simple transactions is
exemplified by text 29d. The obverse of the document, containing
four entries, resembles the preceding text. However, it also has a
(badly damaged) numerical notation along the edge as well as a
(more or less completely destroyed) summarizing entry on the
reverse. This summarizing entry demonstrates another characteristic of the archaic tablets. In most cases, such entries can be
identified as totals, with an accompanying sign summarizing an
economic category. The latter is also the case with the present
tablet. We are aware that the sign 𝅘 (NINDA) was used as a
comprehensive sign for the distribution of various kinds of cereal
rations, suggesting that this tablet probably represented an internal
administrative document from a distributing unit charged with the
control of issued rations, as was possibly also the case for the three
preceding texts. In the present case, however, the value of the

Figure 31. Archaic documents attesting to a continuous grain accounting over a period of eight years.

33

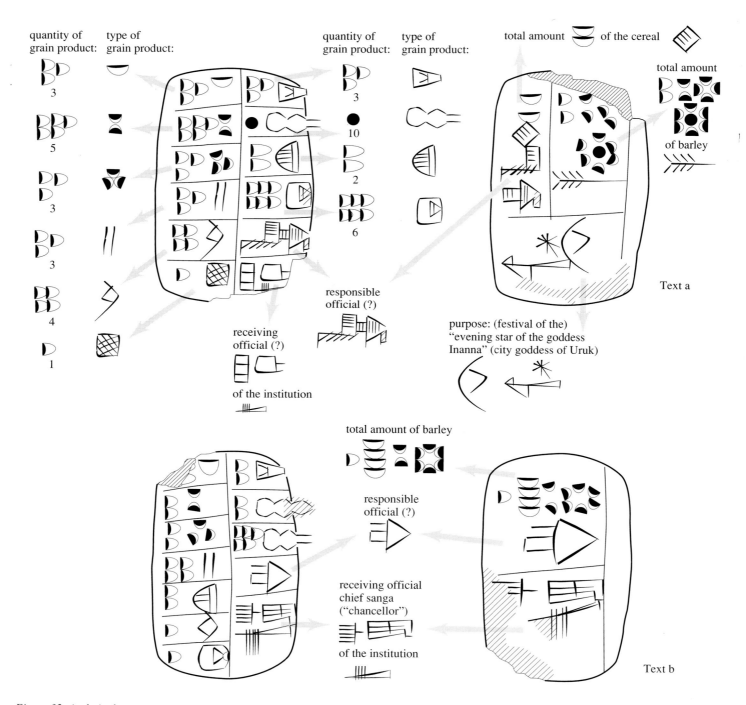

quantity of grain product:

type of grain product:

quantity of grain product:

type of grain product:

total amount of the cereal

total amount of barley

responsible official (?)

receiving official (?)

of the institution

purpose: (festival of the) "evening star of the goddess Inanna" (city goddess of Uruk)

Text a

total amount of barley

responsible official (?)

receiving official chief sanga ("chancellor")

of the institution

Text b

Figure 32. Archaic documents attesting to the calculation of "theoretical" values of grain use in the production of cereal products.

entry on the reverse is much higher than the total of the entries on the obverse. Although this phenomenon is not often seen, the number of its occurrences is still high enough to rule out an erroneous entry made by the scribe.

It should be kept in mind, however, that summarizing notations on archaic tablets are not identical with arithmetical summations, but rather reflect the actual accounting procedures of recording either accumulated or distributed goods. Because documents only inherited their true function in the context of their use, there was no reason to make explicit occurring divergences from the formal arithmetical sum by altering the layout. Apparently we have here just such a divergent case, although because of the poor preservation of the tablet it remains unclear how that total was achieved. It may be that the sum on the reverse represents the grand total of rations after each delivery was made five times, that is, that the entry on the tablet edge refers to the number of times the amount of each entry on the obverse was spent before the final amount was calculated on the reverse.

The four tablets in figure 29 reflect accounting procedures of a lower or middle level in the archaic administrating hierarchy. It is as a rule easier to detect the function of tablets relating to operations—transfers of large quantities of goods or the like—of higher administrative echelons. Such tablets were not necessarily closely connected with specific procedures and contain therefore often more complete information about these procedures than the records from lower administrative levels.

The fragment shown in figure 30 belongs to a text produced at a high organizational level. On the obverse we have a list of several field areas, of which only one entry is preserved. Apparently, it relates to various agricultural areas near the city of Uruk, where the text was found. The reverse of the text probably contained two different notations of cereals (one concerning barley, the other emmer) together with the sum of the two. Partially preserved is the entry pertaining to an amount of emmer. This notation records the largest amount of grain known from the entire proto-cuneiform text corpus. From the combination of the entries from tablet obverse and reverse, it may be suggested that the text to which the fragment belongs was either a compilation of seed-grain for registered fields, or a list of the harvested crop delivered to a central administration. To judge by the amount stated, the latter case seems more likely.

The similar tablets nos. 31a and 31b are also texts from a high administrational level (see fig. 31). Both texts, thought to derive from illicit excavations at Tell Uqair located in the vicinity of the ancient city of Kish, demonstrate the continuity of bookkeeping during the archaic period. The texts contain records of medium-sized quantities of grain—probably in connection with field designations—over a period of eight years, as can be seen from the sequential qualification of the entries with the signs ⟶, ⟶ and so forth for the first year, the second year, and so on. There is a close connection between these texts, which may be postulated not only by the fact that they relate to a period of eight years, but also by the fact that they display identical signatures and, insofar as the fragmentary state of the tablets permits, partially identical entries. However, the relationship between the two tablets is above all underscored by the identical grand totals of both texts (3 ▷ 2 ●, corresponding to about 16,000 liters of grain). Unfortunately, we do not as yet understand the administrative procedures and the nature of the relationship the texts refer to, so that the meaning of the respective entries and the reason for the accounting period of eight years, assuming this was no coincidence, must for the time being remain a matter of speculation. The reasonable interpretation that the cereal notations recorded seed and the fodder grain for registered fields does not seem very helpful for the solution of this problem.

The archaic texts, finally, also document early types of information processing which led to "theoretical" amounts in the form of future calculations, debit posts, standardized obligations, and similar nonempirical accounting procedures.

Simple examples illustrating such accounts are furnished by the tablets in figure 32. The obverse sides of both texts contain, as in the case of the text in figure 29, entries with quantities of cereal products rendered in notations using the bisexagesimal system. Contrary to normal procedure, neither text results in a total of these figures, but instead on the reverse of the tablets the calculated total of the grain needed for the production of the products registered on the obverse. Thus, both tablets contain the calculation of hypothetical values in the simplest form of technical bookkeeping. Unfortunately, since the implicit amounts of grain required for the production of the respective products are not in all cases known, we are unable to reconstruct the exact method by which the calculation was carried out. On the other hand, we will encounter in the next chapter more complicated computations of hypothetical grain use whose calculation methods could in fact be deciphered (see figs. 38–39).

P.D./R.E.

8. The Administrative Activities of Kushim

To date, the archaic texts of the Erlenmeyer collection present more than any other corpus a valuable opportunity to study the basic techniques of archaic accounting and related institutional and individual activities. In this respect, a number of texts bear a particular sign combination, read KU (𒆪) and ŠIM (𒁶), which together probably form the designation of a specific person, but which, on the other hand, may denote some sort of institution or economic unit. Indeed, since the archaic texts only mention individuals in their administrative function, never with their individual characteristics, it is often extremely difficult to decide whether such sign combinations denote an individual, his office or an entire institution. Nevertheless, there is reason to believe that this sign combination in fact specifies a person called KU ŠIM (𒆪𒁶). In the following this assumed individual will therefore be referred to as "Kushim," bearing in mind that during the archaic period written signs probably had no phonetic value as may be implied by the present transliteration into sign readings known from later periods. Regardless of whether an individual of this name really did exist, the economic functions remain the same.

The Responsibilities of Kushim

Kushim is mentioned in altogether 18 tablets, providing enough data to acquire a good idea about his responsibilities. On several occasions, he is specified as SANGA (𒊕). From later texts we know that the Sumerian official sanga was usually charged with the administration of a temple or a palace. We are probably dealing therefore with an administrative official, that is, with the SANGA Kushim (or possibly the SANGA of Kushim).

Kushim was apparently entrusted with the administration of a storage facility containing the basic ingredients for the production of beer. Several texts bearing his name deal with barley. Although this observation does not of itself allow of any further conclusion, since barley is a product with a wide variety of uses, almost all texts signed exclusively by Kushim concern two products—malt and cracked barley or barley groats—from which all the known beer types of the archaic period were brewed. In fact, since some of the texts directly record the production of beer, it seems very likely that the storage facility managed by Kushim was a redistributive unit, above all concerned with the basic ingredients of beer.

Kushim's importance is underlined not by his title as SANGA alone. It can also be deduced from the large measures of cereal products he managed. On one occasion, a tablet (*MSVO* 3, 29) documents an amount of about 135,000 liters of barley (fig. 33).

This tablet belongs to the category of administrative texts that only carry one important entry. Such texts usually specify the amount of a certain product and occasionally give additional information about its quality, origin, location or connected responsibilities, and the like. In the present case, the product is qualified by the sign ŠE (𒊺) as being barley. Next to that sign, another one records a period of 37 months. In addition to Kushim's signature, there are three more signs on the tablet, one of which was erased and later replaced by another. These three signs together probably state the function of the document in question. Unfortunately, we still do not understand the signs well enough to explain the definite type of transaction carried out by Kushim here. But the fact that the given amount of cereal is very large and that it is quoted in connection with an accounting period leads to the assumption that we are here confronted with a balanced account covering the entire period in which the granary was supplied with barley as a raw material for beer production.

The signs ⌵, ▷, •, ◗, and ◖• represent standardized cereal measurements, of which the smallest unit ⌵ probably represented ca. 4.8 liters, the following signs being natural multiples of this unit. The arithmetical relationship between each sign is the following:

▷	=	5	⌵,	or about 24 liters
•	=	6	▷,	or about 144 liters
●	=	10	•,	or about 1,440 liters
◗	=	3	●,	or about 4,320 liters
◖•	=	10	◗,	or about 43,200 liters

Similar or even identical signs occur in conjunction with the time notation, although in this context they have different values. In this case, ▷ stands for "1" and "•" for 10. Since these signs were inscribed inside the sign U$_4$ (◇), we know that they represent months, in this case administrative months, each consisting of 30 days. The signs add up to 37 months.

The quoted span of 37 months opens the door to more intriguing deliberations. Because the administrative texts operate with years of 12 months, the balanced account covers a period of exactly 3 years and one month. This phenomenon seems to offer the possibility that the later usage of a three-year intercalation cycle to adjust the lunar to the solar calendar was already employed during the archaic period.

The text also suggests that during this period certain tendencies toward exaggerated bureaucracy were in place. The amount of roughly 135,000 liters is in fact recorded to an exactness of a measure of 5 liters. This painstaking accuracy stands in complete

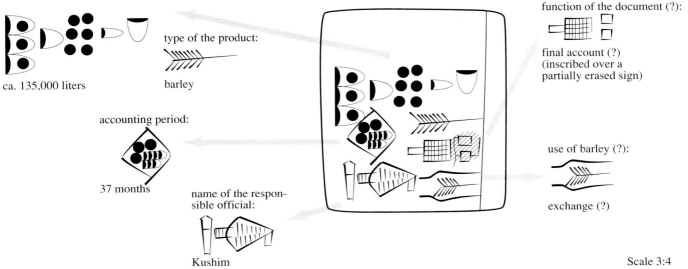

quantity of the product:

ca. 135,000 liters

type of the product:

barley

accounting period:

37 months

name of the responsible official:

Kushim

function of the document (?):

final account (?)
(inscribed over a
partially erased sign)

use of barley (?):

exchange (?)

Scale 3:4

Figure 33. The documentation of economic products.

contradiction with the numerous arithmetical errors that can be found in many texts (see below the discussion of the tablets *MSVO* 3, 55 and 11, with figs. 35 and 39).

The Basic Operation in Archaic Bookkeeping: Summations
The barley controlled by Kushim left his granary in part unprocessed. Such a transaction is testified by the text *MSVO* 3, 64 (fig. 34). The text gives a good example of the basic arithmetical operation in archaic bookkeeping, which consists of simple additions of a number of equal entries. The obverse of the tablet has 4 entries, each respectively recording a specific amount of grain using the ŠE system discussed above. Each entry also quotes the title of an official. Three of these officials are well known to us from a school text, the so-called professions list (see chap. 14), and from various other administrative texts. The reverse side of the tablet states the usual sum of the entries, again in connection with the sign ŠE ($\gg$) for barley. It is also accompanied by the sign BA ( ), which in later texts was used to specify a certain type of distribution. There are many instances in the archaic texts in which this sign had the same meaning. The tablet thus records the allocation of barley to the officials quoted on the obverse. The purpose of the allocations is probably more closely described by the sign , the meaning of which, however, is still unknown.

Photo of the tablet in figure 33.

37

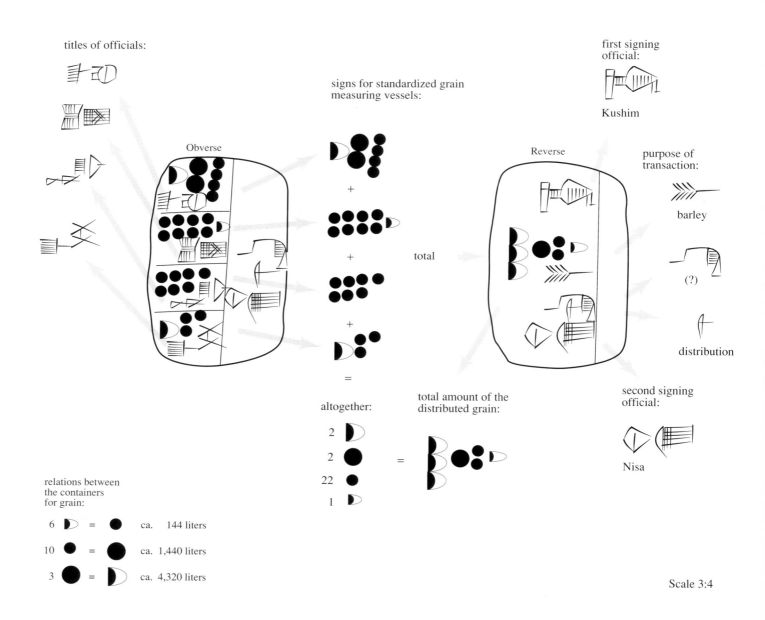

titles of officials:

signs for standardized grain measuring vessels:

first signing official:

Kushim

Obverse

+

+

total

+

=

Reverse

purpose of transaction:

barley

(?)

distribution

altogether:

2

2

22

1

total amount of the distributed grain:

=

second signing official:

Nisa

relations between the containers for grain:

6 = ca. 144 liters

10 = ca. 1,440 liters

3 = ca. 4,320 liters

Scale 3:4

Figure 34. Barley disbursements to four high-ranking officials.

38

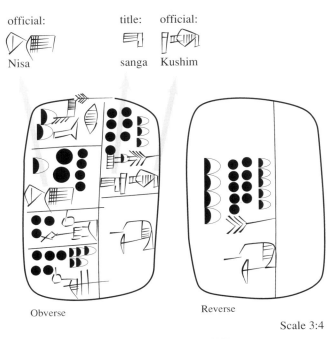

official: title: official:

Nisa   sanga   Kushim

Obverse   Reverse

Scale 3:4

Figure 35. Barley for the officials Kushim and Nisa.

The procedure of addition is simple. In summing up the signs in the entries on the obverse side, we have the following results:

   2 units of the size   ▷

+ 2 units of the size   ●

+ 22 units of the size   •

+ 1 unit of the size   ▷

Bearing in mind the relationship between these units noted above, the sum on the reverse amounts to following notation:

   3 units of the size   ▷

+ 1 unit of the size   ●

+ 2 units of the size   •

+ 1 unit of the size   ▷

In this text, Kushim's signature is accompanied by that of another official, Nisa, represented by the sign combination NI SA (◁ ▤). His name is also well known from a number of texts of the Erlenmeyer collection; he in fact frequently occurs as a co-signatory in documents concerning barley allocations.

A very similar text is to be found on the tablet *MSVO* 3, 55 (fig. 35). In this unsigned text, Kushim and Nisa, the signatories of the previous text, are, among others, qualified as the receivers of barley allocations. This text is incidentally one of those that designate Kushim a SANGA (▤). Moreover, it contains one of the earlier mentioned arithmetical errors: the sum on the reverse disregarded the three ▷ of the last entry on the obverse which the scribe had apparently overlooked.

Accounts of Barley Groats and Malt

With tablets *MSVO* 3, 52 and 51 (figs. 36–37), we return to Kushim's proper field of accountability. These documents, both bearing his signature, state the amounts of the mentioned raw materials, malt and barley groats, needed in beer production.

The given amount of malt quoted in the first of the documents is the largest known for this product in an archaic text. Moreover, the numerical sign ◕ which was used to denote that quantity is to date only known from this text. As to the nature of the documents, they are probably both accounts about allocations (⊢) in which only the calculated sums of the distributed quantities are given.

There were apparently two methods employed to record the different products. In the first case, they could be specified by the applied numerical system. On the other hand, ideographic signs could be added to give a simple specification of the product in

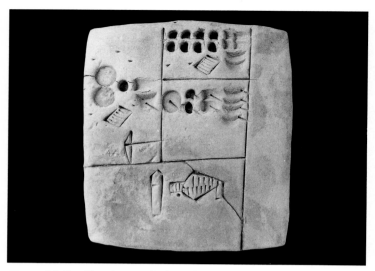

Figure 36. Bookkeeping on the ingredients needed to brew beer, barley groats, and malt.

Photo of the tablet in figure 37.

grand total of barley groats and malt, noted with numerical signs from both systems

barley groats of a specific type, qualified with the sign 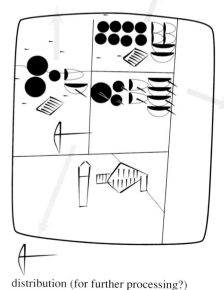 as well as with particular numerical signs: ●⌐D-◡

malt, qualified with particular numerical signs: ◓●↩◡

distribution (for further processing?)

Scale 3:4

question. The specification of barley groats and malt is a typical example of the former method. Both categories are connected to a specific numerical system, each exclusively denoting either of the goods. Furthermore, the category "barley groats" could be more specifically qualified by the sign ◈, although the exact meaning of this sign is still unknown. This constitutes an example of the second method of specifying a product.

Both numerical sign systems applied for the depiction of quantities of barley groats and malt are graphic derivations from the basic system use to specify cereal measures. In the case of barley groats, the signs were marked with slight dots of the stylus. The basic original signs ◡, ▷, ●, and ● were thus transformed to ◡̇, ▷̇, ●̇, and ●̇. In the case of malt, the same signs were marked with an oblique dash (◡̷, ▷̷, ●, and ●). The relationship between the stated amounts expressed by the differing signs remained, however, identical, thus suggesting that the applied numerical sign systems employed the same capacity measures used by the basic numerical sign system for cereals as a whole.

The two texts differ in complexity. The first one (fig. 36) contains one entry concerning barley groats and another concerning malt. Both entries were added together to form a total, despite the differing graphic forms of the numerical signs. As this and comparable texts reveal, the notation for the total included signs from both numerical sign systems. These summations also speak for the homogeneity of the capacity measures represented by corresponding signs.

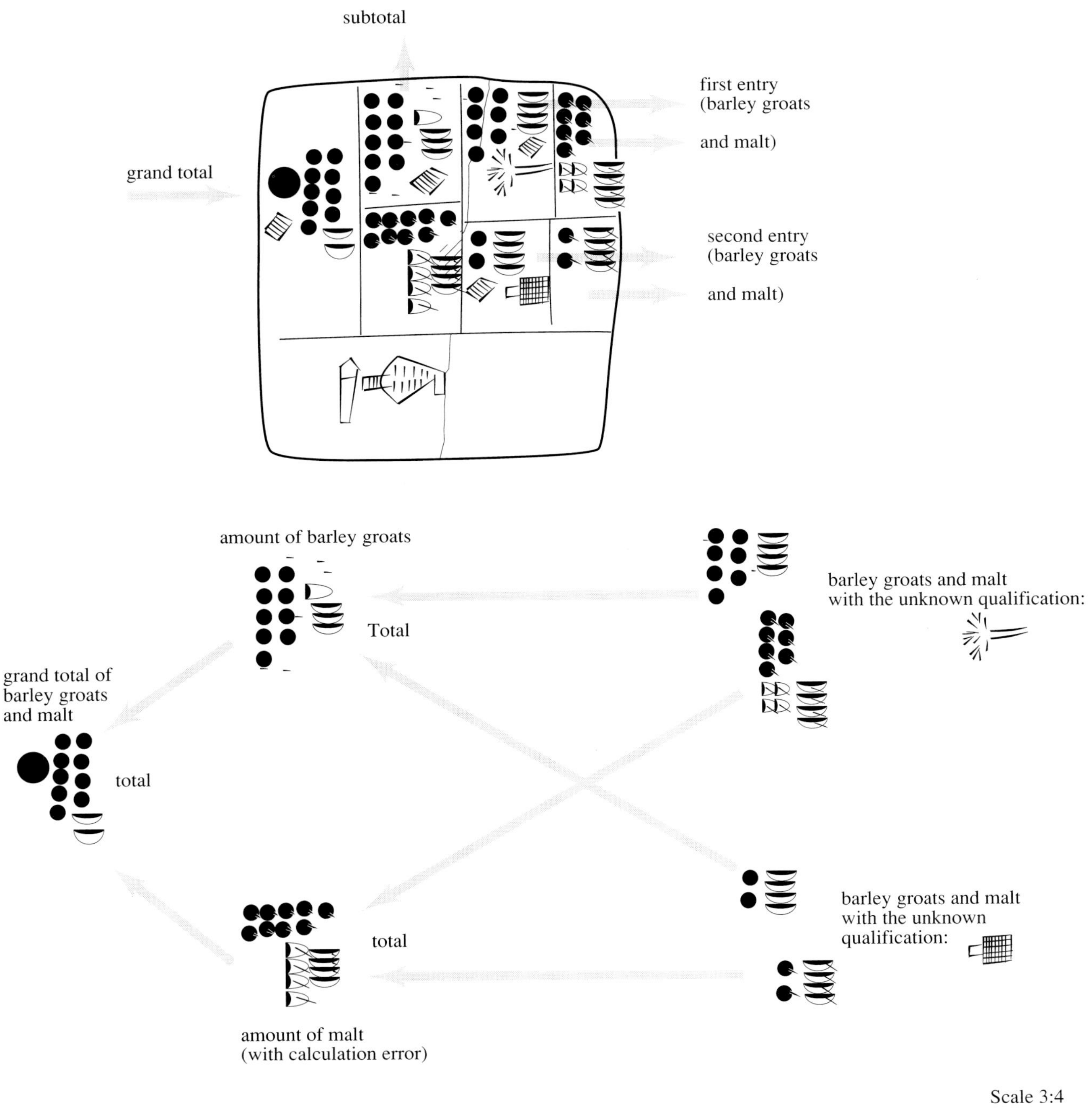

subtotal

first entry
(barley groats

and malt)

grand total

second entry
(barley groats

and malt)

amount of barley groats

barley groats and malt
with the unknown qualification:

Total

grand total of
barley groats
and malt

total

total

barley groats and malt
with the unknown
qualification:

amount of malt
(with calculation error)

Scale 3:4

Figure 37. Bookkeeping on the ingredients needed to brew beer, barley groats, and malt.

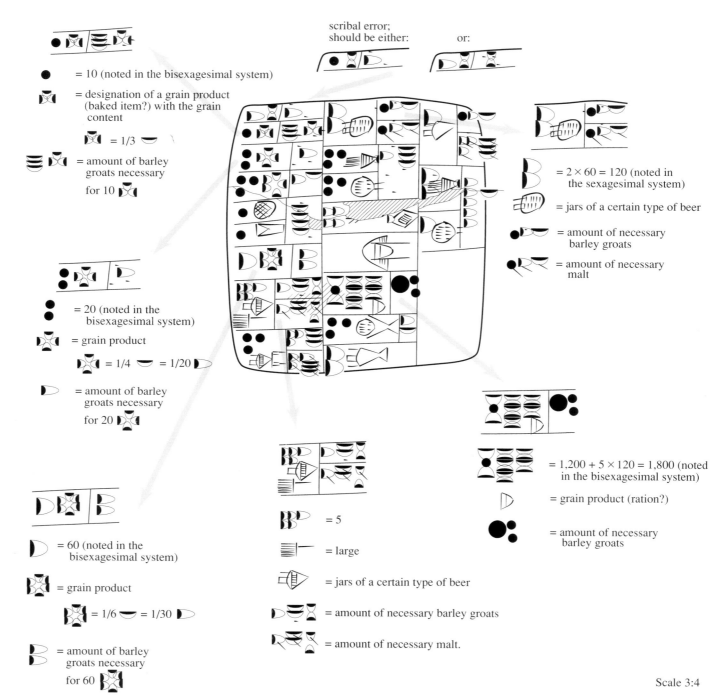

Figure 38. Calculation of the amounts of the ingredients needed in the production of dry cereal products and beer.

The following labels appear around the central figure:

scribal error; should be either: or:

• = 10 (noted in the bisexagesimal system)

= designation of a grain product (baked item?) with the grain content

= 1/3

= amount of barley groats necessary for 10

• = 20 (noted in the bisexagesimal system)

= grain product

= 1/4 = 1/20

= amount of barley groats necessary for 20

= 60 (noted in the bisexagesimal system)

= grain product

= 1/6 = 1/30

= amount of barley groats necessary for 60

= 5

= large

= jars of a certain type of beer

= amount of necessary barley groats

= amount of necessary malt.

= 2 × 60 = 120 (noted in the sexagesimal system)

= jars of a certain type of beer

= amount of necessary barley groats

= amount of necessary malt

= 1,200 + 5 × 120 = 1,800 (noted in the bisexagesimal system)

= grain product (ration?)

= amount of necessary barley groats

In the second text (fig. 37), the quantities for both products are further differentiated according to an additional criterion. In this case, the respective entries are followed by the signs NAGA (![sign]) and DUB (![sign]), the meanings of which are, however, not understood. The summations are formed in two consecutive steps. In the first step, the amounts of barley groats and malt are added together separately, then the grand total of all entries was calculated.

In this text as well, the scribe made a mistake in his totals. In adding both quantities of malt, he forgot to include the four units ![sign] in the subtotal.

Calculations in the Production of Beer and Other Cereal Products
One of the most important texts of the Erlenmeyer collection (*MSVO* 3, 2, fig. 38) discloses exceptional information about the use of the cereal products accounted for by Kushim. A scribe, probably a staff member of Kushim's office, had noted down his calculations pertaining to the exact ingredients required for nine different cereal products and eight different kinds of beer in a tabular compilation. Some of the products are noted with the respective amounts of cereals contained in them. These ingredients are denoted by the signs ![sign], ![sign], ![sign], ![sign], and ![sign]. Others are denoted by more specific ideograms such as ![sign] and ![sign]. In this text, five different numerical systems were used (see chap. 6), the bisexagesimal system for the cereal products, the sexagesimal system for the beer containers, and three different systems for the measures of cereals. One of the latter was used for the specification of the quantities of the cereal ingredients contained in the products; the other two are those already discussed in connection with barley groats and malt. Not only the formal aspects of the compilation but also the fact that it is unsigned reveals that the text represents some sort of supplementary annotation to the proper administrative documents. Such documents have often been regarded as school texts, although the available documents from the administrative archive of Kushim now clearly testify that such calculations were part of regular administrative practice.

Texts containing calculations of the cereal ingredients needed for certain products belong to the most complicated arithmetical texts of the archaic period. To date, only a very few texts have been found in which such calculations were systematically carried out for various cereal products, for types of beer and so on. We know of only one text (now in the Iraq Museum, Baghdad) with features comparable to those of text *MSVO* 3, 2. One of the remarkable things about these texts is that they inform us directly about the ingredients of different cereal products. In fact, it was the study of such texts that provided the basic proofs for the decipherment of the cereal measures used in the present publication. Their special value is also to be seen in the light they shed on the developmental stage of arithmetical techniques in the period immediately after the invention of writing.

The structure of the calculations is demonstrated by the following three examples taken from the text in question.

1. The fourth line in the first column records an amount of barley groats needed for the production of 30 units of the final cereal product (represented by the triple repetition of the sign ● , the sign normally used for "10"). The final product is represented by the numerical sign ![sign]. The total amount of barley groats needed, which is represented by the sign combination ![sign], is obtained when ![sign] is multiplied by 30.
2. The seventh line of the first column informs us about how much barley groats and malt (in this case equal amounts of both products) was needed for the production of five jars with a type of beer, represented by the signs ![sign] ![sign]. This line, therefore, documents the composition of this type of beer.
3. In the fifth line of the second column, the equivalent amount of barley for 1800 daily cereal rations (sign ![sign]) was calculated. The use of the sign ![sign] points therefore to the size of such rations (approximately 0.8 liter). The figure 1800 is rendered in the bisexagesimal system, containing the sign ![sign] for 1200 and ![sign] for 120, which was used exclusively to quantify cereal products.

As in many other cases the present text contains an error. For a unit of the cereal product ![sign] the scribe had written in the first text line sign ![sign], corresponding to ten times the necessary amount of the ingredient barley groats. Although this calculation is a fairly easy one, and the remaining, more complicated calculations seem to be otherwise correct, we must assume that the detected error is merely due to a mental lapse on the part of the scribe. For the correct reading, one has to replace the sign for "one" (![sign]) with the sign denoting "ten" (●).

Beer Production and Accounts of Cereal Ingredients
Finally, the documents from the administration of the official Kushim provide a rare example of a direct accounting connection between different texts. During the archaic period, running accounts apparently already existed. However, the texts are so fragmentary that the continuity of such accounts can only very rarely be traced. It should therefore be viewed as an unusual coincidence that two texts from the Erlenmeyer collection refer at two different stages to one and the same transaction, thereby clearly documenting the continuity of archaic bookkeeping as a whole.

Text *MSVO* 3, 6 (fig. 39b) documents the production of beer for four administration officials, among them a person with the

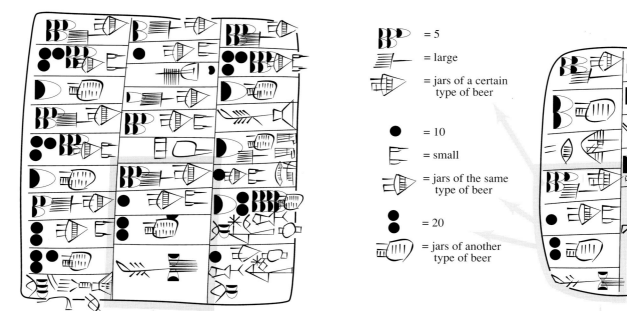

= 5

= large

= jars of a certain
type of beer

= 10

= small

= jars of the same
type of beer

= 20

= jars of another
type of beer

Text a obverse

entries concerning the same beer distribution to the same person called:

signing
official

grand total of
the necessary
barley groats

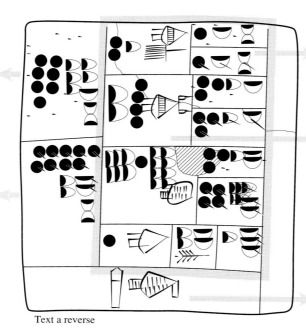

calculated amounts of
barley groats and malt for
each type of beer entered
in separate cases

separate summations of
the number of jars of the
different types of beer entered
on the obverse

grand total of
the necessary
malt

signature of the official
in charge of beer production:

Text a reverse

Scale 3:4

Figure 39. Account on barley groats and malt used in beer production.

Photos of the texts a–b in figure 39 (with reverse of text b).

denotation ⟶ 𝍢 as well as the "head of the SANGA's," the 𝍢 𝍢 𝍢. The last four cases of the first column state, for example, that the person called ⟶ 𝍢 received five large (𝍢) and ten small (𝍢) jars containing a special type of beer (𝍢) as well as 20 jars containing another type of beer (𝍢). The difficult reverse of the tablet probably contains references connected to the labor time which various named brewers required for the production of the beer.

Text *MSVO* 3, 11 (fig. 39a) shows how calculations similar to those in text *MSVO* 3, 2 were dealt with in order to calculate the amounts of necessary cereals for the present and other allocations of beer. The obverse makes reference to allocations partly to different individuals and partly destined for use at various occasions during a period of several days, perhaps some sort of religious festival. Among the entries are to be found references to deliveries for the person ⟶ 𝍢 as well as for the "chief SANGA" mentioned in text *MSVO* 3, 6.

On the reverse of the tablet, the sum of the jars is given for each beer type and then the amount of barley and malt requisite to their respective production was recorded. These were calculated in the same manner as in text *MSVO* 3, 2 (see fig. 38). The text is again signed by Kushim.

This last text as well contains some calculation errors. In his totals, the scribe forgot to include the five large jars. Furthermore, the final amount of barley groats calculated for the beer jars of the type 𝍢 is too low, the amount of malt too high. This is rather surprising, since this beer type is constituted of equal amounts of barley groats and malt. The error should have been noticed immediately, since the recorded amounts are not the same.

P.D./R.E.

9. The Development of Bookkeeping in the Third Millennium B.C.

As writing continued to evolve, language-related specifications were added to the entries of administrative documents to clarify their function and their relationships; such information was, as a rule, provided by tablet format in the archaic periods of writing. This welcome assistance is extremely useful for the understanding of documents that continued to be compiled in a very formalized manner. Whereas during the archaic age the addition of further information concerning product quantities was restricted to placing a numerical sign at a predetermined place within the text format, such information was incorporated into grammatically structured sentences in later Old Sumerian texts from pre-Sargonic Lagash, as exemplified by the tablet in figure 40.

This text apparently had the same bookkeeping function in the production of cereal products as the two much older archaic texts discussed at the end of chapter 7 (fig. 32). Each of the first four cases of the tablet contains an entry on a specific amount of bread, with further specification of its cereal ingredients. Depending on whether the numbers related to the loaves of bread or to their cereal ingredients, different numerical signs were used. The number of bread loaves is rendered in archaic signs, whereas the cereal amounts were written with the cuneiform script. The relationship between these entries was, however, expressed not only by this formal difference, but also in language. Language-based information did not, however, of its own guarantee that the text was commonly understandable—a phenomenon to which most will testify who have been confronted with modern accounting ledgers—since the ancient books complied with a specific subject-related terminology.

The second entry of the tablet may, for example, be read in the following manner: "40 ninda ka gu$_7$ ba.an.né 50 du$_8$." The term "ba.an.né" is a phonetic notation of the grammatical locative-terminative element "-e" attached to the cereal measure "bán." We know this to be true since in a similar text the word was represented by the ideogram bán (⍟ ; in Old Sumerian metrology this measure, equal to six sìla, seems to have corresponded to ca. 10 liters). The sign du$_8$ is, due to context, to conventional understanding of the Sumerian word "ninda," and to the second millennium B.C. correspondence du$_8$ = Akkadian epû, provisionally translated "baked." With some reservation one would therefore translate the sentence: "40 kagu-breads baked at the rate of 50 per bán."

We understand the meaning of this formulation mainly because other texts contain more complete information about the subject referred to here in formulated language. In one such text, for example, we find the formulation "ninda ba.an.né 30 du$_8$ 90 zì.bi 3(bán).am$_6$," which may be translated "breads: for each bán 30 (loaves) are baked(?), 90 (loaves). The flour involved: 3 bán." The

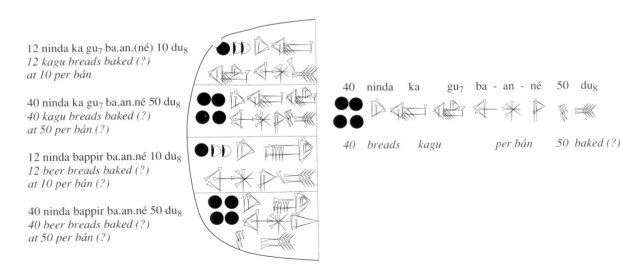

12 ninda ka gu$_7$ ba.an.(né) 10 du$_8$
12 kagu breads baked (?)
at 10 per bán

40 ninda ka gu$_7$ ba.an.né 50 du$_8$
40 kagu breads baked (?)
at 50 per bán (?)

12 ninda bappir ba.an.né 10 du$_8$
12 beer breads baked (?)
at 10 per bán (?)

40 ninda bappir ba.an.né 50 du$_8$
40 beer breads baked (?)
at 50 per bán (?)

40	ninda	ka	gu$_7$	ba - an - né	50	du$_8$
40	*breads*	*kagu*		*per bán*	*50*	*baked (?)*

Figure 40. Old Sumerian text demonstrating the early use of grammatical forms in administrative documents.

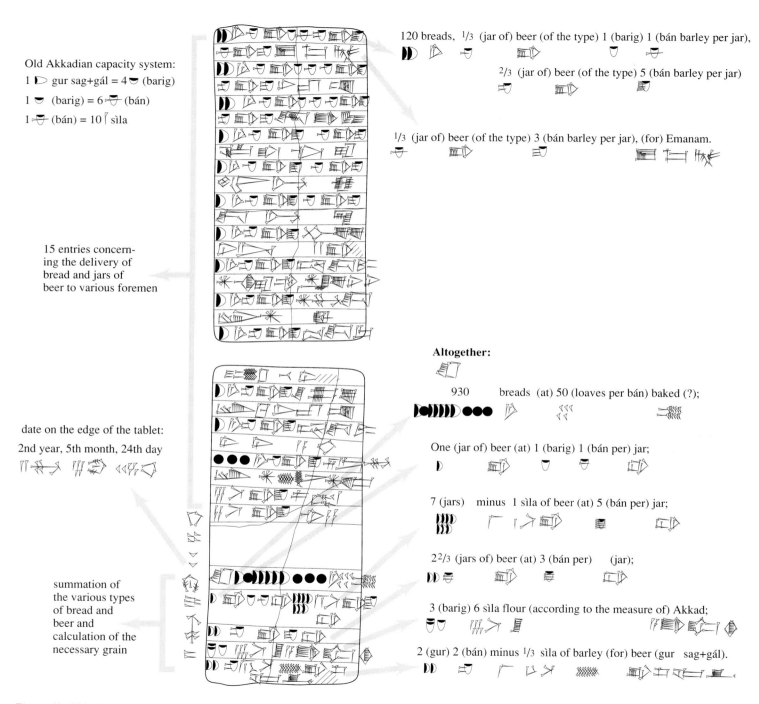

Old Akkadian capacity system:
1 ⬭ gur sag+gál = 4 ⬬ (barig)
1 ⬬ (barig) = 6 ⬱ (bán)
1 ⬱ (bán) = 10 ⌐ sìla

15 entries concerning the delivery of bread and jars of beer to various foremen

date on the edge of the tablet:
2nd year, 5th month, 24th day

summation of the various types of bread and beer and calculation of the necessary grain

120 breads, 1/3 (jar of) beer (of the type) 1 (barig) 1 (bán barley per jar),

2/3 (jar of) beer (of the type) 5 (bán barley per jar)

1/3 (jar of) beer (of the type) 3 (bán barley per jar), (for) Emanam.

Altogether:

930 breads (at) 50 (loaves per bán) baked (?);

One (jar of) beer (at) 1 (barig) 1 (bán per) jar;

7 (jars) minus 1 sìla of beer (at) 5 (bán per) jar;

2 2/3 (jars of) beer (at) 3 (bán per) (jar);

3 (barig) 6 sìla flour (according to the measure of) Akkad;

2 (gur) 2 (bán) minus 1/3 sìla of barley (for) beer (gur sag+gál).

Figure 41. Old Akkadian example for a developed form of theoretical calculations of grain quantities required in bread and beer production.

arithmetically verifiable notations lead to the following meaning of the formulation: from one bán of flour, 30 loaves of bread of the category "ba.an.né 30 du₈" can be baked. Hence 3 bán of flour are needed for 90 loaves of bread.

A document from the final phase of the Old Akkadian period (approx. 2250 B.C.) with very similar contents is shown in figure 41. The text represents a compilation of the delivery of bread and beer rations, stating the amounts of cereals necessary for their production.

The text begins with a list of 15 individuals, probably the receivers of the recorded amounts of bread (ninda, sign ⟁) and jars of beer (kaš, sign ⟐). The quality of the beer is specified through the addition to the sign kaš, denoting the jar, of a notation stating the amount of grain required in brewing one jar of the given beer. As usual for this type of text, the list begins with entries concerning the individuals receiving larger rations; notations concerning those receiving smaller amounts follow afterwards. At the end of the account, the breads and the beer jars are totaled according to type. Finally, the grand total of the flour and barley used was recorded. A check of the calculation reveals that the amount of flour corresponds exactly to the flour used for the production of the bread, the amount of barley is virtually identical with the amount used for the different beer products (a small difference is probably the result of a scribal error). On the left edge of the tablet, the text was dated exactly to the day, an accounting rule attested from this period on.

Perhaps the most important accounting operation introduced during the third millennium B.C. was the balancing of theoretical debit postings with real production. The previous examples have shown that both bookkeeping procedures can be traced back to the archaic period, but just when debits and credits began to be compared systematically is not known. Some features seem to indicate that these or similar techniques were already in use during the archaic age, as probably demonstrated by the reverse of the texts *MSVO* 3, 67, and 75 (see also *Frühe Schrift*, catalogue nos. 4.67 and 4.75). The earliest evidence for the existence of such techniques originates from the Old Sumerian period.

The three tablets shown in figure 42 date from this period. All three offer evidence for this technique and at the same time are among the earliest examples for a series of postings in consecutive years. The first tablet (*RTC* 57, fig. 42a) dates to the third year of the "city ruler" (énsi) Enentarzi of Lagash and specifies two amounts of grain (barley and white emmer) of an official called Lugal-pirigtur. The following formulation "the barley is the property of the ensi of Lagash" states that the cereals came from the royal granaries, or were harvested on royal fields, requiring later reimbursement. The second tablet (fig. 42b) recorded that Lugal-

pirigtur delivered certain amounts of both cereals to the royal household in the following year. The amounts are approximately the same as the ones given to him the year before. Incidentally, we also are told that Lugal-pirigtur was the sanga ("administrator") of the "white temple." The third tablet (fig. 42c), finally, gives the differences between the disbursed and reimbursed amounts of grain. Since the sanga returned less than was handed out to him, the differences were booked as LÁ+A, meaning "deficits," and were posted to his debit account. Later texts disclose that such deficits were carried over to the following year and that they were liable to later reimbursement.

In the Ur III period, the accounting of expected and real performances reached its most developed form. The administrative texts of this period document a continuous calculation of all labor performance together with theoretical credits and duties. Accounts relating to the balancing of expected and real labor performances were drawn up at regular intervals on the foremen of the state-controlled labor force (see fig. 43). The accounting period usually covered a 12-month-year, each month being 30 days long. As a rule, the accounting balances of the foremen were "overdrawn," since it seems the expected performances were fixed as the maximum of what a foreman could reasonably demand of his workers. Such deficits were noted with the sign combination LÁ+NI in the Ur III period, without doubt the same bookkeeping terminus as the Old Sumerian expression LÁ+A already seen in connection with the preceding text. Occasionally, a "surplus" (diri) was produced. In this case as well, the credit balance was carried over and posted into the account of the following period, so that each balancing period was part of a continuous bookkeeping file. Accounting procedure, of course, required that an eventual surplus be posted into the credits section, a deficit into the debits section of the following account.

A precondition for the feasibility of such global balancing of all expected and real performances was the standardization and calculability of the expected performances, as well as a means of comparing all performances. Because the economy of the Ur III period was still based predominantly on natural payment and exchange, an innovation was required for the realization of such control through a statewide recognized system of accounting. The introduction of unifying norms of performance and of a system of value equivalence was in fact the consequence by which the normed natural performances became comparable to each other.

Although we are often only able to trace the performance standards and value equivalences through calculation of account entries, there can be no doubt of the existence of explicitly formulated norms which were strictly adhered to. They can be reconstructed from conversions of labor performances and pro-

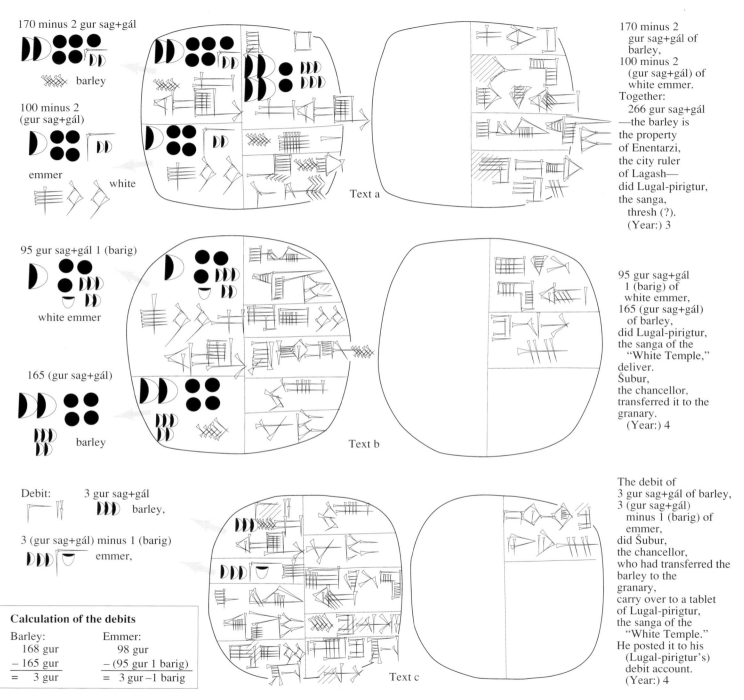

170 minus 2 gur sag+gál

barley

100 minus 2
(gur sag+gál)

emmer   white

Text a

170 minus 2
gur sag+gál of
barley,
100 minus 2
(gur sag+gál) of
white emmer.
Together:
266 gur sag+gál
—the barley is
the property
of Enentarzi,
the city ruler
of Lagash—
did Lugal-pirigtur,
the sanga,
thresh (?).
(Year:) 3

95 gur sag+gál 1 (barig)

white emmer

165 (gur sag+gál)

barley

Text b

95 gur sag+gál
1 (barig) of
white emmer,
165 (gur sag+gál)
of barley,
did Lugal-pirigtur,
the sanga of the
"White Temple,"
deliver.
Šubur,
the chancellor,
transferred it to the
granary.
(Year:) 4

Debit: 3 gur sag+gál
barley,

3 (gur sag+gál) minus 1 (barig)
emmer,

Calculation of the debits

Barley:	Emmer:
168 gur	98 gur
− 165 gur	− (95 gur 1 barig)
= 3 gur	= 3 gur −1 barig

Text c

The debit of
3 gur sag+gál of barley,
3 (gur sag+gál)
minus 1 (barig) of
emmer,
did Šubur,
the chancellor,
who had transferred the
barley to the
granary,
carry over to a tablet
of Lugal-pirigtur,
the sanga of the
"White Temple."
He posted it to his
(Lugal-pirigtur's)
debit account.
(Year:) 4

Figure 42. Old Sumerian examples testifying to continuous bookkeeping.

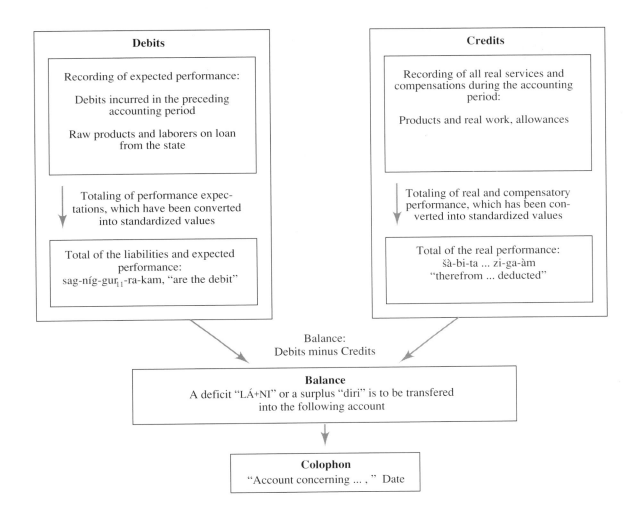

Debits	**Credits**
Recording of expected performance: Debits incurred in the preceding accounting period Raw products and laborers on loan from the state	Recording of all real services and compensations during the accounting period: Products and real work, allowances
↓ Totaling of performance expectations, which have been converted into standardized values	↓ Totaling of real and compensatory performance, which has been converted into standardized values
Total of the liabilities and expected performance: sag-níg-gur₁₁-ra-kam, "are the debit"	Total of the real performance: šà-bi-ta ... zi-ga-àm "therefrom ... deducted"

Balance:
Debits minus Credits

Balance
A deficit "LÁ+NI" or a surplus "diri" is to be transferred
into the following account

Colophon
"Account concerning ... , " Date

Figure 43. Flow chart revealing the structure of the accounts concerning foremen of labor gangs in the Ur III period.

ducts into equivalent products specific to the respective sector of the economic organization. Depending on the economic sector, the means of comparison or the measure of standardized norms and duties could be silver, barley, fish, or "laborer-days," that is, the product of the number of workers multiplied by the number of days they worked. The reconstruction of the conversions established the fact that they were based on specified conversion factors for different labor performances and produced goods.

An example of the fully developed bookkeeping of the Ur III period is given by the tablet in figure 44. It contains the annual balance of a foreman to whom a group of 37 female workers was assigned. It is dated to the fourth regnal year of Šu-Sin. The laborers were primarily occupied with the milling of grain, but could be charged with other jobs. According to the normal method of balancing, the account can be divided into three sections, the "debits," the "credits," and the "balance" (see fig. 45).

Figure 44. Neo-Sumerian account concerning the labor performance of female workers in a mill.

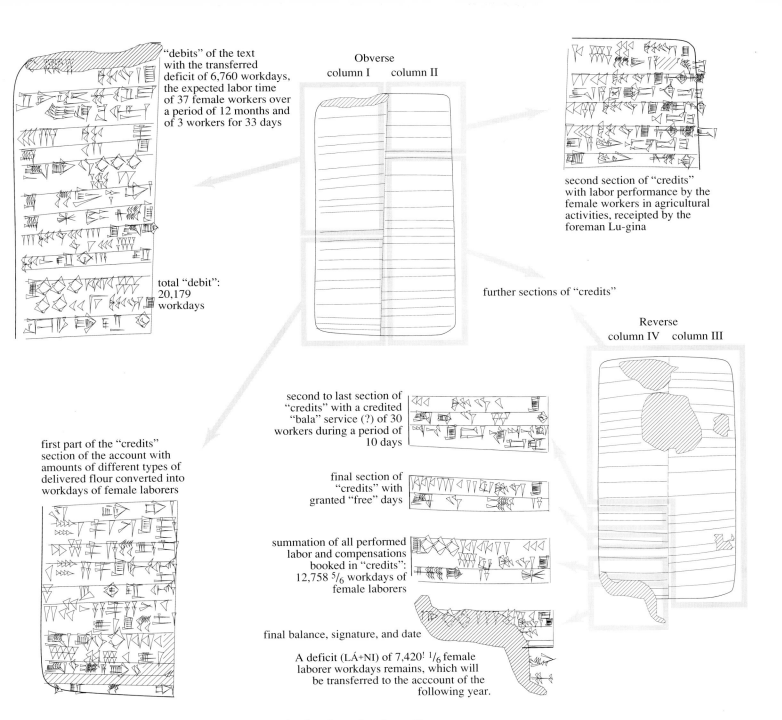

"debits" of the text with the transferred deficit of 6,760 workdays, the expected labor time of 37 female workers over a period of 12 months and of 3 workers for 33 days

total "debit": 20,179 workdays

Obverse
column I   column II

second section of "credits" with labor performance by the female workers in agricultural activities, receipted by the foreman Lu-gina

further sections of "credits"

Reverse
column IV   column III

first part of the "credits" section of the account with amounts of different types of delivered flour converted into workdays of female laborers

second to last section of "credits" with a credited "bala" service (?) of 30 workers during a period of 10 days

final section of "credits" with granted "free" days

summation of all performed labor and compensations booked in "credits": 12,758 $^5/_6$ workdays of female laborers

final balance, signature, and date

A deficit (LÁ+NI) of 7,420$^!$ $^1/_6$ female laborer workdays remains, which will be transferred to the acccount of the following year.

Figure 45. Structure of a neo-Sumerian account concerning female workers in a mill.

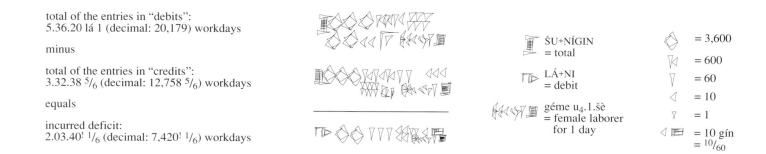

total of the entries in "debits":
5.36.20 lá 1 (decimal: 20,179) workdays

minus

total of the entries in "credits":
3.32.38 $^5/_6$ (decimal: 12,758 $^5/_6$) workdays

equals

incurred deficit:
2.03.40! $^1/_6$ (decimal: 7,420! $^1/_6$) workdays

ŠU+NÍGIN = total	◇	= 3,600
	⋈	= 600
LÁ+NI = debit	V	= 60
	◁	= 10
géme u₄.1.šè = female laborer for 1 day	▽	= 1
	◁ ▦	= 10 gín = $^{10}/_{60}$

Figure 46. Balancing procedure in the text illustrated in figure 44.

Under the "debits," the deficit carried over from the previous year is given, in this case a debit of 6,760 "female laborer days." The expected performance of 37 female laborers over a period of 12 months of 30 days each follows, amounting to 13,320 female laborer days. Finally, the performance of three additional female laborers over a period of 33 days is included, resulting in 99 female laborer days. These three postings add up to the total annual debit of 20,179 female laborer days.

The section concerning the "credits" begins with the amounts of flour produced by the milling team converted into female laborer days. Work performances carried out in agricultural enterprises by the laborers under another foreman called Lu-gina follow, as well as several other jobs, among which is noted the so-called bala service, a labor duty regularly occurring in such balances, whose exact meaning remains unclear. This section ends with the calculation of so-called free days, also booked as labor performance. The foreman is usually compensated with one free day in six work days for every female worker. The sum of these performances, here converted into female laborer days, and the compensatory "free days," add up to 12,758 $^5/_6$ days in total.

The final "balance" therefore states an increased deficit of 7,420 $^1/_6$ female laborer days (see fig. 46), which of course would then be booked with the debits of the following year. From other texts we know what drastic consequences such continuous control of deficits meant for the foreman and his household. Apparently, the debts had to be settled at all costs. The death of a foreman in debt resulted in the confiscation of his possessions as compensation for the state. One consequence of such a confiscation was that the remaining members of the household could be transferred into the royal labor force and required to perform the work formerly supervised by the deceased foreman.

Such were the working conditions of the foremen to which the administrative texts referred. So-called inspection texts regularly report on large numbers of escaped laborers. In view of the total control the laborers were subjected to, it is not difficult to imagine why they tried to flee.

P.D./R.E.

10. Surveying and Administrating Fields

Irrigated land has always constituted an important part of the restricted natural resources of Mesopotamia. Among the economic documents from all periods, we encounter a large number of texts that deal with the measurement and central administration of arable land. In order to establish the size of a field surface, two different standards were employed, the linear measure based on ninda, a metrological unit approximately equivalent to 6 meters, and the surface measure šar (garden), the equivalent of one square ninda. Whereas the units of length were organized in the sexagesimal number system, surface or field measurements formed part of an extremely irregular system probably tied to an ancient tradition of sowing and harvest units which only at a later stage was connected with the surface unit šar. The surveying of fields was based exclusively on length measurements, and from the obtained measurements the areas of the mostly quadrangular, though often irregularly shaped fields were calculated. This was usually done by multiplying the averages of opposite sides. From the viewpoint of modern geometry, this procedure results only in approximate values because it does not take into account the precise geometrical form of a field. For the Mesopotamian scribe, however, this procedure constituted the area concept, thus forming the basis of a peculiar, early form of geometry.

Archaic Field Accounts

Calculations of areas from length measurements are already attested by documents from the archaic period (see figs. 47–49). The best-preserved of these tablets, *MSVO* 1, no. 2 (figs. 47a and 48a), was discovered in an administrative building at a mound in northern Mesopotamia with the modern toponym Jemdet Nasr. It contains entries relating to length measurements and the areas of five fields. Each of the listed fields is accompanied by a particular sign combination. Three of the combinations are well known from other texts to represent the titles of high-ranking officials. Especially noteworthy is the combination ⸗ ▷, also attested in tablets from the Erlenmeyer collection (see fig. 34), meaning "the city ruler's wife." Two distinct signs qualify the recorded lengths, a horizontal stroke for the field length and a vertical stroke for its width. Both signs soon fell into disuse and were replaced by special administrative terms relating to the field dimensions (see fig. 54).

Following the length measurements, another case with the sign GAN$_2$ (▥), the pictographic representation of an irrigated field, records the size of the respective calculated areas. In the case of the second and third fields, the numbers are so exact that there can be no doubt that these areas were calculated. In the other three instances, however, inaccuracies probably stemming from difficulties in the method of multiplying occurred.

The reverse of the tablet exhibits a simpler operation, but the administrative procedure behind this operation is unclear. Apart from the sum of the calculated field areas of the obverse side of the tablet, the reverse also contains a case in which twice that area is recorded and qualified as ⸗ ▥ , the "field of the city ruler." In the final case of the text, all values are subsumed in a grand total. Since this kind of calculation is found on other tablets, such as the badly damaged, but from the point of view of account format practically identical tablet *MSVO* 1, no. 3 (see the text reconstruction in fig. 48), one can propose that the documented procedure constitutes a regular method of surveying and allocating agricultural land for high officials of the state bureaucracy, above all for the city ruler and his wife.

The identification of the archaic signs for length and width of fields provided the key to the understanding of the text shown in figure 50, probably the oldest evidence known of the calculation of field areas. The badly fragmented tablet contains only numerical signs and the ideograms denoting length and width. Obverse and reverse reveal the same format. Both display two only slightly different length and two slightly different width values each, which is a typical feature of later texts on quadrangular fields. The reconstruction of the text shown in figure 50 is based on the original in Heidelberg and on older photographs showing an additional fragment which today is lost. We believe this very plausible reconstruction demonstrates that in each case the calculation of the field surfaces resulted in the unrealistically large and "round" number of 10 šar. This gives credence to our conclusion that the text is a school text from the earliest days of writing containing "difficult" exercises on surface calculation.

One of the few archaic texts that clearly refer to the reason measurements and calculations of fields were made during this period was purchased by the Oriental Institute of the University of Chicago (see fig. 51). Such calculations apparently served among other things for the calculation of the amount of grain required to sow a given field. On one side of the tablet an area of 1 ◉ ("bur'u"), on the other the amount of 25 ● of grain are recorded. Relative to the area, this would add up to 25 ▧ per iku. Using the absolute value we have determined for this capacity unit, we would have the amount of $25 \times 0.8 = 20$ liters of grain per iku. A comparison of this amount with measures known from corresponding records in later texts suggests strongly that the figures on the obverse of this tablet represent the grain needed to sow the given field area on the reverse of the tablet.

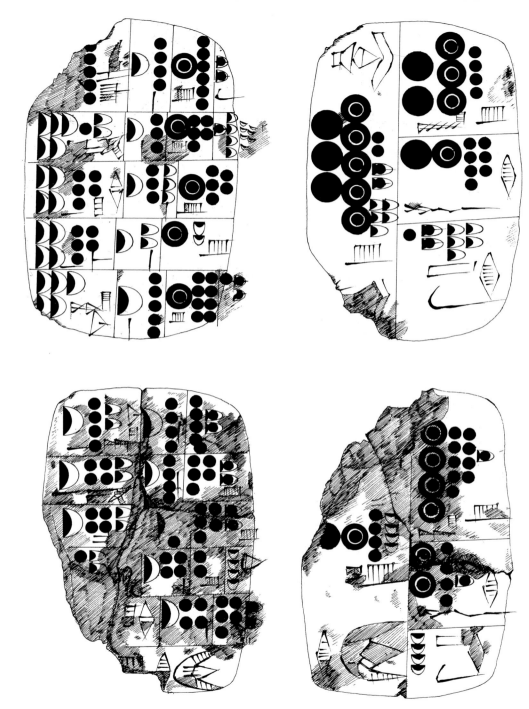

Figure 47. Archaic tablets with calculated field areas.

56

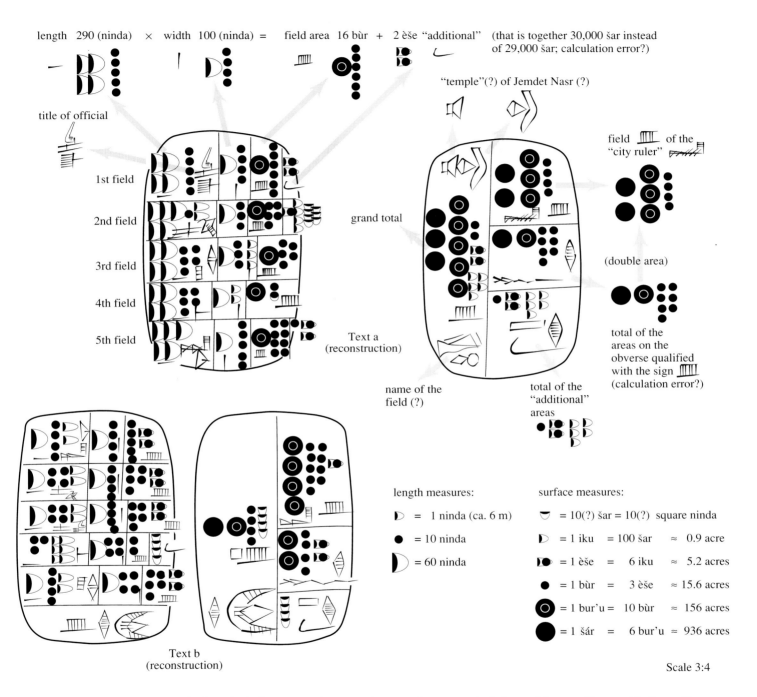

length 290 (ninda) × width 100 (ninda) = field area 16 bùr + 2 èše "additional" (that is together 30,000 šar instead of 29,000 šar; calculation error?)

title of official

1st field

2nd field

3rd field

4th field

5th field

grand total

Text a
(reconstruction)

name of the field (?)

Text b
(reconstruction)

"temple"(?) of Jemdet Nasr (?)

field [⫼] of the "city ruler"

(double area)

total of the areas on the obverse qualified with the sign [⫼] (calculation error?)

total of the "additional" areas

length measures:

◖	= 1 ninda (ca. 6 m)	
●	= 10 ninda	
◗	= 60 ninda	

surface measures:

◡	= 10(?) šar	= 10(?) square ninda	
◗	= 1 iku	= 100 šar	≈ 0.9 acre
◖◗	= 1 èše	= 6 iku	≈ 5.2 acres
●	= 1 bùr	= 3 èše	≈ 15.6 acres
◎	= 1 bur'u	= 10 bùr	≈ 156 acres
⬤	= 1 šár	= 6 bur'u	≈ 936 acres

Scale 3:4

Figure 48. Certain reconstruction and a hypothetical reconstruction, assuming error-free area calculations, of the texts illustrated in figure 47.

57

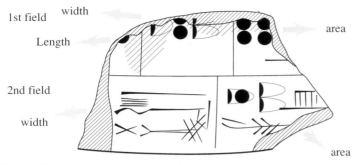

1st field width

Length

2nd field

width

area

area

Figure 49. Fragment of a surveying document.

The Administration of Allotment Fields in the Fara Period (ca. 2600 B.C.)

Much better information about the purpose of field measurements is conveyed by documents from the Early Dynastic period, of which the earliest well understood examples date to the so-called Fara period. The tablet shown in figure 53 was unearthed at Fara (ancient Šuruppak). It has 104 entries on allotment fields, each entry stating the size of the field in question together with a name or title, to which an activity-related specification was often added. Among the persons listed we find two tradesmen, several scribes, a fisherman, and many other "professions." These persons were probably in the service of a temple or palace and were compensated for their affiliation with a field to secure their subsistence.

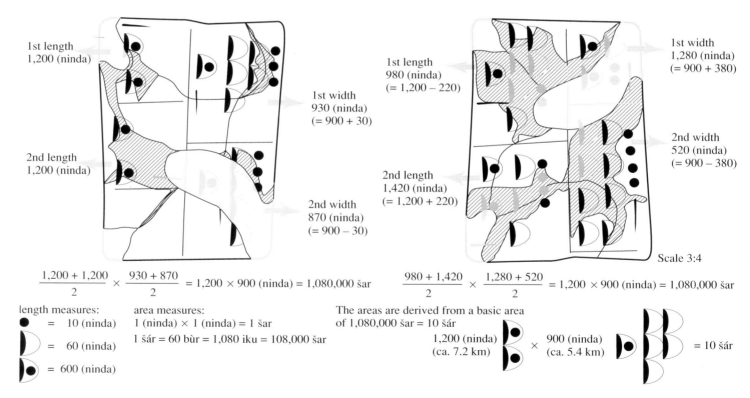

1st length
1,200 (ninda)

2nd length
1,200 (ninda)

1st width
930 (ninda)
(= 900 + 30)

2nd width
870 (ninda)
(= 900 − 30)

1st length
980 (ninda)
(= 1,200 − 220)

2nd length
1,420 (ninda)
(= 1,200 + 220)

1st width
1,280 (ninda)
(= 900 + 380)

2nd width
520 (ninda)
(= 900 − 380)

Scale 3:4

$$\frac{1,200 + 1,200}{2} \times \frac{930 + 870}{2} = 1,200 \times 900 \ (\text{ninda}) = 1,080,000 \ \text{šar}$$

$$\frac{980 + 1,420}{2} \times \frac{1,280 + 520}{2} = 1,200 \times 900 \ (\text{ninda}) = 1,080,000 \ \text{šar}$$

length measures:
● = 10 (ninda)
) = 60 (ninda)
)● = 600 (ninda)

area measures:
1 (ninda) × 1 (ninda) = 1 šar
1 šar = 60 bùr = 1,080 iku = 108,000 šar

The areas are derived from a basic area of 1,080,000 šar = 10 šar
1,200 (ninda) (ca. 7.2 km) × 900 (ninda) (ca. 5.4 km) = 10 šar

Figure 50. Reconstruction and interpretation of a school text containing unrealistic "practice exercises" on field area calculations.

The size of the fields varied between 2.5 and 10 iku (the iku equals approximately 0.8 acre). Their entire area amounts to 3 bur'u 7 bùr 1 èše (672 iku, about 600 acres). Besides the total area, the necessary seed grain (barley) of 21 gur.maḫ is recorded. Since one gur.maḫ was fixed at 480 sìla during the Fara period (1 sìla is equivalent to approximately 1 liter), the seed grain per field amounts to 15 sìla (ca. 15 liters) per area unit iku.

A second document also belongs to this compilation of allotment fields and the seed grain needed for them (fig. 52). In this short text, three grain deliveries from two different storage facilities are recorded, their sum exactly corresponding to the amount of seed grain registered in the preceding text. We can therefore assume that a central seed grain supply administered by the large granaries existed in the Fara period. Aside from the figures relating to grain, a large field surface is noted which in fact is only 7 iku larger than the total surface of the stated allotment fields. This difference may have been the result of a mistake in the scribe's calculations.

The difference in the orthography of the unit bur'u in the two texts is remarkable. The list of the three seed grain deliveries contains the older sign ◉, which also occurs in the previously mentioned archaic texts. (figs. 47–50). In the compilation of the allotment fields, on the other hand, we have the younger writing

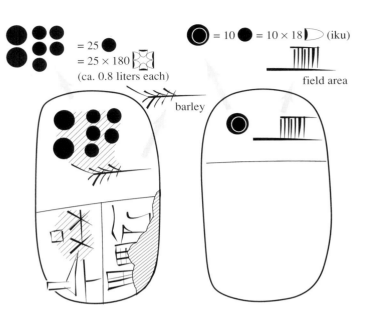

Figure 51. Archaic document on the amount of barley needed for a specific field area.

Figure 52. Text with a deduction of seed grain for the allotment fields mentioned in the text illustrated in figure 53.

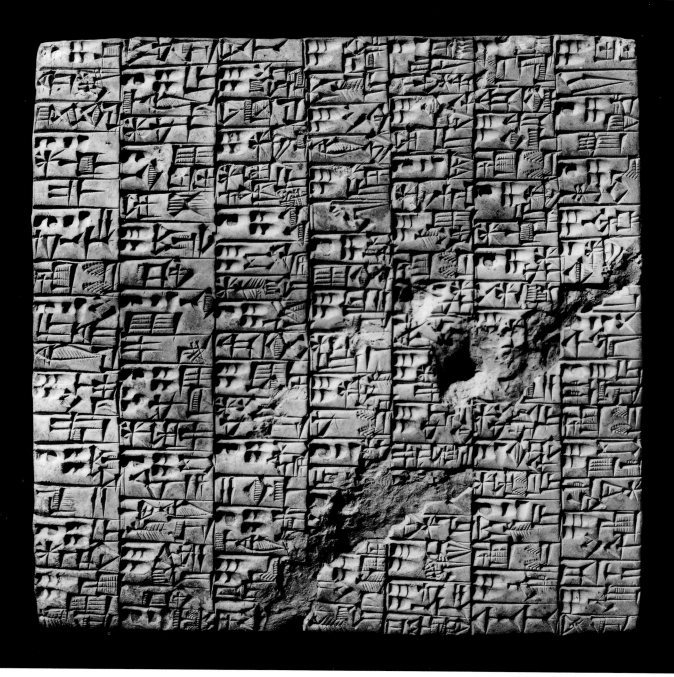

Figure 53. Text listing fields allotted to more than one hundred members of an economic unit.

61

column I:

1 (UŠ) 1 ½ (éš) 5 gi, equal lengths;

3 (éš) 6 gi, equal widths;

field area involved: 1 (bùr) 1 (èše) 1 ½ iku. It is plowed.

1 (UŠ) 3 (éš), equal lengths!;

1 (UŠ) 1 ½ (éš) 5 gi, equal widths!;

first part of column III:

It is "royal domain."

1 (UŠ) 1 ½ (éš) 3 gi, equal lengths;

7 gi, equal widths;

field area involved: 2 ½ ⅛ iku, fallow.

Column II:

field area involved: 4 (bùr) minus 2 ¼ iku.

1 (UŠ), equal lengths;

3 (éš), equal widths;

field area involved: 1 (bùr).

The fixed bala(?):

2 (bùr) ½ iku, plowed.

Altogether: 8 (bùr) 1 (èše) minus ¼ iku.

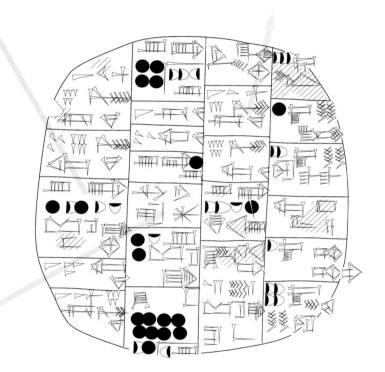

Old Sumerian measures in the province of Lagash

length measures:

= 1 gi = ½ ninda (ca. 3 m)
= ½ éš = 10 gi
= 1 éš = 20 gi
= 1 UŠ = 6 éš

field area measures:

= 1 iku = 1 square éš
= 1 èše = 6 iku
= 1 bùr = 3 èše
= ½ iku
= ¼ iku
= ⅛ iku (?)

Figure 54. Survey measures given in an Old Sumerian text.

column I:

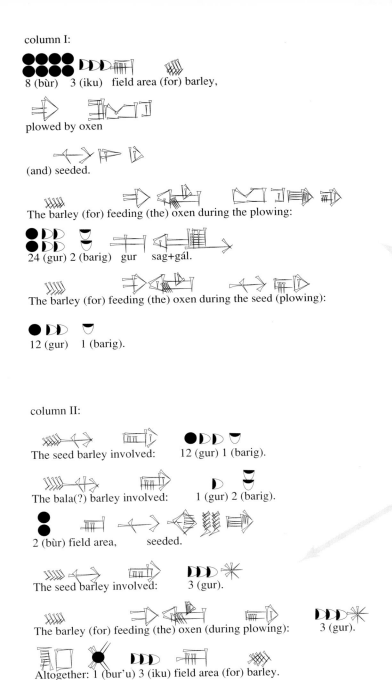

8 (bùr) 3 (iku) field area (for) barley,

plowed by oxen

(and) seeded.

The barley (for) feeding (the) oxen during the plowing:

24 (gur) 2 (barig) gur sag+gál.

The barley (for) feeding (the) oxen during the seed (plowing):

12 (gur) 1 (barig).

column II:

The seed barley involved: 12 (gur) 1 (barig).

The bala(?) barley involved: 1 (gur) 2 (barig).

2 (bùr) field area,   seeded.

The seed barley involved: 3 (gur).

The barley (for) feeding (the) oxen (during plowing):   3 (gur).

Altogether: 1 (bur'u) 3 (iku) field area (for) barley.

first part of column III:

⌈The barley⌉ involved: 56 (gur) 2 (barig) gur sag+gál

It is "royal domain"

of the field   "da.UL₄.ka."

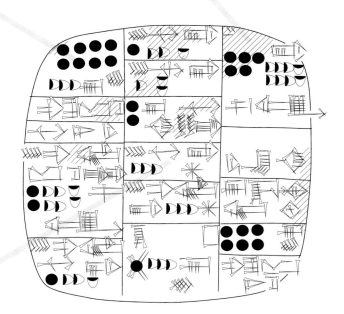

Old Sumerian measures in the province of Lagash

field area measures:			grain capacity measures:		
◗	= 1 iku (ca. 3,600 m²)		◡	= 1 barig	= 6 bán
◖●	= 1 èše	= 6 iku			= 36 sìla (ca. 54 l)
●	= 1 bùr	= 3 èše	◗	= 1 gur	= 4 barig
✳	= 1 bur'u	= 10 bùr	●	= 10 gur	

Figure 55. Calculation of the amount of barley for the cultivation of a field recorded in an Old Sumerian text.

♣, which itself was later replaced by its cuneiform correspondene (see figs. 58–59). The texts were thus probably compiled by two different scribes whose orthographic usage reflected an incomplete stage of standardization in the writing of numerical signs.

Old Sumerian Administrative Field Texts from Lagash (ca. 2400 B.C.)

The Old Sumerian texts from the archive of Lugalanda and UruKAgina, the last two rulers of the first dynasty of the province of Lagash, are still more informative concerning the purpose of the habit of measuring fields than those from the Fara period.

The texts of this archive distinguish among three different forms of disposition over the fields. Most fields are denoted níg.en.na, meaning "domain of the ruler." Then there are the šuku fields, that is, "allotment fields" for the palace staff, and fields designated as APIN.lá, meaning "leased farmland." The texts in figures 54–56 deal predominantly with the administration of the "domain of the ruler," which stood under the direct control of the central administration and covered its domestic demands. The texts provide information about field cultivation, the amount of expenditures, yields and current rights of disposition, all topics which were continuously and painstakingly recorded in the accounts.

The text in figure 54 is interesting above all for the details of surveying it contains. The first part of the text gives the dimensions of four fields as well as their areas, which were precisely calculated from these measures.

After the entries with lengths and area measures, a series of entries follow concerning smaller vegetable gardens, mainly planted with various kinds of onions and leeks. These entries contain as a rule the number of furrows together with the designation of the vegetable planted, followed by entries containing one of two personal names, Sagatuka and Gu'u, both probably representing two individuals from the palace personnel who either enjoyed the right of cultivating the land or were in some way or other responsible for the vegetable beds. The text closes with the remark that the fields belonged to the category "domain of the ruler" as well as with the name of the tract of land the fields belonged to, plus the name of the "chancellor" who was responsible for the surveying.

The entries containing the measures of the fields use a terminology which at that time had become the standard terminology of surveyors. In referring to length the term ús ("side," sign ⟐) was used, and for the narrow side located along the irrigation canal the term sag ("head," sign ⟐). The qualifying term sá ("to be equal," sign ▽) expresses the condition that the opposite sides of a field were of the same length. The calculated surface was then, as in the case of the archaic texts, qualified with the semantic indicator GÁN ("field," sign ▱).

The text shown in figure 55 provides a profound insight into the way the measured and calculated field areas served as a basis for economic planning. The first section of the text records calculated figures of several amounts of grain required to plow and sow given fields qualified as "domain of the ruler" on a tract of

Figure 56. Old Sumerian record for the distribution of seed grain.

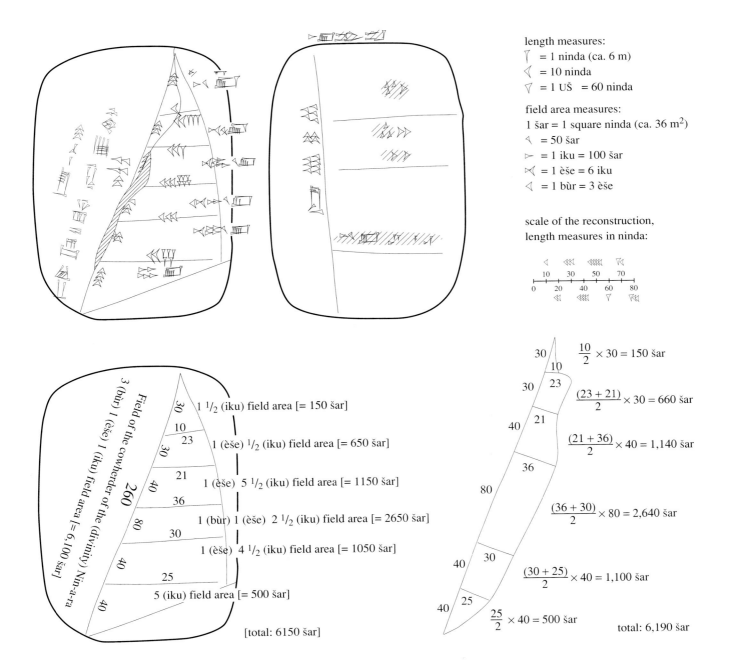

length measures:
$\vee$ = 1 ninda (ca. 6 m)
$\langle$ = 10 ninda
$\triangledown$ = 1 UŠ = 60 ninda

field area measures:
1 šar = 1 square ninda (ca. 36 m²)
$\triangleleft$ = 50 šar
$\triangleright$ = 1 iku = 100 šar
$\bowtie$ = 1 èše = 6 iku
$\triangleleft$ = 1 bùr = 3 èše

scale of the reconstruction,
length measures in ninda:

10 30 50 70
0 20 40 60 80

3 (bùr) 1 (èše) 1 (iku) field area [= 6,100 šar]
Field of the cowherder of the (divinity) Nin-a-ra

260

30   1 ½ (iku) field area [= 150 šar]
10
23   1 (èše) ½ (iku) field area [= 650 šar]
30
21   1 (èše) 5 ½ (iku) field area [= 1150 šar]
40
36   1 (bùr) 1 (èše) 2 ½ (iku) field area [= 2650 šar]
80
30   1 (èše) 4 ½ (iku) field area [= 1050 šar]
40
25   5 (iku) field area [= 500 šar]
40

[total: 6150 šar]

30    $\frac{10}{2} \times 30 = 150$ šar
10
30   23
      $\frac{(23 + 21)}{2} \times 30 = 660$ šar
40   21
      $\frac{(21 + 36)}{2} \times 40 = 1{,}140$ šar
      36
80
      $\frac{(36 + 30)}{2} \times 80 = 2{,}640$ šar
40   30
      $\frac{(30 + 25)}{2} \times 40 = 1{,}100$ šar
40   25
      $\frac{25}{2} \times 40 = 500$ šar   total: 6,190 šar

Figure 57. Field plan from the Ur III period and a reconstruction of the calculations of the field areas as well as the actual shape of the field recorded on the obverse.

65

Figure 58. Field plan from the Ur III period with survey measures of a large agricultural estate.

Figure 59. Field plan from the Ur III period.

land called "da.UL$_4$.ka." The figures were calculated from the area measures using specific arithmetical relations that can be reconstructed from the document. These relations are:

24 sìla of barley per iku, fodder for the oxen used for first plowing

12 sìla of barley per iku, fodder for the oxen used for seed plowing

12 sìla of barley per iku as seed grain

The reverse contains entries using the same relations for another field belonging to a different tract of land; further, Sagatuka, the same person who was connected with the vegetable gardens in the previous text, is named as the official responsible for the work. We may infer from his professional title sag.apin, meaning "plowmaster," that he was the foreman of the workers who carried out the various jobs mentioned in the text.

The text in figure 56 records an amount of barley delivered to a "plowmaster" called Inimanizi to be used for a particular field as seed grain and as fodder for the oxen that pulled the seed plow. The total quantity of barley recorded in this text amounts to 8 gur sag+gál. Since the text also notes the area of the field (2 bùr and 2 èše), we can also here reconstruct a relation on which the calculation was based, resulting in 24 sìla of barley per surface unit iku. This total corresponds to the expected amount of 12 sìla of fodder for the oxen plus 12 sìla of seed grain already derived from calculations in the previous text.

Field Plans from the Ur III Period (ca. 2100–2000 B.C.)
In the Ur III period, field administration was improved by better documentation of the results of surveying. From this period on, sketched plans of the fields were included with the documents, annotated with length measures and calculated area measures like a modern land register. Similar plans have been found referring to buildings and, in rudimentary form, even to entire cities.

The field plans from the Ur III period provide for the first time detailed information about the location of the fields relative to each other. The tablet in figure 57 contains one of the simpler examples of such field plans. It gives the measures of the "field of the cattle herdsman of (the deity) Ninara." The left side of the field, which was probably the side along the main irrigation canal, formed the base line of the surveying procedure. For each segment of the field, the length of the section on the base line, the distance to the outer border line and the calculated area were recorded. In addition, the total length of the base line is given, although this length (260 ninda, approx. 1.5 km) had no relevance for the area calculations. Furthermore, the name of the field as well as the total of its calculated areas rendered in rounded iku are registered in the plan.

The particular areas are only given with an exactness of half an iku. Peculiar is the incorrect calculation of the fifth section from the top, an error for which there are, however, numerous parallels in other field plans. Instead of recording the correct and round figure of 11 iku (= 1 èše 5 iku) the scribe arrived at a value of ten and one half iku. Such irregularities are probably the result of the fact that before the invention of the sexagesimal place value system, which seemingly was introduced only a short time later, no simple method to perform multiplications was known. The reverse of the tablet bears a preliminary sketch of another field, in which, however, a series of entries was erased.

Plans of this type demonstrate that surveying was in fact based exclusively on measuring lengths. The rendered shapes of the fields are not true geometrical representations of the fields. They are not in scale and do not even represent the actual shapes of the respective fields in a qualitatively accurate manner. In spite of these peculiarities, which are to the modern eye real deficiencies, such field plans did fulfill their intended function, because the area calculation procedure, being based exclusively on length measurements, disregarded, too, the actual shapes of the fields. Thus the distortions in the rendering of the sketches did not have any real effect on the calculated areas. The field plans allowed for a fast identification of the relevant values needed for area calculations and they showed furthermore how these measured figures had to be combined in order to achieve a correct result.

The surveying procedure of irregularly shaped fields essentially involved the following steps:

The field was first divided into sections, each of which either formed the approximate shape of a right-angled triangle or a rectangle. For relatively small fields, the criteria by which such sections were defined were probably connected to the topography of the terrain. The base line was usually a straight canal or riverside from which, according to the variations in width, the field could be divided into trapezoidal sections. In the case of larger fields, the procedure was somewhat different. Here the method consisted of staking off a large quadrangle, referred to as "temen," approximately corresponding to the shape of the field. The parts of the field that projected beyond or within the boundaries of the temen were subdivided into sections in the same manner as demonstrated for the smaller fields. In the case of excessively large fields the temen could consist of several adjoining quadrangles together conforming to the approximate shape of such a field.

The next step was to measure the dimensions of the various sections of the field. Apparently, a long reed (Sumerian gi, sign ⊢⟫⟫) stick or some sort of measuring rope (Sumerian éš, sign ▤) served the surveyor for this purpose. Both instruments in fact yield the name-giving terms for the Old Sumerian length units gi (approximately 3 meters) and éš (approximately 60 meters), respectively. The etymology of the otherwise prevailing (especially during the Ur III period) length unit ninda (about 6 meters) remains obscure.

In the case of more moderate-sized sections of the field, it was usually considered sufficient to measure the distances between the section points on the base line and their respective distance from the often irregularly running outer boundary of the field, the latter assumed to be the same length as its corresponding base line. In the case of larger fields, all four sides of the temen were thoroughly measured, the dimensions of the remaining areas being established in the same way as with small fields. The measured lengths were then entered into the plan so that it represented the relative positions of the measured lines necessary for the calculations of the areas.

Each section of the field was then calculated. Triangular surfaces such as might appear at the end of a field were calculated by multiplying the measured length at the base line or the measured section of the temen boundary, respectively, by the distance between the base line and the opposite field boundary and then by dividing that value by two. Since the sketched plans leave us in the dark about the exact shape of the fields, we can only presume that the two sides were chosen which approximately stood in a right angle to each other, implying that the result was essentially correct. For the quadrangles of the temen, as is the case of all quadrangles of which all four sides were measured, the area was usually calculated by multiplying the arithmetical means of the opposite sides. Quadrangles along the border of a field were calcu-lated in a similar way, but because in such cases the field boundary was not as a rule measured, the section of the base line was used directly instead of its mean value with the section on the field boundary.

The calculated areas of the sections of the field were then also entered into the plan and, depending on the procedure used to calculate the total area of the field, either simply totaled or according to the field plan added to or subtracted from the area of the temen. That final total was also inscribed on the tablet, usually on the reverse side. Occasionally, distinctions between different soil qualities were also noted in the field plan. These areas may then have been totaled separately.

Figures 58 and 59 give the plan of a complicated surveying of a large field, approximately 5 km long and 4 km wide. The measured temen is formed by a variety of different rectangles. It is surrounded by a border of smaller areas measured separately.

The procedure of calculating the surface of such complicated temens is somewhat odd. It is known from only two texts, one of which is illustrated in figures 58–59. The various sections of the temen were calculated as if the opposite sides were of identical length. The calculation was carried out twice, the first time with the measurements of one side, the second time with the measurements of the other side. In this manner two values relating to each section of the temen were obtained. Both were entered into the field plan next to their respective field segments, the second value always upside down relative to the first value. The calculation circled—so to speak—around the field, yielding values for each field section. The final step was then to calculate their mean values!

P.D./R.E.

11. Bookkeeping on Labor

The centrally organized exploitation of economic resources, as testified by the administrative texts of the third millennium B.C., among other elements consisted of the control and management of the labor force required in agricultural production and specialized workshops. According to the ancient documents it seems a substantial part of the population from the archaic period was already at this early stage dependent on the institutions that controlled these resources.

The nature of this state of dependence remains today a matter of controversy among historians. One of the unanswered questions is whether the individuals in the labor force should be called slaves or whether they should be regarded as having simply restricted freedom. Regardless of questions of terminology, however, the fact that the administrative institutions relatively freely controlled large numbers of laborers cannot be contested. Individuals ascribed to this social group are already referred to in the earliest texts from the late fourth millennium B.C. from the script phase Uruk IV. Toward the end of the third millennium, state control over economic resources probably reached its apex during the Third Dynasty of Ur, a measure of strict control which remained unequalled during the remainder of the pre-Christian era. Accounts from the Ur III period provide us with the most exhaustive and detailed written material pertaining to the centrally directed use of laborers in Mesopotamia.

The largest group of preserved administrative documents relating to dependent laborers consists of inventories and written calculations concerning the distribution of rations to this work force. The size of these rations was fixed early at an amount of food approximating the minimum level of subsistence and was subject to only minor fluctuations throughout the entire third millennium B.C., suggesting that they merely served to keep the work force in production. Grain and grain products were distributed on a monthly basis, wool and fats annually, while other nutrients were distributed more irregularly, for example on the occasions of a religious festival. The distribution of rations was assumed in part by the central granaries and storehouses, in part by the foremen of labor troops, usually consisting of between five and fifty individuals.

An important contribution to the discussion concerning the size of the rations during the earliest period of written evidence (approx. 3100 B.C.) is offered by certain archaeological artifacts dating to that period. Among the characteristic finds from the late Uruk period are large quantities of sherds and completely preserved vessels of a rather modest and undecorated bowl type, commonly referred to as the "beveled-rim bowl" (see fig. 11). This bowl, apparently mass-produced following a simple molding technique, was early assumed by archaeologists to be evidence for the existence of a rationing system. According to this interpretation, the vessel played a role in the distribution of a specified amount of barley, which corresponded to the approximate daily nutritional needs of a grown individual. According to the calculations made by Hans Nissen based on the sherd assemblage from archaic layers of Uruk, the capacity of the beveled-rim bowls corresponded on average to a volume of about 0.8 liters of barley. Indeed, this amount is practically identical with the size of a daily ration for laborers attested by the administrative documents of later periods.

The pictographic representation of the beveled-rim bowl, the sign ▷ (NINDA), was a key factor in the decipherment of the archaic rationing system attested in the earliest written records. The establishment of the mean volume capacity of the beveled-rim bowl was also a crucial clue in our determination of rough absolute values in the archaic numerical sign system ŠE (see chap. 6 above).

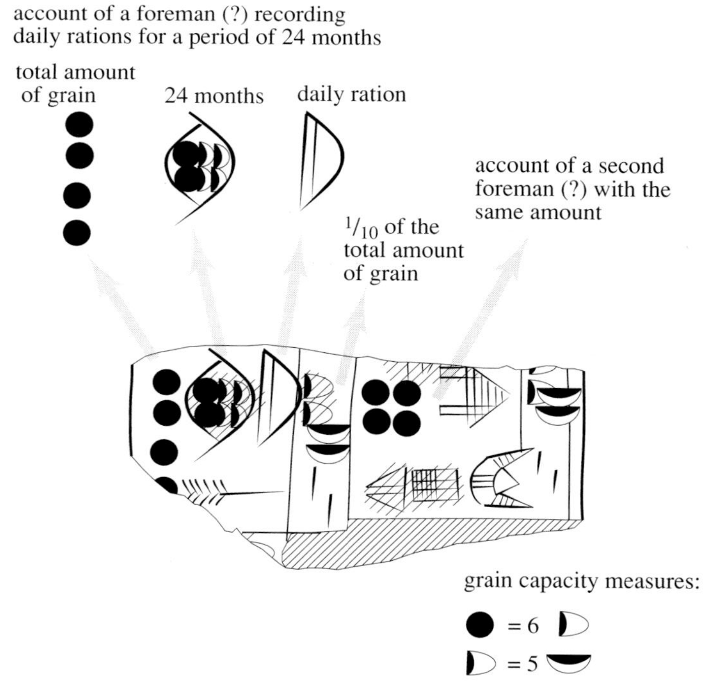

Figure 60. Posting of cereal rations for a period of 24 months in an archaic text fragment.

The tablet fragment in figure 60 exemplifies the role of the beveled-rim bowl within the rationing system of the archaic period. The first entry of the text records four of the signs •, each of which represented six units of barley (sign ⫸, ŠE) of the size ▷. The sign ◇ (U₄), a pictographic denotation of the sun rising in a valley, follows, within which the numerical notation 2 • 4 ▷ denoting the number 24 was inscribed. The complete sign combination means "24 months." The following sign NINDA representing the beveled-rim bowl states that the registered amount of grain was for rations. The total amount of 4 •, that is, 24 ▷ of barley, reveals that one monthly ration amounted to 1 ▷. Moreover, since one accounting month always corresponds to 30 days, it is easily seen that a *daily* ration was represented by the sign ▷, equal to ¹/₃₀ of the amount of barley represented by the numerical sign ▷ (see the representation of the numerical sign systems in chap. 6). In fact, the equivalence between the pictographic sign ▷ and the numerical sign ⊠ can be deduced from a sufficient number of texts in particular from the northern Babylonian settlement Jemdet Nasr that it seems justified to assume that the numerical sign corresponded to the volume of one beveled-rim bowl, that is, to a daily ration of 0.8 liters of barley. Hence, in the case of grain the basic unit ▷ stood for a capacity measure of about 24 liters (= one monthly ration).

For reasons of completeness, it may be added that in the second case preserved on the tablet in figure 60 the same amounts are given and that both entries are followed by a subcase recording an amount one tenth the size of that given in the first entry. Although we are not certain about the true meaning of such supplementary entries, which are attested in a number of other documents, it is possible that they specified the rations earmarked for the work gang foremen (compare the contemporary proto-Elamite text in figs. 64–65, according to which for each group of 10 laborers one foreman with one grain ration was registered).

The simple arithmetic relationships in these and similar archaic texts may be evidence that the structure of the archaic system of capacity measures resulted from the rationing system, with the following correspondences:

daily ration ▷	⊠	equivalent to approximately 0.8 liter
"weekly" (six day) ration ⌣	= 6 ⊠	
monthly ration ▷	= 5 ⌣	
half-year ration •	= 6 ▷	

The total number of archaic texts from which, as in the present case, the use of the sign ▷ can be interpreted as a daily ration is,

however, very small. Most noteworthy is especially the manifest lack of clear connections between the texts bearing records on grain rations on the one hand and such instances stating the disposition of laborers on the other. The reason for this may be seen in the circumstance that the rations generally were not distributed to the laborers nor the foremen directly, but rather came first into the hands of high-ranking officials, each of whom

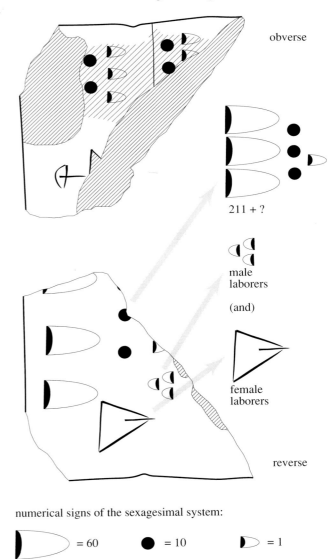

obverse

211 + ?

male laborers

(and)

female laborers

reverse

numerical signs of the sexagesimal system:

◗ = 60   ● = 10   ▷ = 1

Figure 61. Account of more than 211 male and female laborers.

71

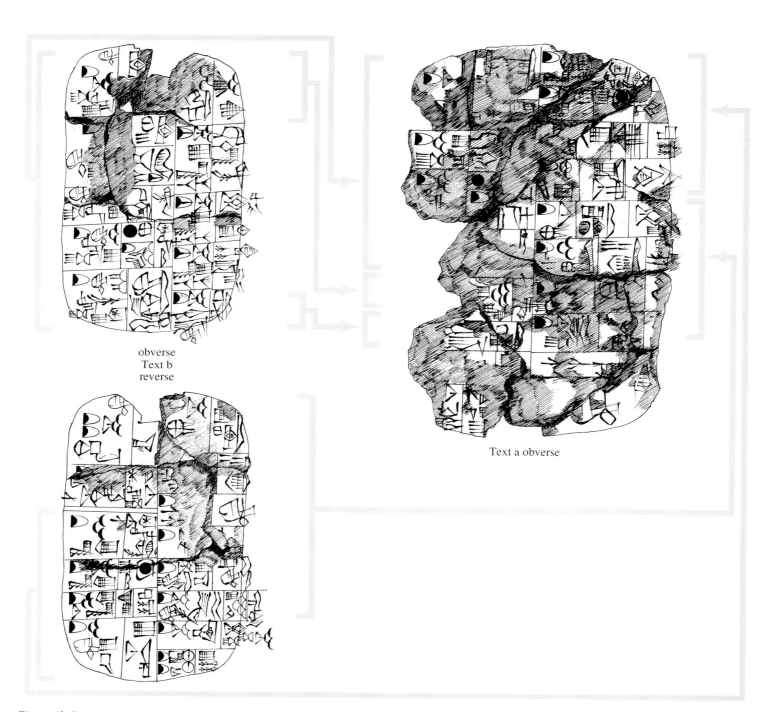

obverse
Text b
reverse

Text a obverse

Figure 62. Posting of single entries (texts b and c) concerning prisoners into a final account (text a).

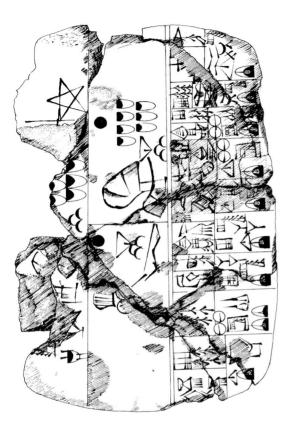

Text a reverse

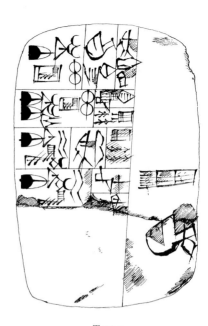

Text c

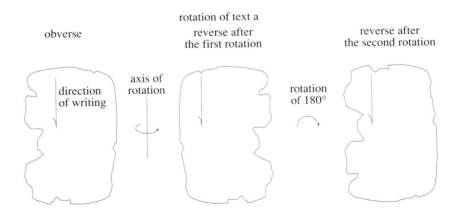

obverse

direction of writing

axis of rotation

rotation of text a reverse after the first rotation

rotation of 180°

reverse after the second rotation

was responsible for the welfare of a group of laborers from a certain field of activity (see corresponding examples in chaps. 7 and 9). Laborers as state property, moreover, would receive rations regardless of their particular employment, so that the concept of "wages" need not enter this discussion.

Texts disclosing information on individually named laborers, with an extra entry giving the total of the persons involved, are comparatively numerous. Such laborers were specified by the signs ▷ (MUNUS) and ◁ (KUR). Both signs are probably pictographic representations of human genitalia, the first sign designating the female and the second the male laborer or, on a more general level, "woman" and "man." That interpretation is supported in particular by the appearance of the compound sign ▷◁, which on a more general level represented both male and female laborers in the same way as the sign combination ◈▷ (AB₂+GU₄, "cow+bull") was used in the texts on livestock to imply "cattle" (see chap. 12). There has, however, been some confusion caused by the fact that in later tradition the same sign combination ▷◁ acquired the meaning "female slave," with the reading géme; the "male slave" was represented by the sign combination nita (man) + kur, usually explained as "male (prisoner of war from the) mountains(/foreign lands)."

Few texts from the archaic period convey an impression of the size of the work force under central administration. In figure 61, a text fragment is displayed which reveals that the size of that labor force was in fact quite substantial during the archaic age. To judge by the preserved remainder of the text, the account consisted of individual entries on the obverse side, each recording some 20–30 individuals, and a final total on the reverse of at least 211 individuals qualified by the sign combination ▷◁.

In some archaic texts, individuals registered with the signs ▷ and ◁ are more precisely qualified with the signs ◇ (SAG+MA) and ‖ (ERIM or BIR₃). The latter sign originally depicted a yoke and was used in later texts as well as in figurative art iconographically for "yoke." It apparently also received a metaphorical meaning to denote captives of war fettered in a yoke. It was probably only after the loss of its immediate pictographic meaning that the sign came to represent "military troop" and later "soldier/laborer" (Sumerian reading érin).

Later cuneiform tradition leaves us in the dark about the semantics of the sign ◇ (SAG+MA) in the archaic period. The sign ◇ (SAG) is the pictogram of a human head. It represented, *pars pro toto*, a human being. In combination with the sign ▷ (NINDA) for "ration," for example, it forms the sign GU₇ (see fig. 12) of the more general sense "disbursement." The sign ⌣ (MA) is the pictogram for a cord used to hang fruit to dry and was employed in the archaic texts alone or further qualified with

additional strokes (gunification) to denote certain categories of fruit. The sign combination ◇ (SAG+MA) could therefore possibly have meant "human being around whose neck a rope has been tied," bringing to mind the image of a captive being led away. Regardless of the exact meaning of both signs it seems established that the sign ‖ (ERIM) as well as ◇ (SAG+MA) were used to qualify persons who, owing to war or some other social or political aggression, had fallen into captivity and consequently been subjected to forced labor.

Three closely related texts from the administrative building of Jemdet Nasr offer a good description of the way books were kept on captives employed in forced labor. At the same time, they provide a convincing example for the practice of setting up balance sheets based on individual documents. Figure 62 depicts the relationship of the documents 62b–c with the complete accounting in text 62a.

The first two texts 62b–c contain in consecutive cases of each column entries concerning the registered captives. Each case is divided into two or three, in one case even four subcases. In the first, the number of the registered laborers was recorded. Usually only one individual is given, in fewer cases two. The signs SAL (▷) or KUR (◁), which qualified these numerical notations, expressed the genders of the laborers; some of the entries, however, contain for unknown reasons the sign combination ▷◁. Many of the laborers listed are further specified as "captives" by the sign ◇ (SAG+MA). The first subcase of each entry contains a sign combination that probably names the individual responsible for the captives. In the two following subcases, the names of the registered laborers are presumably stated and finally, in the last subcase, the name of the person who assumed control of the registered laborers is given.

Some of the laborers mentioned in the texts are accompanied by specific numerical signs. Instead of the sign ▷ these individuals were qualified with the sign ▷, that is, the regular sign of the sexagesimal system S for the unit "one" crossed with the stroke characteristic of the numerical system S' (for a survey of the numerical sign systems see chap. 6). Implications for the function of these modified numerical signs can be drawn from the method by which the single entries of both texts were transferred to the—badly damaged—final balance account 62a (compare the examples of such transfers on the obverse of the tablet in fig. 62 left with those on its reverse in fig. 62 right).

This balance sheet again lists all the entries from both individual documents, totaling 27 male and female laborers. Once the scribe had filled the obverse side of the tablet, he turned it over (according to the orientation chosen in the figure) by making a half rotation around its vertical axis and then completed another column on its reverse. The following correlation demonstrates that the entries on the final balancing tablet correspond exactly to the entries of both texts from which it was drawn, albeit in a different sequence: the scribe here differentiated by recording on the obverse all the individuals qualified with the numerical sign ▷, on the reverse all those qualified with the numerical sign ▷.

Text no.	col.	case		Text no.	col.	case
62b obv.	I	1–5	=	62a obv.	I	1–5
	II	1	=		I	6
	II	2	=	rev.	I	3
	II	3	=		I	5
	II	4	=		I	4
	II	5	=	obv.	I	7
rev.	I	1–2	=		I	8–9
	I	3–6	=		II	1–4
	II	1–6	=		II	5–8
	II	7–8	=	rev.	I	1–2
62c obv.	I	1–4	=		I	6–9

After having booked the entries, the scribe proceeded by turning the tablet upside down, recording two subtotals within the central column of the reverse. In a last step he entered the grand total of the recorded laborers in the left column of the reverse. The first subtotal records exactly those 17 individuals who were noted on the obverse and qualified with the numerical sign ▷. These people are qualified as male and female laborers (▷◁) of the category ✹ (SAG+MA). The remaining ten laborers recorded with the numerical sign ▷ on the reverse of the tablet are noted separately in the second subtotal, where they are characterized through the addition of the sign ‖ (ERIM).

We do not understand the exact purpose of this differentiation. In administrative texts relating to domestic animals, the same numerical sign ▷ was generally used to book an animal that had died during the accounting period. Consequently, one might be tempted to suggest that the ten laborers referred to in the present context were indeed dead. On the other hand, we cannot rule out the possibility that the sign was merely used to stress an as yet unspecified functional difference between the two groups of laborers. As a matter of fact, such use of explicitly different numerical signs is well documented in later accounting tradition.

Dating to approximately the same time as the Uruk III period texts from Mesopotamia are a number of administrative texts of similar contents which come from Susa and are written in the so-called proto-Elamite script. Although this script remains for the most part undeciphered, we are able to make often far-reaching conclusions about the contents of the proto-Elamite texts, based on their formal similarity to proto-cuneiform tablets, that is, to the archaic texts from Mesopotamia, in particular insofar as the structure of documented accounts and the similar use of certain signs for objects in bookkeeping are concerned.

The proto-Elamite texts exhibit two features that clearly distinguish them from the proto-cuneiform documents, relating to sign form and text layout, respectively. One essential difference to the archaic texts from Mesopotamia is that the proto-Elamite documents were written in a linearized script, which on a superficial level tends to blur the formal and structural similarities between the two text corpora. The first signs on a proto-Elamite tablet have by and large the same function as the proto-cuneiform "subscription" (that is, signature), usually inscribed together with the final total on the reverse side of an archaic account tablet from Mesopotamia. As already demonstrated, such signatures supplied information relating to the type of transaction recorded as well as the responsibilities of the individuals involved in that particular transaction. Following the introductory sign combinations, which generally express the purpose of a proto-Elamite tablet, are individual entries, one after the other, without regard to the formal arrangement of the tablet into columns. Each entry normally includes an ideographic notation followed by a numerical one, thus diverging again from the strict sequence used in the proto-cuneiform texts. The principle of recording the total on the reverse side of the tablet, however, is adhered to by the proto-Elamite scribes.

The obverse of the proto-Elamite tablet in figure 63 lists in several columns altogether seven labor troops. The list itself is remarkably similar to the compilation on the proto-cuneiform text shown in figure 61; the proto-Elamite sign ▷, moreover, corresponds in all probability to the graphically similar sign ◁, meaning "male laborer," from the proto-cuneiform script. The number of laborers belonging to each group listed in our proto-Elamite account varies between 44 and 147. In front of each number relating to the size of a group either one or two other signs were written which, according to our findings, refer to the foreman of the gang.

In proto-Elamite texts, the numbers relating to registered individuals formed part of a numerical system which was restricted in use to the distributional area of the script itself, a region approximately identical with later Persia. Hence, that system is not to be found in the contemporary archaic texts of Mesopotamia. Apparently it was only applied in conjunction with the registration of labor gangs and herds of domestic animals. It actually constitutes the only known decimal system of this region

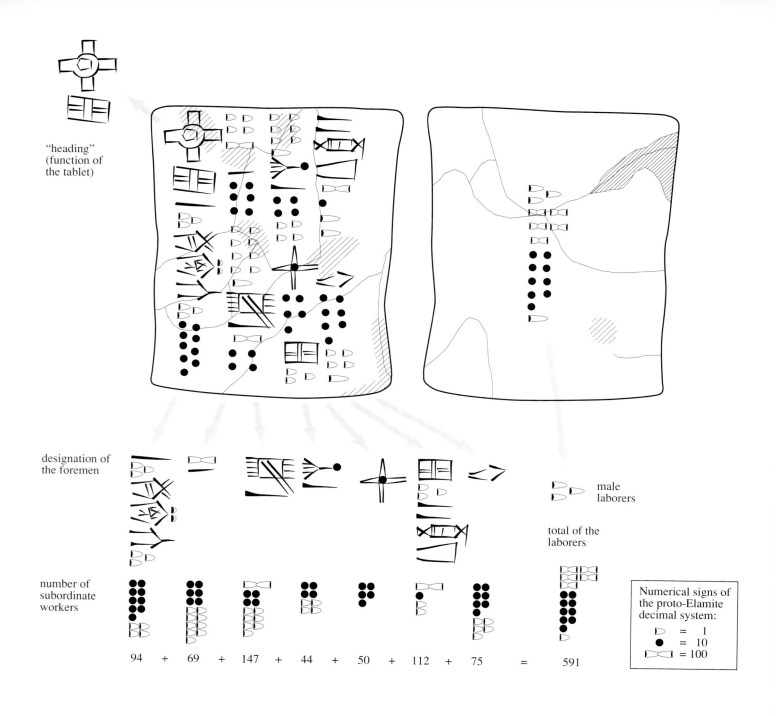

Figure 63. Proto-Elamite account of 591 workers.

from the archaic period. The following signs of this system have been identified:

$$\rhd = 1$$
$$\bullet = 10$$
$$\bowtie = 100$$
$$\underset{\sim}{\asymp} = 1{,}000$$
$$\underset{\bullet}{\asymp} = 10{,}000$$

The signs of this system for the numbers 1,000 and 10,000 seem to have been borrowed from the proto-cuneiform bisexage-simal system and ascribed here new numerical values. This suggests that the system originally only consisted of the numbers 1, 10, and 100 and was only expanded at a time when centraliza-tion of the economic administration led to the necessity of record-ing increasingly larger numbers of laborers and domestic animals.

The structure of a second proto-Elamite example is illustrated in figures 64–65. In this account, laborers and grain rations are treated simultaneously. It reveals with a certain degree of clarity the hierarchical structure of the labor gangs known from texts dating to the later Old Sumerian period.

Two individuals stood at the top of the hierarchy attested by this text. Both probably functioned as chief supervisors of the registered laborers. Of special interest are the people under the control of the first supervisor, since it seems that they actually formed together a full force of laborers, whereas the second supervisor only administered the remainder of the listed workmen. The first labor force can be qualified as a century, since it con-sisted of ten gangs, of ten laborers each plus one foreman, thus forming together 11 individuals per gang. That number was recorded after the name of every foreman. The reverse side of the tablet with the totals accordingly records a sum of 111 laborers for the first chief supervisor, that is, the total of all gangs together with their respective foremen and the chief supervisor himself.

The fact that all the members of the three hierarchical groups were preceded by the sign $\rhd$ is in agreement with the summary of the laborers, foremen, and chief supervisor in a grand total. Such comprehensive qualifications of laborers from different hierarchical levels are well known from later Mesopotamian sources. Such is, for instance, the case for the Sumerian term guruš during the period of the Third Dynasty of Ur. In the summations on the reverse side of the proto-Elamite tablet, the two chief supervisors are additionally qualified by the sign $\rightarrowtail$. This sign most likely served to underscore the special status of the two indi-viduals, corresponding semantically and graphically to the Sumeri-an sign ugula for the foremen of laborers (both signs likely representations of sticks).

The cereal rations are always specified for two labor gangs together, that is, for 22 individuals. Following the two entries, each consisting of the sign $\rhd$, the name of the foreman and the numerical notation $\bullet \rhd$ corresponding to the eleven persons of each gang, the sign $\gtrless$, probably the proto-Elamite sign for "grain ration," was inscribed, and finally the amount of barley distributed to the 22 individuals. The barley quantity is expressed in the proto-Elamite capacity system for grain which corresponds to the ŠE system of the archaic texts from Mesopotamia. For two complete gangs, an amount of 1 $\bullet$ and 5 $\rhd$ was required. Since in the capacity system 1 unit of $\bullet$ replaces 6 units of $\rhd$, every labor-er received an amount represented by $1/2 \rhd$. This amount probably corresponded to the monthly ration of a laborer. Assuming that the capacity units in Susa were of the same size as those in archaic Mesopotamia, this amount would correspond to half of what a la-borer was given in Mesopotamia as attested by the archaic text in figure 60 and others. The laborer in proto-Elamite Susa would thus have received only about 12 liters per month. There are, however, a number of indications that the capacity systems in the two regions were based on different unit sizes despite their identical numerical structure.

We are ill informed about the type of tasks assigned to the labor gangs whom we find documented in the proto-Elamite texts. In particular, we do not know whether their work was carried out in the immediate neighborhood of the city or on an interregional basis. From the Fara period, the period following the archaic age, however, there is enough evidence to confirm the existence of regionally organized and directed work projects. This is, for exam-ple, attested by the tablets represented in figure 66, both of which were found in the ruins of Fara, the ancient city of Šuruppak. Both texts are compilations of "conscripted work forces" (corvée workers? Sumerian lú dab$_5$) from nearly all the politically im-portant cities of the Fara period: Uruk, Adab, Nippur, Lagash, Umma, and Šuruppak itself. For example, the first of these two tablets may be transliterated and translated in the following manner (text 66a; the sexagesimal number notations of the original appear in the translation converted into decimal numbers; see chap. 6):

Obverse:

I	2.20 guruš	140 laborers,
	lú dab$_5$ Unug^{ki}	corvée workers from Uruk,
	3.35 Adab^{ki}	215 (from) Adab,
	1.14	74
II	Nibru^{ki}	(from) Nippur,
	1.50 Lagaš^{ki}	110 (from) Lagash,
	1.06 Šuruppak^{ki}	66 (from) Šuruppak,

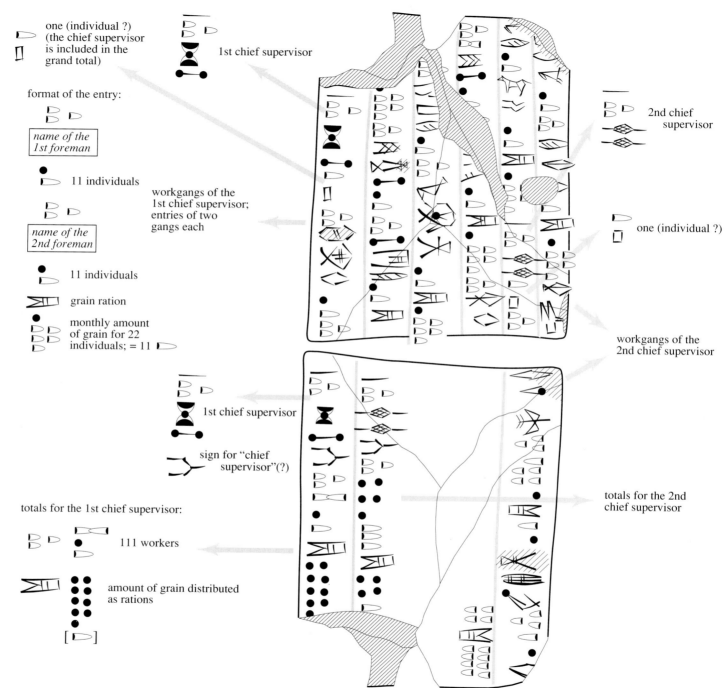

one (individual ?) (the chief supervisor is included in the grand total)

1st chief supervisor

format of the entry:

name of the 1st foreman

11 individuals

name of the 2nd foreman

11 individuals

grain ration

monthly amount of grain for 22 individuals; = 11

2nd chief supervisor

one (individual ?)

workgangs of the 1st chief supervisor; entries of two gangs each

workgangs of the 2nd chief supervisor

1st chief supervisor

sign for "chief supervisor"(?)

totals for the 2nd chief supervisor

totals for the 1st chief supervisor:

111 workers

amount of grain distributed as rations

[ ]

Figure 64. Proto-Elamite tablet containing an account of cereal rations for the labor gangs of two supervisors.

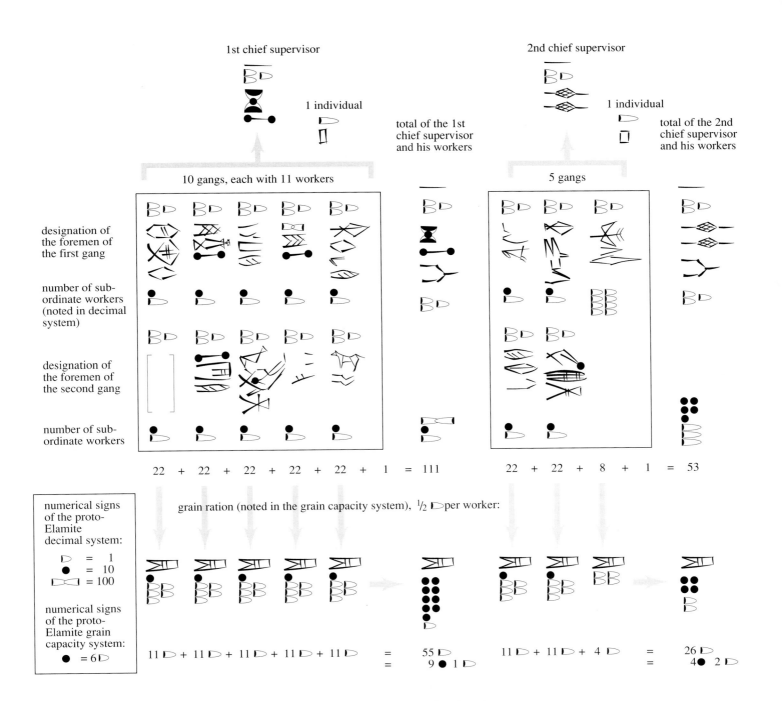

Figure 65. Reconstruction of the calculations contained in a proto-Elamite account of grain rations.

Figure 66. Accounts registering numbers of laborers drafted from different cities, dating to the Fara period.

Reverse:

III 2.08 Umma^{ki} 128 (from) Umma.
IV AN.ŠÈ.GÚ Together:
  11.00 lá.10 guruš 660 minus 10 laborers,
  lú dab₅ ki.en.gi corvée workers from Sumer.

The total given in this text is evidently erroneous, since 83 laborers remain unaccounted for. In the second text (text 66b) with similar contents the total is correct:

Obverse:

I 3.02 guruš 182 laborers
  Unug^{ki} (from) Uruk,
  3.12 Adab^{ki} 192 (from) Adab,
  1.34 Nibru^{ki} 94 (from) Nippur,
II 1.00 Lagaš^{ki} 60 (from) Lagash,
  56 Šuruppak^{ki} 56 (from) Šuruppak,
  1.26 Umma^{ki} 86 (from) Umma,
  lú dab₅.dab₅.ba they are corvée workers

III ki.en.gi from Sumer
  DU.DU given over to (?)
  šu.sum DUDU.
Reverse:
IV ŠU.NÍGIN Total:
  11.10 guruš 670 laborers,
  lú dab₅.dab₅.ba they are corvée workers.

The purpose of the conscription of the laborers listed here is, unfortunately, also unclear. Since it seems that state formation was not at an advanced developmental stage during the Fara period, it would be unlikely that economic administration should have exceeded regional dimensions or that it could have achieved the centralism known from later periods, which would in fact have allowed for the establishment of labor gangs in cities located at a considerable distance from the administrative center. Problems did, however, already exist during the Early Dynastic I period which could have been alleviated if interregional measures in the organization of the labor force had been available. The problems

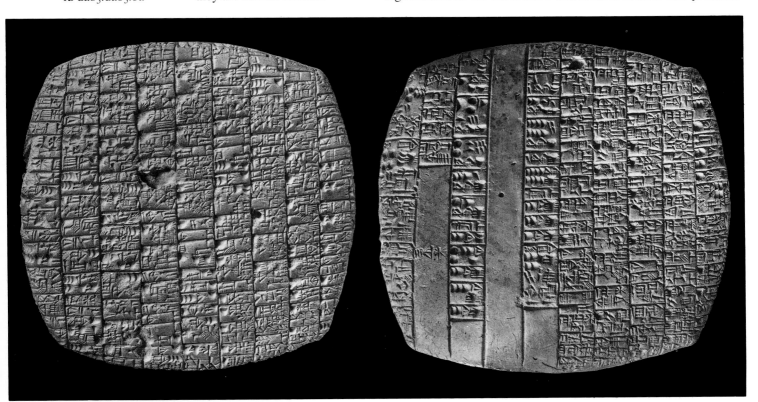

Figure 67. Old Sumerian text listing the disbursements of barley rations.

especially concerned the functioning of the irrigation network that has been attested in that period; it is rather unlikely that this network could have been built or maintained without the implementation of interregional coordination of the labor forces from the various urban centers, all of which will have been interested in successful water flow.

The texts from the Old Sumerian period are more explicit about the food rations of laborers than are our archaic examples. They also offer an insight into a new dimension of the administration of labor: we find here the earliest indications of the calculation of work performances on the basis of standardized performance expectations.

One example from which rations can be traced in detail during that period is offered by the tablet in figure 67. It is dated to the fifth regnal (lugal) year of UruKAgina. The text contains several lists of barley rations destined for laborers of different categories. Unfortunately, the specifications of the categories are difficult to interpret and must therefore remain untranslated. The rations were apparently distributed via middlemen whose names are recorded. These middlemen functioned for the most part as foremen of the registered laborers. The text entries are of the following type (reading from the beginning of column 1):

10 igi.nu.du$_8$	10 igi-nudu (laborers) with barley
še ba 1(barig) 2(bán)	rations of 1 (barig) 2 (bán) each,
⸢ Ur.nu	(of which) Ur-nu and
⸢ U$_4$.é.nam	U-enam
nu.kiri$_6$.me	are fruit gardeners and
⸢ Ur.^{d}AB.ir.nun	Ur-AB-irnun and
⸢ Igi.dingir.šè	Igi-dingir-še
DÙ.A.TAR.me	are DUATAR (laborers).
še.bi 3 (gur) 1 (barig)	The barley involved: 3 gur
2 (bán) gur sag+gál	sag+gál, 1 (barig), 2 (bán),
Dingir.a.mu	(responsible:) Dingir-amu.

The text contains numerous similar entries, all regarding the distribution of barley rations to responsible officials, with a special notation stating the type of laborer they were destined for. Apart from the undetermined categories "igi-nudu" and "DUATAR," there are personal designations relating to gender (nita = man; mu$_{10}$ = woman), age (šà-du$_{10}$ = child, literally "sweetheart") and to professions (sagi = cup-bearer; muḫaldim = cook; dub.šar = scribe; šu.i = barber, etc.). On the reverse face of the tablet, the laborers and the rations were totaled separately according to their respective categories. A final notation ⫴.ba.am$_6$, signifying "it is the third distribution," states that the barley rations booked were distributed in the third month of the current year. This conclusion can be drawn from the fact that in comparable texts such notations generally refer only to the first through the twelfth distribution. Very few texts record a thirteenth ration, probably accounting thus for an intercalation.

The sizes of the registered monthly rations vary between 2 bán and 2 barig (i.e., 12 bán). The great majority of the rations, however, amount to figures between 1 barig and 1 barig 2 bán, hence between 6 and 8 bán. In the Old Sumerian period one bán was the equivalent of 6 sìla. Assuming that during this period one sìla had a capacity of ca. 1.5 liters—the later unit bán contained 10 sìla of approximately 1 liter each—the majority of the Old Sumerian monthly rations ranged from 54 to 72 liters of barley. These figures agree with the later, well-documented monthly rations of the Ur III period amounting as a rule to 60 liters (1 barig) per laborer guruš.

The indications mentioned earlier of expected performances, which can be found in texts from the Old Sumerian period for the first time, are difficult to understand. Later texts, however, especially those from the Ur III period, are more informative about how such expected performances were calculated. Such later evidence makes it easier to interpret the meager references to labor quotas in the Old Sumerian texts.

Performance expectations were usually formulated specifically for each type of work as quantitatively defined work duties. Such obligations consisted of, for example, the amount of barley a laborer had to harvest, a certain quantity of fish a fisherman had to deliver, or a specified volume of soil a laborer employed at a construction site was expected to excavate in a workday. Here as well, foremen were responsible for the accomplishment of the tasks. The extent of the performance was fixed according to the sex and age of the individual doing the work and was in the same way as in later periods certainly based on optimal performance.

The Old Sumerian text illustrated in figure 68 constitutes an early example relating to performance expectation. The text records obligations connected with work on an irrigation canal. A typical entry of the text is the following:

11 lú	11 laborers
lú.1.šè	for each laborer
kin kùš.⸢.ta	one cubit of work
i.ši.ti	assigned. The work
kin.bi ⸢ gi kùš 5 × ⸢	involved: 1 "reed," 5 cubits.
Ur.^{d}Še.nir.da	(Responsible:) Ur-Šenirda.

On the reverse side of the tablet the tasks to be performed are totaled:

ŠU.NÍGIN ¹/₂ éš	total: 1/2 "measuring cord,"
kùš 4 × ⸢ kin dù.a	4 cubits, performed work,
e.zi.de₆ GÁN Ù.gig	dike construction of the
	field Ugig
é.ᵈNin.tu.ka	at the Nintu temple.
En.ig.gal	Eniggal,
nu.bànda	the chancellor,
mu.dù	constructed the building.

The distances rendered in "cubits" (1 kùš ≈ ¹/₂ m), "reeds" (1 gi = 6 kùš) and "measuring cords" (1 éš = 20 gi) apparently refer to the running length of raised dike. Since the text does not allude to the depth and shape of the canal, there is no possibility of reconstructing the extent of the work involved. In this respect, the texts of the Ur III period are more revealing. For tasks connected with the removal of earth in canal constructions it was normally fixed at $1/6$ of a volume šar (approximately 3 cubic meters) per laborer and day and at $1/16$ of a volume šar (about $1/8$ cubic meter) in the erection of a mud wall. The length measurements given in the current text may be based on the same order or labor performance.

Although the Old Sumerian texts contain clear indications of standardized performance expectations, we must assume that the complete control of labor performance theoretically fixed to quotas was not exercised before the Ur III period .

A tablet from Umma (fig. 69) documents in an unusually precise way the full recording of human labor achieved during this early period. It contains the balance of a foreman called Ur-Šara over a period covering approximately one year lasting from day 23 of month 3 in the forty-eighth regnal year of Shulgi to day 7 in month 2 of the first regnal year of the following ruler Amar-Suen. The foreman was in charge of 36 female laborers—one of whom died during this period—in a grain processing workshop. The main activity of the laborers consisted of milling several types of cereals to flour. According to the text they were, however, also assigned other tasks. The account deals on the one hand with raw as well as finished products which were, with extreme accuracy, converted into the standard value units of barley, on the other hand with the labor time of the millers, in this case to an exactness of $10/60$ of a work day in the total balance.

The structure of the balance follows that of regular neo-Sumerian "debit-credit balances" (chap. 9), with the peculiarity that depending on the type of labor the product was converted to one of two means of comparison, barley or labor time. The account is divided as usual into two distinct sections. The first section running from the beginning of the text to the fifth line of

Figure 68. Old Sumerian text citing labor quotas in canal construction.

the second column (in translation I 1 to II 5) deals predominantly with quantities of processed raw materials, the number of employed laborers and the time they were employed. This section forms the "debit" part of the account since raw materials as well as the labor force, expressed in (female) laborer days (géme u$_4$.1.šè, grammatically speaking a terminative, thus literally: "female laborers for one day"), had to be balanced at the end of the accounting period against real delivered products and the work actually performed. In the second section of the text, the "credits," all finished products produced within the stated period are noted, plus the theoretical time of work necessary for their processing, the other jobs performed, all of which were totaled at the end of the section. The final step was then to calculate the difference between debits and credits. The amounts of grain and work days calculated as deficits were then recorded as such (Sumerian LÁ+NI); these probably formed the first entry of the "debit" section (sag.níg.gur$_{11}$.ra[k]) of the account of the following period. In some cases, such deficits had to be cleared directly, a procedure

Figure 69. Account of Ur-Šara, an Ur III foreman of female laborers in a grain mill.

84

Account on female laborers in a grain processing workshop (see fig. 69):

I 1) 193 gur, 2 (bán) 5 sìla barley (measured according to the) royal
(standard),
38 gur emmer
33 gur 4 (bán) wheat
from Ir.
3 gur, 4 (barig) 1 (bán) 5 sìla barley,
1 gur, 3 (barig) 4 (bán) 5 sìla spelt (?),
1 (barig), 4 (bán) emmer
from Lugal-ušur
3 gur barley
10) restored deficit of Bida.
1 (barig), 4 (bán) 4 sìla spelt
from Nin-melam.
Together, the equivalent barley: 308 gur, 3 (barig) 3 (bán) 8 sìla.
36 female laborers, (each of whom received) 3 (bán per month), from
the completed day 23 of the month "Barley brought to the
quai" (month 3 of the Umma calender) of the year "Ḫarši
and Kimaš were destroyed" (Šulgi 48)
until the completed day 7 of the month "Bricks cast in
moulds" (month 2 of the year following "Ḫarši and Kimaš
were destroyed" (Amar-Suen 1),
II 1) the work performance involved is 11,304 female laborer days.
31 $^{10}/_{60}$ female laborer days, work performance of the "free" days of
the deceased female laborer.
This constitutes the debit.

Therefrom:
1,884 (days), work performance of the "free" days of the female
laborers.
185 gur, 2 (barig) 4 (bán) minus $^{1}/_{2}$ sìla dabin flour.
18 gur, 3 (barig) 1 (bán) 4 sìla sig-flour,
10) 35 gur, 4 (barig) 1 (bán) 5 sìla "pounded" flour,
4 (barig) 1 (bán) dabin flour, loss (?), flour "filled" into the house,
the work performance involved is 7,226 days.
2 gur, 1 (barig) 4 (bán) 1$^{1}/_{2}$ sìla eša flour,
4 (bán) 4 sìla fine, ground bread (?),
the work performance involved is 37$^{1}/_{3}$ days.
(the document bears) the sealing of Lu-dingira.
22 $^{1}/_{2}$ (volume-)šar of excavation work, per (female) digger 10
(volume-)gín (per day), the work performance of the female
laborers involved is 270 days
(the document bears) the sealing of Ur-Namnunka.
III 1) 238 (female laborer days as) work performance of the female
laborers who winnowed barley, the tablets involved are 3,
(the documents bear) the sealing of Ir.
30 female laborer days of the female laborers who loaded flour onto
the barge,
(the document bears) the sealing of Šeš-ani.

19 female laborer days carrying straw to the temple of Šulgi,
(the document bears) the sealing of Akala.
4 female laborers, (each) 47 female laborer days, the work
performance involved
10) is 188 days,
(the document bears) the sealing of Šara-zame.
27 female laborers in 7 days went to the bala(-service)
27 female laborers in 3 days returned from the bala(-service),
the work performance involved is 270 days.
96 female laborer days of the female laborers who were at the
weaving-mill,
(the document bears) the sealing of ADU.
30 female laborer days of the female laborers who . . . the sieve of
the dabin flour,
20) (the document bears) the sealing of Ur-zu.
240 female laborer days, female laborers of the ar‹za›na flour,
(the document bears) the sealing of Lugal-nig-lagare.
Dead: Nin-ḫegal, from the month "House of the sixth month"
(month 8) of the year
IV 1) "Ḫarši and Kimaš were destroyed" (Šulgi 48) until the
completed day 7 of the month "Bricks cast in moulds"
(month 2) of the year following "Ḫarši and Kimaš were
destroyed" (Amar-Suen 1),
the equivalent work performance is 187 days.
Total: 186 gur, 1 (barig) 4$^{1}/_{2}$ (bán) sìla dabin flour,
total: 54 gur, 2 (barig) 3 (bán) minus 1 sìla sig-flour,
total: 2 gur 1 (barig) 4 (bán) 1$^{1}/_{2}$ sìla eša flour,
total: 4 (bán) 4 sìla fine, ground bread (?),
10) total, the equivalent barley: 300 gur, 1 (barig) 1 (bán) 6$^{1}/_{2}$ sìla,
total: 10,715 female laborer days
deducted.

Deficit: 8 gur, 2 (barig) 2 (bán) 1$^{1}/_{2}$ sìla (barley),
deficit: 620$^{10}/_{60}$ female laborer days,
this is the deficit.
Account of Ur-Šara, foreman of milling, in the month "Bricks
cast in moulds" (month 2) of the year following "Ḫarši and
Kimaš were destroyed" (Amar-Suen 1)

which is attested by corresponding administrative documents (the so called LÁ+NI su.ga texts = "replaced deficit").

We do not present here all the details on which the calculations in the text are based. These calculations can, however, be fully reconstructed, since practically no mistakes were made by the original bookkeeper, with the exception of some insignificant imprecision in the results.

The text reveals more than just interesting aspects concerning bookkeeping structure. It also provides insight into many details of the living conditions of the laborers themselves, as well as into the methods by which their performances were regulated. In this respect, for instance, we learn that the female laborers only spent about 70 percent of their working time with the grinding of flour. During the remaining time, they were employed for various other tasks, including trench work, the loading of flour onto barges, the transportation of baled straw to the temple, and various jobs in the

Figure 70. Account of Lu-sa-izu, an Ur III foreman of female laborers in a grain mill.

Account on the female laborers (fig. 70):

I 1) 216 gur, 3 (barig) 5 (bán) 5 sìla barley (measured according to the)
       royal (standard),
35 gur emmer,
16 gur wheat
    from Ir.
3 gur barley from the restored deficit of the fattener Bida.
Together, the equivalent barley: 286 gur, 3 (barig) 5 (bán) 5 sìla.
36 female laborers, (each of whom received) 3 (bán per month), from
       the completed day 23 of the month "Barley brought to the
10)   quai" (month 3 of the Umma calender) in the year "Ḫarši"
       (Šulgi 48) until the completed day 20 of the month "Dumuzi"
       (month 12),
       the work performance involved is 9,612 female laborer days,
       from Ur-Urtab.
36 female laborers, (each of whom received) 3 (bán per month), from
       the completed day 20 of the month "Dumuzi" (month 12) in
       the year "Ḫarši" (Šulgi 48) to the completed day 8 in the
       month "Bricks cast in moulds" (month 2), in the year
       following "Ḫarši"
20)   (Amar-Suen 1),
II 1)   the work performance involved is 1,728 female laborer days,
       from Dingira.
123 $^{1}/_{3}$ (days), work performance of the "free" days of the deceased
       female laborers.
3 female laborers, each 48 days,
       the work performance involved is 144 (days)
Total: 11,607$^{1}/_{3}$ female laborer days.
       This constitutes the debit

       Therefrom:
1,914 (female laborer days) work performance of the "free" days of
       the female laborers.
184 gur, 2 (barig) 5 (bán) dabin flour,
10) 17 gur, 2 (barig) 1 (bán) 5 sìla sig-flour,
16 gur, 3 (barig) 1 (bán) "pounded" flour,
       the work performance involved is 6,559 $^{1}/_{2}$ days.
1 gur, 1 (barig) 3 (bán) 6 sìla fine pea-flour,
       the work performance involved is 49 $^{1}/_{2}$ days.
3 (barig) 1 (bán) fine, ground ninda of the type zigiduḫḫum,
       the work performance involved is 9$^{1}/_{2}$ days
18 gur šagina pea-flour,
       the work performance involved is 675 days.
       (In charge:) Basag, the šagina.
20) 1 gur, (barig) 8 sìla flour, loss (?), flour "filled" into the house.
       (The document bears) the sealing of Lu-dingira,
       the work performance involved is 37 (days),
22$^{1}/_{2}$ (volume-)šar of excavation work, per (female) digger 10
       (volume-)gín (per day), the work performance of the female

laborers involved is 270 days.
       (The document bears) the sealing of Ur-Namnunka.
232 (female laborer days as) work performance of the female
       laborers who winnowed barley, the tablets involved are 3,
       (the document bears) the sealing of Ir.
24 female laborer days of the female laborers who loaded flour onto
       the barge,
       (the document bears) the sealing of Lu-Šara, the son of Alla.
10) 19 female laborer days carrying straw to the temple of Šulgi,
       (the document bears) the sealing of Akala, the nubanda.
276 female laborers, labor performance during milk processing.
       (The document bears) the sealing of ADU, the cook.
222 (female laborers), labor performance of the female laborers who
       did not attend the bala(-service) but in the city . . . ,
       (the document bears) the sealing of ADU.
25 female laborers in 7 days went to the bala(-service), in 3 days
       returned from the bala(-service), the work performance
       involved is 250 days.
20)   Dead: Geme-. . ., from the month "nesag offering" (month 4) on.
       Dead: Geme-Ninurta,
       Dead: Luzi, daughter of Ili-bani,
       Dead: Nin-lama, female slave of Adalal from the month "Šulgi"
       (month 10) on.
       Dead: Išib-Urbartab, from day 20 of the month "Dumuzi"
       (month 12) on,
       the work performance involved is 740 (days),
IV 1)   in the year "Ḫarši was destroyed" (Šulgi 48) until the
       completed day 8 of the month "Bricks cast in moulds"
       (month 2) of the year following "Ḫarši and Kimaš were
       destroyed" (Amar-Suen 1),
       334 days of the arzana female laborers.
       (The document bears) the seal of Lugal-nig-lagare.
Total: 19 gur, 1 (barig) 3 (bán) 6 sìla šagina pea flour,
       the bala barley involved: 1 gur, 4 (barig) 3 (bán) 9$^{1}/_{2}$ sìla 6 gín,
       total: 185 gur, 3 (barig) 5 (bán) 8 sìla dabin flour,
10) total: 34 gur, 2 (bán) 5 sìla sig-flour,
       total: 3 (barig) 1 (bán) ground zigiduḫḫum ninda,
       the bala barley involved: 3 (barig) 1 (bán),
       the barley involved: 276 gur, 2 (barig) 2 (bán) 3 $^{1}/_{2}$ sìla 6 gín,
       total: 11,611 $^{1}/_{2}$ female laborer days,
       deducted.

Deficit: 10 gur, 1 (barig) 3 (bán) 1 $^{1}/_{3}$ sìla 4 gín barley,
surplus: 4 $^{10}/_{60}$ female laborer days,
Account of Lu-sa-izu in the month "Bricks cast in moulds" (month 2)
       in the year
20) following "Ḫarši was destroyed" (Amar-Suen 1).

textile manufactory. Other jobs are also mentioned though they are in some cases insufficiently specified to be comprehensible, while in other cases they are not qualified at all. Once a task was accomplished, it was verified with the seal of the foreman in charge of the work and consequently posted to the credit account of Ur-Šara as a task fulfilled by his female laborers outside of the workshop controlled by him.

Exactly $1/6$ of the (female) laborer days forming the expected performance of the 36 milling laborers in his "debit" section was posted in the first line of his "credit" account and qualified as "free" days ($u_4.du_8.a$); the same compensation for male laborers was usually only $1/10$ of the debited work days. These credited free days were hence treated by the foreman as days in which real work had been performed. From the fact that male and female laborers were treated differently in respect to free days, we may deduce that there was no such thing as a rigid weekly schedule with something comparable to a work-free Sunday. Breaks in work occurred rather on an irregular basis, depending on the work performed and the constitution of the workers. A comparison between the nominally booked work-free periods—whether or not they were really honored by the foremen of work gangs—and modern vacation norms makes apparent that such periods hardly exceeded the minimum time required for the regeneration of the laborers' strength.

At the beginning of the eighth month of Shulgi's forty-eighth regnal year, one of the female laborers in this account called Nin-ḫegal died. The 187 days following her death included in the "debit" section of the account had thus to be included in the "credits." Although this procedure was unassailable from the point of view of accounting, it seems somewhat curious that the work days no longer fulfilled by a deceased laborer should appear in "credits" as days of accomplished work. The circumstance that the free days booked as performed work in the beginning of the "credits" section of the account, moreover, had to be recovered for the state, since clearly a dead woman could not enjoy free days; accordingly, the free days corresponding to a period of 187 workdays were posted at the end of the "debit" section of the account. No detail of this text exemplifies so drastically the high level of formalization achieved by bookkeeping of labor performance during the Ur III period.

The factors of conversion contained in the text—of various types of grain into barley as a means of comparison, of cereal ingredients into their equivalents expressed in barley, or of cereal products into the work time necessary for their processing—also deserve special attention. A comparison of the conversions attested in the present text to those known from other texts leads to the conclusion that the procedure was in fact standardized, at least on a local level, allowing for an overall control and conversion of the performed work.

The text illustrated in figure 70 provides a special opportunity for such a comparison. This account, also from Umma, records the labor performance of a female laborer group under the control of another foreman for exactly the same period as that noted in the previous text (fig. 69). The foreman, called Lu-sa-izu, was also in charge of 36 female laborers occupied in a grain processing workshop. From a formal point of view, the text has a more complex structure and the exact reconstruction of its documented calculations is somewhat problematic, although the same conversion factors were applied in this text as those known elsewhere. The first text for example, contains the following implicit relations:

1 unit measure of zíz (emmer) =	1 unit measure of še (barley)
1 unit of gig (wheat) =	2 units of še
1 unit of ìmgaga (spelt) =	2 units of še

The first two relations are also used implicitly in the second text. These conversion factors, through which different kinds of cereal categories could be converted into the equivalent values expressed in barley, are not restricted to the period of the Ur III Dynasty. They seem to have largely remained the same down to the Neo-Babylonian reign of Nabonidus.

In the conversion of processed flour, the following relations were applied in the first text:

1 unit measure of dabin (flour) =	1 unit measure of še (barley)
1 unit of zì-sig$_{15}$ =	2 units of še
1 unit of zì-gaz$_x$ =	2 units of še
1 unit of ninda-àr-ra-sig$_5$ =	1 $1/2$ units of še
1 unit of eša =	2 units of še

In this case as well, the second text confirms the first three relations; moreover, it contains two additional conversion factors concerning flour not given in the first text. Finally, the work times required to process a unit measure of the noted grain products are the same in both texts:

for dabin	10 sìla per day
for zì-sig$_{15}$	10 sìla per day
for zì-gaz$_x$	10 sìla per day
for ninda-àr-ra-sig$_5$	20 sìla per day
for eša	20 sìla per day

P.D./R.E.

12. Bookkeeping on Animal Husbandry

Numerous administrative documents from practically every period of the third millennium B.C. provide valuable information about the organization of livestock breeding. They document the general outlines of a systematic economic control of domestic animals, especially cattle, sheep, goats, equids—above all donkeys—and pigs. Exploitation of the animals' labor potential as well as the products obtained from them took many forms. According to the documents, this diversity formed one of the most important pre-conditions for the expansion of economic wealth in Mesopotamia and its neighboring regions during the third millennium.

Cattle were held in small herds, as a rule no more than fifteen or twenty head, in the vicinity of urban centers. The main economic value of cattle lay more in their function as a source of traction power required in agricultural plowing than in the production of such dairy goods as fats and cheese. Still less important was their role in the supply of meat, the consumption of which was mainly restricted to the priesthood during cultic ceremonies and to other high-ranking state officials.

Of special economic relevance was the exploitation of large numbers of medium-sized herds of sheep and goats. According to traditional practice, the herds moved seasonally between the summer and winter pasture lands located in the Zagros Mountains and the Mesopotamian flood plain, respectively. The continuously growing urban population of Mesopotamia, in increasing numbers no longer directly dependent on agricultural production for its subsistence, heightened the demand not only for basic cereal commodities but also for textiles. The demand for the latter was almost exclusively met by textiles woven from sheep and goat wool, which, as a matter of interest, also constituted the most heavily traded commodity in the commercial exchange with the periphery of Mesopotamia. The herds controlled by the urban centers were also the chief source of cheese and other dairy products as well as meat.

According to ancient documents, donkeys were a significant factor in economic life as burden and traction animals.

Pig breeding enjoyed by comparison a subordinate, although often underrated role in the third millennium economies. Osteological evidence has proven that shortly after the process of domestication of sheep and goat was completed pigs increasingly found their way into the domestic life of the earliest settled households of the Near East. In fact, pigs retained a certain economic importance over a long period of time. Administrative documents regularly refer to pigs and seem to indicate that the practice of pig breeding reached its highest degree of development during the Old Sumerian period.

The Designation of Domestic Animals in the Archaic Administrative Texts

The archaic precursors of the cuneiform signs designating domestic animals were already identified some time ago. The signs representing cattle, for instance, were pictographic. The age and the function of an animal was expressed by adding to these ideograms specific qualifying signs. The signs designating the gender of young animals AMAR, namely KUR ( ) and SAL ( ), probably represented the male and female sexual organs; the sign GA ( ) stands for a "milk" jar.

	GU$_4$	either bull or ox (representation of the head of a bull or ox with horns)
	AB$_2$	cow (representation of a head of a cow, the horns pointing downwards)
	AMAR	calf (head of a calf without horns)
	KUR+AMAR	bull calf
	SAL+AMAR	heifer calf
	AB$_2$ GA	milk cow
	AMAR GA	suckling (calf)

The signs for sheep and goat have an abstract character. The signs, though, have certain common features: the cross +, the circle ◯ and the lozenge ◇ barred by a diagonal line (as a qualification for the male sex). Again, young animals are specified through adding certain qualifying strokes or complete signs to the basic signs representing the species referred to.

	U$_8$	ewe
	UDUNITA	ram
	UD$_5$	nanny-goat
	MAŠNITA	billy-goat
	KIR$_{11}$	female lamb
	SILANITA	male lamb
	EŠGAR	female kid
	MAŠ	male kid

Cattle, in the general sense of the term including bulls, oxen, cows and calves, were summarized under the composite sign (AB$_2$+GU$_4$), sheep and goats under the sign (UDU).

The sign (ANŠE) was used to denote the ass. Pigs were represented by the signs (ŠUBUR) and (ŠAH$_2$). There seems to be no written evidence from the archaic script phases Uruk IV and III concerning the practice of ass breeding. Such texts are well

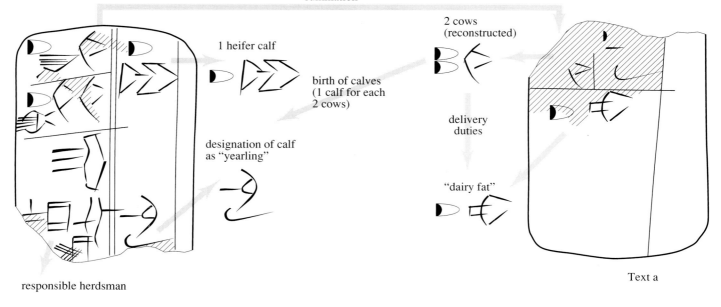

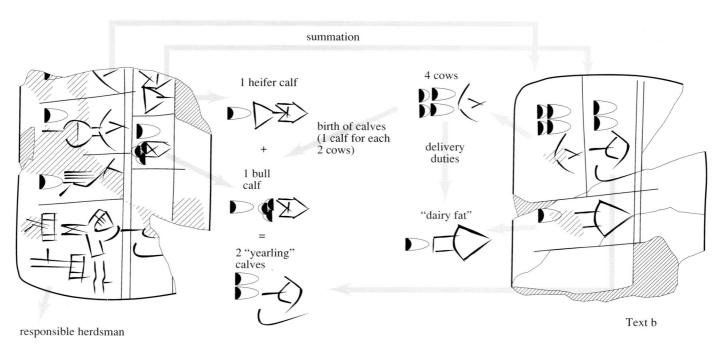

Figure 71. Archaic annual accounts of dairy cattle.

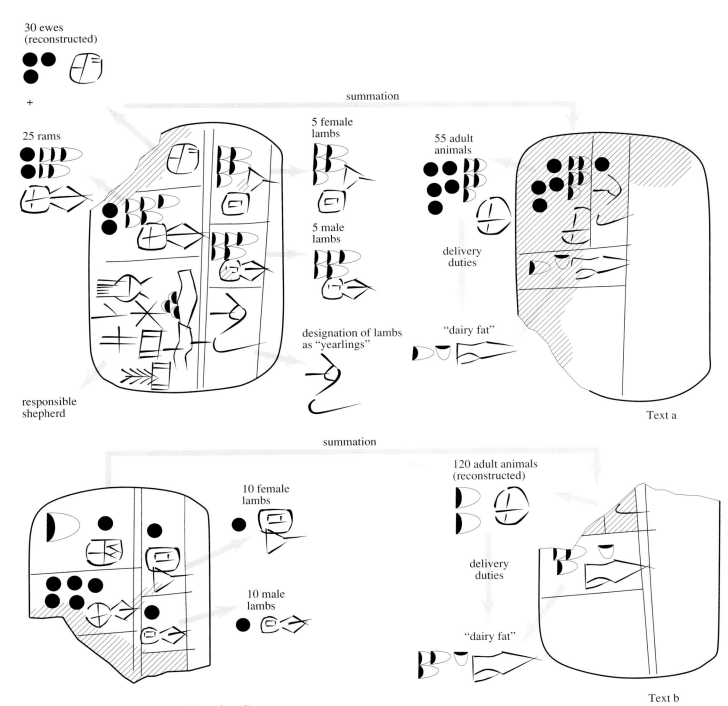

Figure 72. Archaic annual accounts of sheep breeding.

30 ewes
(reconstructed)

+

25 rams

responsible
shepherd

summation

5 female
lambs

5 male
lambs

designation of lambs
as "yearlings"

55 adult
animals

delivery
duties

"dairy fat"

Text a

summation

10 female
lambs

10 male
lambs

120 adult animals
(reconstructed)

delivery
duties

"dairy fat"

Text b

known, however, beginning with the later Fara period. The archaic texts do testify to the existence of developed pig herding in the earliest phases of script development. A text from Uruk (W 23948, published in *BagM* 22 [1991] 57) refers to two herds of 95 fattened pigs, 29 of which were piglets born within the accounting period (see fig. 26).

Domestic animals were generally categorized not only according to sex but also according to age. In case no age-category specification existed, accountants of the archaic and following periods could revert to number signs usually employed in the recording of years. In the archaic period, the concept of year was represented by a pictogram representing the sun together with a number of horizontal lines, depending on the number of years he wished to record:

$\rightarrow$ 1 year $\Rightarrow$ 2 years $\ggg$ 4 years   etc.

A similar method served for the rendering of the age of any given domestic animal:

$\dashv\!\models$	ŠUBUR+1N$_{57}$	one-year old pig
$\Rrightarrow\!\models$	ŠUBUR+3N$_{57}$	three-year old pig
$\dashv\!\rightleftharpoons$	ŠAḪ$_2$+1N$_{57}$	one-year old wild pig
	etc.	

This procedure was above all used in connection with cattle and pigs, since the age of both species was relevant for their exploitation in specific tasks in the field, for example, in plow traction or in food production consisting either of dairy products or meat.

The Archaic Administration of Animal Herds

The archaic tablets shown in figures 71–72 represent each an annual account of an animal herd under the responsibility of one herdsman. Together, the texts exhibit a text format used specifically in the administration of animal herds.

The object of bookkeeping in the first two texts (fig. 71) is a small number of cows. In the first text (71a), the annual productivity of two cows ($\diamond$) was recorded. The meanings of the qualifying signs in both cases are unknown. According to the documents, one of the cows gave birth to a heifer calf within the accounting period. The cows were apparently tended by an individual noted in the third case of the text. In this as well as in the following text, the name of the herdsman was recorded with an additional designation, apparently relating to his function. Of particular interest is the qualification of the herdsman with the sign $\ggg\!\boxminus$ (ŠE+NAM$_2$) , which may have meant "fattener" or "fattening stall."

In the missing first case of the reverse side of the tablet, the adult cows were in all probability noted again in a summary together with the calf which then would appear in a separate notation. A registered jar of the type $\triangleright$ (DUG$_b$) forms the last entry of the text, referring to the (expected) delivery of a certain amount of a dairy product obtained from the milk produced during the accounting year.

On the second of the two tablets (71b), which has the same format, four cows are recorded together with two calves. The calves were recorded separately according to the their sex. As was the case in the first text, the reverse of the tablet summarizes the adult animals separately from the young ones.

Here again, in the last entry a jar of the type $\triangleright$ (DUG$_b$) was booked. Archaic and later documents seem to suggest that this sign designates an amount of a dairy product, hereafter referred to as "milk fat." For the lack of clarifying evidence, nothing more can as yet be said about this product. The recorded amount probably satisfied a delivery quota set by a central authority—the owner of the cows—for every milk-producing animal. There is some evidence suggesting that the rendered jar originally had a liquid capacity of between 6 and 8 liters and that the owner of the cows consequently collected yearly 3 to 4 liters of milk fat per milk cow.

In both texts, the calves were qualified with the notation $\rightarrow$ $\subset$ (U$_4$+1N$_{57}$ BAR). The first part of this sign combination, the sign for "year" already explained above, apparently served to document the birth of the calves during the accounting year. The sign $\subset$ (BAR) is also known from the field texts of Jemdet Nasr discussed in chapter 10. In that text category it was used as a qualification of surfaces along the "outer" limits of certain fields (see fig. 48). In the present case a similar interpretation would seem to support a translation of the entire notation "additional (animals) in the current year."

Two other texts in figure 72 are also accounts disclosing the same structure. Each account again covered an administrative year but referred to flocks of sheep, for each of which responsibility was assigned a particular shepherd. The first column of the obverse side of each tablet relates to the ewes and rams belonging to each flock which, as opposed to the recorded cattle in the previous two texts, were not further qualified. In the following, third case, the responsible shepherd is named. The parallelism to the structure of the cattle texts is strengthened by the fact that one of the two shepherds was qualified $\ggg\!\boxminus$ (ŠE+NAM$_2$), "fattener" (?). Moreover, in the second column the lambs were yet again separately registered according to their sex. We learn in these texts that approximately one third of the ewes recorded had lambed in the accounting year.

In addition, the reverse side of both documents contains a final compilation of the flocks, including separate summations of the adult sheep and the lambs plus an extra entry concerning the delivery of an amount of "dairy fat." In this case as well as in documents pertaining to goats the sign ⟜ (KISIM) represented this product, hence depicting a different type of jar from that referred to by the pictogram which occurred in connection with "milk fat" deliveries of the cow herders. The absolute size of the depicted jar is unknown. Its capacity will certainly not have been significantly below that of the jar represented by the sign ⟚ (DUG_b), since both documents (72a–b) reveal that just one jar of the KISIM corresponded to the expected fat deliveries—the "user fees" of the goatherders—to the authorities for as many as fifteen to twenty ewes.

Summarizing accounts covering a certain accounting period are particularly informative concerning the general features of economic organization in the archaic period. Unfortunately, such texts are extremely scarce. Two tablets from Uruk (W 15785,a10 [unpublished] and W 20274,1 [obverse published in *ATU* 2, pl. 18]) nevertheless provide a good glimpse of the scale of the flocks controlled by the state. These accounts record a total of 1,418 and 1,380 sheep, respectively.

Archaic Documents on the Processing of Animal Products
The modalities by which the processing of animal products was organized complied with the centralized structure of the administration of livestock herds itself. Final accounts such as the texts shown in figure 73 give testimony to this centrality. In both texts, relatively large amounts of animal products are registered in more or less identical sequence. The first entry in the first text reveals much about the quantity of the products being processed. In this entry, the same dairy product (⟚), already seen in the annual balances discussed above (fig. 71), was recorded. In this case, however, the quantities shown correspond approximately to 26 times the annual expected deliveries for small herds of between 2 and 4 milk cows.

Unfortunately, the majority of the signs representing animal products in both texts are as yet not fully understood. What can be said, however, is that the first half of each text concerns textiles exclusively, except for the mentioned dairy product occurring in one of the texts. The textiles were either of wool, goat hair, or some other fleece or fur. Although the quantities of the registered textiles are relatively small, it may be assumed that the quality of the fabrics was high. Later sources often refer to the extreme labor requirements in the production of higher quality textiles, which thus could only be produced in low quantities at high production costs.

In the second part of both texts follows a list with an array of animal products, each recorded in very large quantities. Among the products there are some that were characterized with the sign ▌ (Sumerian: ŠE₃). The meaning of this object designation sign is unclear; it apparently represents a widely available product which could be processed from different animal species. In the texts 73a–b it appears in context with the signs for goat (✛▌) and sheep (⊞▌); in other texts it may occur together with the sign for bull or ox (◇▌), or even that for pig (⟝▌). It may be that the sign referred to a specific kind of processed dung, perhaps used as fuel. Should this identification prove to be correct, then the first text recorded 1,263 units of goat's dung and 171 units of sheep dung, and in the preserved part of the second text 1,223 units of goat's dung.

Of considerable significance is the sign ▷◁ (GA'AR), which according to later cuneiform tradition was replaced by the phonetically written ga.àr, normally translated "cheese" but literally meaning pounded or stamped milk. We suspect that this cheese, pressed into the shape of a small cake, was processed in extremely large amounts and that it could be stored over relatively long periods of time. This product was not counted in the sexagesimal, but rather in the bisexagesimal system, a numerical sign system which, according to our analysis, was used for rations of mass-produced comestibles. The texts record 6,480 and 18,120 units of the product, the latter notation being the largest number attested in the bisexagesimal system.

Cattle Herding in Proto-Elamite Documents
The proto-Elamite texts, written during approximately the same period as the archaic administrative texts from Mesopotamia, have, regrettably, not been adequately deciphered. Many of the documents, however, seem to point clearly enough to the importance the herding of small cattle held in this region.

A good example of the tablets containing presumed records of animal herds is the text shown in figure 74. The obverse of this text has four entries, each pertaining to one herd with, first, the name of the herdsman, followed by the designation of the animals (⤙) and their number. According to the present state of research, the proto-Elamite sign ⤙ corresponds semantically and graphically to the proto-cuneiform sign UDU (⊞), the collective term comprising all categories of sheep and goats. The reverse lists again the type of animals recorded and the total of all four herds, adding up to 65 animals.

That total, by the way, illustrates again the noteworthy difference between the proto-Elamite way of recording animals and the corresponding method in archaic Mesopotamia. Whereas in the proto-cuneiform tablets animals and humans were noted in the

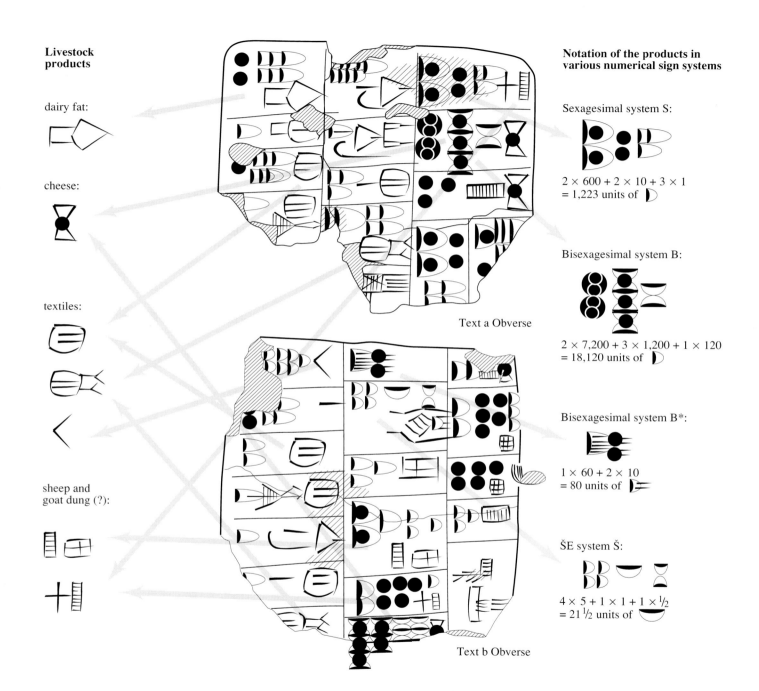

Livestock products

dairy fat:

cheese:

textiles:

sheep and goat dung (?):

Text a Obverse

Text b Obverse

Notation of the products in various numerical sign systems

Sexagesimal system S:

$2 \times 600 + 2 \times 10 + 3 \times 1$
$= 1,223$ units of

Bisexagesimal system B:

$2 \times 7,200 + 3 \times 1,200 + 1 \times 120$
$= 18,120$ units of

Bisexagesimal system B*:

$1 \times 60 + 2 \times 10$
$= 80$ units of

ŠE system Š:

$4 \times 5 + 1 \times 1 + 1 \times \frac{1}{2}$
$= 21\frac{1}{2}$ units of

Figure 73. Archaic accounts of livestock products.

94

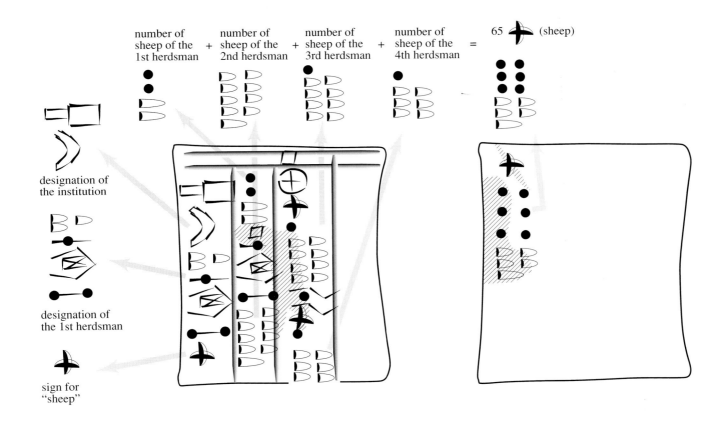

Figure 74. Proto-Elamite administrative document concerning four herds of sheep.

sexagesimal system, comparable notations in the region coinciding with the distributional area of the proto-Elamite texts, corresponding approximately to later Persia, seem to have employed a decimal system exclusively. Accordingly, in order to represent the total of 65 animals, the proto-Elamite scribe repeated six times the sign for "10" (●) instead of writing the sign for "60" (◗).

Old Sumerian Accounts of Livestock Products
The interpretation of the proto-cuneiform and proto-Elamite administrative documents relating to matters of herd management and

use of livestock products is aided by the evidence supplied by Old Sumerian texts from the archive of the southern Babylonian city Girsu. Among these texts, which date predominantly to the first half of the twenty-fourth century B.C., there are similar documents recording the (expected) delivery of dairy products of the herdsmen tending state- or temple-owned animals. Figure 75 shows one of these tablets, dated to the fifth regnal year of the "énsi" Lugalanda, the penultimate ruler of the province of Lagash in the Old Sumerian period. The tablet records the annual delivery quotas of a number of herdsmen in charge of smaller herds of

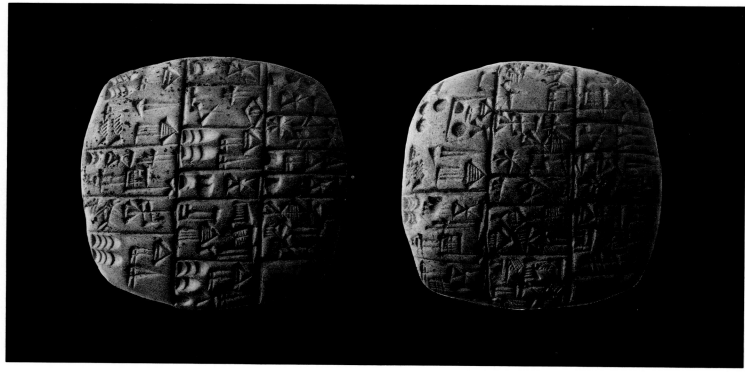

Figure 75. Old Sumerian account of dairy products.

varying size, consisting of five to fifteen milk cows. The quotas were fixed in units of a dairy product, probably a butter-like product, designated ì áb sè.ga, literally "thrown dairy fat" and the product ga'ar (⋈ ; = *LAK* 490), "cheese."

The following translation of the text demonstrates that for the Old Sumerian period the function of such accounts is clearly understood:

I	8 dug ì áb sè.ga	8 jars of thrown dairy fat,
	2 (gur) ga'ar gur sag+gál	2 gur sag+gál of cheese,
	Nam.dam	(from) Namdam.
	8 dug ì	8 jars of (thrown dairy) fat,
	2 (gur) ga'ar	2 (gur) of cheese,
	Me.sàg.nu.di	(from) Mesag-nudi.
	6 dug ì	6 jars of (thrown dairy) fat,
	1 (gur) 2 (barig) ga'ar	1 (gur) 2 (barig) of cheese,
	Ur.šu.ga.lam.ma	(from) Ur-šugalama.
	5 dug 10 sìla ì	5 jars 10 sìla of (thrown dairy) fat,

1 (gur) 1 (barig) 3 (bán) ga'ar	1 (gur) 1 (barig) 3 (bán) of cheese,
Dingir.šeš.mu	(from) Dingir-šeš-mu.
1 dug ì	1 jar of (thrown dairy) fat,
1 (barig) ga'ar	1 (barig) of cheese,
Lú.kur.ré.bí.ge₄	(from) Lukure-bige.
ŠU.NÍGIN 30 lá 1 dug	Total: 30 minus 1 jar, 10 sìla
10 sìla ì.áb sè.ga	of thrown dairy fat,
7 (gur) 3 (bán) ga'ar gur sag+gál	7 gur sag+gál 3 (bán) of cheese,
ì ga'ar ú.rum	fat and cheese are the property
Bára.nam.tar.ra	of Bara-namtara,
dam Lugal.an.da	the wife of Lugalanda,
énsi	the ruler
Lagaš^{ki}.ka	of Lagash.
e še á giš gi ka.ra.ka.ka	After at the location ...
En.ig.gal	Eniggal,
nu.bànda	the chancellor

gúrum áb mu.ak.a	who carried out the inspection of the cows,
níg.ka₉.bi e.ak AŠ+\\\\\	made the account. (Regnal year:) 5.

The liquid capacity of the "jars" in which the dairy fat was delivered to the administration was standardized and corresponded to 20 sìla, approximately equivalent to 30 liters. They can therefore be considered metrological units specific to that particular product. Cheese of the category "ga'ar" was measured in capacity units as well, thus in a manner different from that of the archaic dairy product "GA'AR" (▷◁) which was counted as discrete units. The change that occurred with this product is unclear; it may have been due to a change in the metrological system or perhaps in the nature of the product itself. All we know is that from the period of the Old Sumerian texts onward cheese quantities were rendered according to the "normal" capacity system which traditionally had been applied in measuring and recording quantities of grain. As already seen in chapter 10, this system had a specific structure in Lagash during this period:

1 sìla	≈ 1.5 liters
1 bán	= 6 sìla
1 barig	= 6 bán
1 gur sag+gál	= 4 barig

Other texts from the Old Sumerian corpus (especially the texts DP 93 and DP 274=275) document the fact that the quantities of dairy fat and cheese yearly due the central administration were determined by the number of cows entrusted to the care of a particular herdsman. Accordingly, 10 sìla of "thrown dairy fat" and 18 sìla of "cheese" (approximately 15 and 27 liters, respectively) per cow were to be delivered yearly. The figures given in the present text are consistent with those just cited, so that the number of milk cows contained in the herds of the recorded herdsmen can be calculated. Thus if we assume that 16 milk cows formed the herd of Namdam, his annual duties would amount to 160 sìla dairy fat and 288 sìla cheese. This corresponds exactly to the 8 jars of dairy fat and 2 gur of cheese registered in the text. Accordingly the following figures have been reconstructed for each herdsman:

Namdam	16 milk cows
Mesag-nudi	16 milk cows
Ur-šugalama	12 milk cows
Dingir-šeš-mu	11 milk cows
Lukure-bige	2 milk cows

Three of the herdsmen are also registered in the texts DP 93 and DP 274 mentioned above. Both texts are dated six years before the text in figure 75. We thus learn that the three herds had in the meantime increased in size. In the herd of Namdam, the number of milk cows had increased from thirteen to sixteen, in that of Mesag-nudi from eight to sixteen, and in that of Ur-šugalama from four to twelve. Since other texts also point to a continuous increase of the herds, this seems to reflect a general policy in cattle breeding.

Cattle-Breeding Strategies during the Ur III Period

One unusual document preserved from the Ur III period discloses crucial information on the calculations carried out in connection with cattle breeding and the expected output of dairy products of that time (see fig. 76). In this document, the annual production of "dairy fat" and "cheese" are calculated over a period of ten years based on the hypothetical growth of a cattle herd consisting, at the beginning of that period, of four milk cows.

The tablet is probably from Drehem, a center for livestock transactions under the administration of the Ur III empire. The ten years treated in the text fall into the reign of Shulgi, a period marked by a rigidly applied central rule during which the empire, at the apex of its territorial expansion, was governed as if it were a single economy. During this time the central bookkeeping had also become increasingly preoccupied with elaborate and complete details, nearly to the point of absurdity.

The present tablet does not belong to the normal bookkeeping documents of the period. The exact purpose of the calculations in this account, rather untypical by standards of normal bookkeeping practice, is not known. The document is designated the "account of Idūa, son of Issu-arik, the manager (sanga) of the temple of (the deity) Ištaran." There is no doubt that the document represents a theoretical calculation of the expected reproduction of consecutive generations of the cows and hence on the concomitant increase of future delivery duties. The text does not refer at the end of the accounting period to an existing herd.

This is demonstrated not only by the arithmetical structure of the text, but also by the unrealistic assumption of a mortality rate of zero, thus allowing for a continuous high milk production even by very old cows. Even at the end of the period, the four cows of the original herd are still alive and, at the *minimum* age of 14 years, included in the calculation, thus still calving at regular intervals and producing the same amount of milk as at the beginning of the accounting period. This calculation will therefore not have referred to a real animal herd, especially so considering the high mortality rate among domestic animals as the result of disease, infections, and the like. It seems quite clear that, for reasons

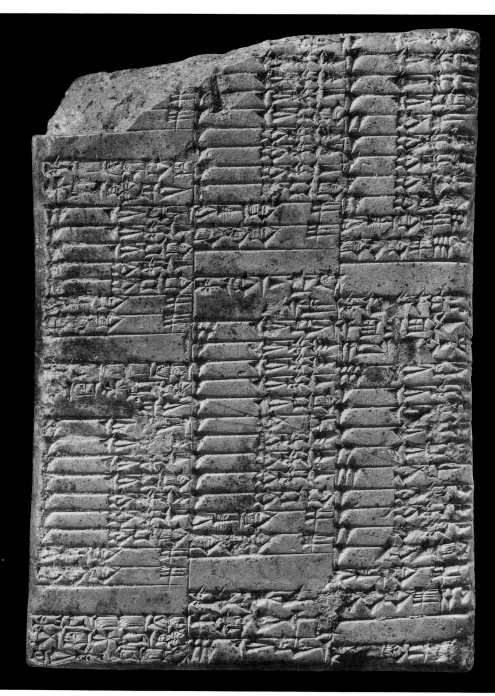

Figure 76. Neo-Sumerian tablet with a calculation of the growth of a herd of cattle.

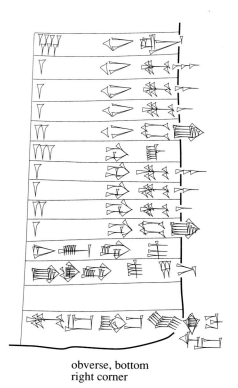

7	áb máḫ
1	áb mu.3×AŠ
1	áb mu.2×AŠ
1	áb mu.1×AŠ
2	áb amar.ga
3	gu₄ gal
1	gu₄ mu.3×AŠ
1	gu₄ mu.2×AŠ
7	gu₄ mu.1×AŠ
1	gu₄ amar.ga
ì.nun.bi	3 (bán)
ga.àr.bi	4 (bán) 5 sìla
mu Ur.bí.lumᵏⁱ ba.ḫul	

7	full-grown cows,
1	three-year-old cow,
1	two-year-old cow,
1	one-year-old cow,
2	sucking heifer calves,
3	full-grown bulls,
1	three-year-old bull,
1	two-year-old bull,
7	one-year-old bulls,
1	sucking bull calf,
the dairy fat involved: 3 (bán),	
the cheese involved:	4 (bán) 5 sìla.
Year: "Urbilum was destroyed" (45th regnal year of Šulgi)	

obverse, bottom
right corner

Figure 77. Excerpt from the text illustrated in figure 76, stating the number of cattle registered in the seventh year of the model calculation.

unknown to us, the text represents a trial or model calculation concerning hypothetical herd growth.

Because of precisely this circumstance, the text provides reliable insights into the categories and rules of bookkeeping practices of that period. Both cows (áb; sign ◇) and bulls (gu₄; sign ⇨) are divided into five age categories:

	amar.ga	suckled animals
	mu.1×AŠ	one-year-old animals
	mu.2×AŠ	two-year-old animals
	mu.3×AŠ	three-year-old animals
	máḫ	adult animals

For every year documented in the text, the exact number of animals is given according to the age categories listed above. The calculation of the expected deliveries of dairy products for each year on the basis of the number of animals in the preceding year is then recorded: for each adult cow (áb.máḫ) 5 sìla of "dairy fat"

(ì.nun) and 7 ½ sìla of "cheese" (ga.àr) was to be delivered. Figure 77, for example, depicts the section of the account dealing with the seventh year in the calculation (obverse, column III, lines 14–27) when the number of milk-producing cows had increased to seven while the calculation of the deliveries was based on the number of milk cows—six—from the sixth year.

The annual reproduction of cattle (fig. 78) was fixed as a rule at an average rate of one newborn calf for every two adult cows. The gender distribution of the calves was also theoretical: the text exhibits a strict adherence to the sequence male-female, and so on. For years in which adult cows were registered in odd numbers, calving success was recorded by dividing this number by two and rounding the result to the next lower number. In the section on the eighth year, the rule does not apply. Apparently due to a scribal mistake, the birth of three instead of the expected four calves is recorded.

At the end of the reverse of the tablet (fig. 79), all cattle were totaled separately according to sex at the conclusion of the 10-year

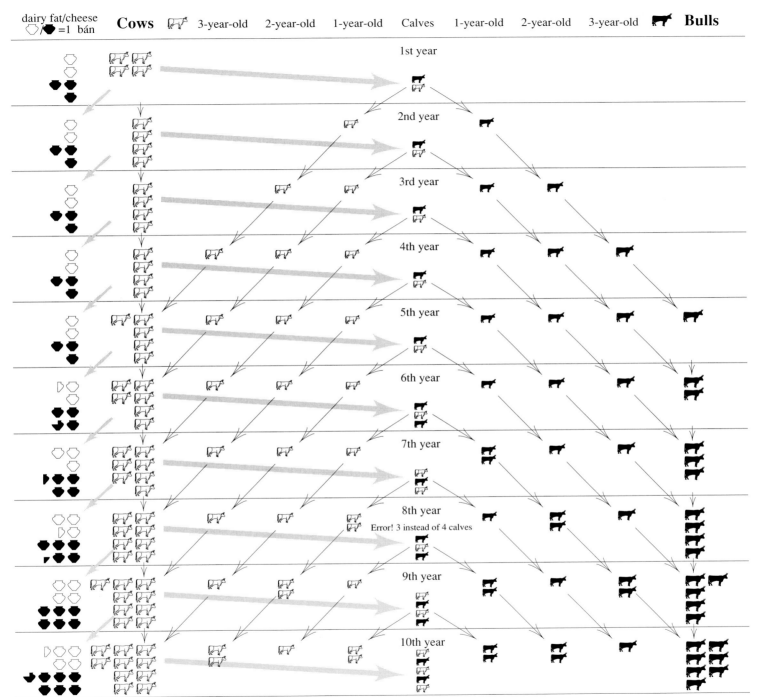

Figure 78. The growth of cattle herd according to the text illustrated in figure 76.

101

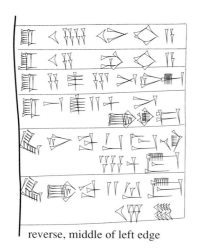

ŠU+NÍGIN	18	áb.ḫi.a
ŠU+NÍGIN	14	gu₄.ḫi.a
ŠU+NÍGIN	4 (barig) 3 (bán) 5 sìla ì.nun	
ŠU+NÍGIN	1 (gur) 1 (barig) 5 (bán) 2½ sìla ga.àr gur	
kù ì.ba	⅓ ma.na 7½ gín	
kù ga.ba	2⅔ gín 15 še	

Together:	18 divers cows,
together:	14 divers bulls,
together:	4 (barig) 3 (bán) 5 sìla dairy fat,
together:	1 (gur) 1 (barig) 5 (bán) 2½ sìla cheese,
the silver (equivalent) of the fat involved:	⅓ mana 7½ gín
the silver (equivalent) of the cheese involved:	2⅔ gín 15 še

reverse, middle of left edge

Figure 79. Summation in the text illustrated in figure 76.

period. In a next step, the total amount of dairy fat and cheese delivered over the entire period was calculated. The amount was then converted into its corresponding value equivalent expressed in silver. The exchange rate was set at 10 sìla of dairy fat or 150 sìla of cheese per shekel of silver (approx. 8.3 g). These figures reveal that dairy fat was considered fifteen times more valuable than cheese, so that its production costs in labor and raw milk will have been much greater than that for cheese. This finding in fact strongly suggests that "dairy fat" in reality was a butter-like product derived from cream, whereas "cheese" was a relatively "cheap" foodstuff (only about twice as expensive as equal measures of barley!) processed from the remaining skimmed milk or directly from the raw milk.

The Scope of the Economic Control of Domestic Animals

The greatest concern of the accounting of farm animals was undoubtedly the control of the herds. Moreover, animal use, delivered products, and occurring expenses were registered in detail.

On the tablet from Drehem in figure 80, the deliveries of 18 individuals were listed in the form of fattened livestock. The animals were transferred to the central authority during the "month of the great feast," which suggests that the deliveries were made in the explicit context of the religious event.

The obverse of the tablet records predominantly the deliveries of seemingly high-ranking officials, as exemplified by the priest of the "temple of (the deity) Nanše." Each of these individuals seems to have been compelled to hand over relatively large numbers of animals. The first person, for example, delivered "1 fattened ox, 6 sheep, 1 billy-goat," the second "1 fattened ox, 9 sheep, 1 billy goat," and the priest just mentioned "1 fattened ox, 3 fattened sheep, 1 fattened lamb, 3 sheep, 2 billy-goats, 1 lamb." The following persons, especially those listed on the reverse of the tablet delivered considerably fewer beasts, for example, just one lamb by the "priest of (the temple of the goddess) Inanna," or two lambs by the "governor of (the city of) Nippur." Some of the persons can be identified as members of the regular palace staff. A lamb, for example, was delivered by a person additionally qualified as a cook.

Fattened livestock are often mentioned in the documents as deliveries for special festivities. In terms of cattle breeding, the supply of fodder was also at all times of some concern for bookkeeping. Written evidence dealing with calculations about fodder, especially for sheep, is in fact already attested in the archaic period. An exact interpretation of this evidence remains, however, for the moment extremely difficult. Beginning with the texts of the Old Sumerian period, a systematic routine of control of the monthly feed requirements of livestock of the central

institutions is evident. The administrative documents in question are accounts of several columns in which the different animal categories were listed separately and, on the basis of defined feed requirements, the amount of fodder given to each animal was booked. Figure 81 shows a text with such entries. The tablet from Lagash dates back to the first regnal year of Lugalanda. In the fourth and fifth columns of the text, entries concerning the fodder destined for fattening pigs (šáḫ; sign ⟨▦⟩) are found. The fodder was given to the care of the swineherd called Lugalpa'e:

8 (gur) 3 (barig) še šáḫ ú,	8 (gur) 3 (barig) barley for the grass(-fed) hogs,
1 (barig) še šáḫ giš.gi Lugal.pa.è	1 (barig) barley for the wild boar, (delivered to) Lugalpa'e.

In the Ur III period, even more care was taken in the accounting of fodder. Even the feed for the fattened birds and rodents destined to be offerings for the temples was recorded in

Figure 80. Neo-Sumerian list of slaughter cattle.

Figure 81. Old Sumerian account of fodder.

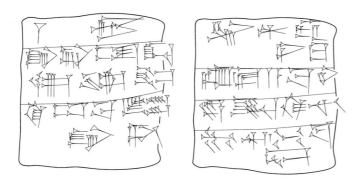

Figure 82. Neo-Sumerian text concerning the use of a nanny goat to suckle a piglet.

the accounts. The tablet in figure 82 conveys an impression of the attention to detail of bookkeeping during this period. The text on the tablet reads as follows.

1 ud₅ ga.bi	One goat, whose milk
zé.da šáḫ gu₇.dè	will be given to a piglet,
ki Ab.ba.sa₆.ga.ta	from Aba-saga
Lú.dingir.ra ì.dab₅	did Lu-dingira receive.
kišib *É-a-ba-ni*	Seal: Ea-bani.
iti Á.ki.ti	Month: Akiti,
mu dingir gu ba.dím	year: "(Amar-Suen) built the throne (for Enlil)" (third regnal year of Amar-Suen, ca. 2044 B.C.).

P.D./R.E.

13. The Education and Profession of the Scribe

Well in advance of the appearance of script in Babylonia at the end of the fourth millennium B.C. (see chap. 4), professional administrators must have been familiar with the problems of recording elementary features of economic transactions using complicated, yet for their purposes efficient non-literary instruments of control. It is difficult to conceive how the application and maintenance of administrative structures were possible without an orderly transmission of expertise and experience, that is, without some sort of organized system for the training of future administrators. Within this circle of experts, a number of experiments were undoubtedly carried out to achieve more efficient methods of control. The idea of writing, which may have resulted from such experiments, in the end proved the most diverse and adaptable instrument of control.

Among those learning to use writing, this new administrative mechanism was transmitted for the first time. The traditional administrative professional thus turned into a literate administrative expert, whom we rather inexactly call a "scribe." No doubt the ability to read and write became the professional qualification of a growing number of individuals in Babylonia. As a rule, these people enjoyed high social status. The origin of that respect is to be seen not only in the inherent connection between writing and its function as a controlling instrument, but also simply in its connection to culture.

The archaic texts give but scant information about the education or professional activity of scribes. The usual Sumerian word for scribe, dub.šar (literally, "tablet-writing"), only occurs in later texts. There is, however, a possibility that the word DUB (proto-cuneiform sign ⌐▤) on its own designated the scribe during this early stage, since it occurs twice in the professions list (see chap. 14) in the sign combination SANGA.DUB. On the other hand, it may be that the sign read SANGA (▤◺) represents the earliest "scribes" (but see the remarks referring to the SANGA Kushim above, chap. 8).

The conspicuous unity in the appearance of the tablets as well as the writing conventions attested in the written evidence from different regions of Babylonia are suggestive of the existence of some kind of regulated system of education. This is most apparent for the tablets from script phase III at Uruk, a phase during which the graphic form of texts from southern Babylonia scarcely differed from those written in the northern settlements Tell Uqair or Jemdet Nasr. For this script phase, one is even tempted to think of a centralized system of education.

We are, of course, not able to reconstruct the exact methods by

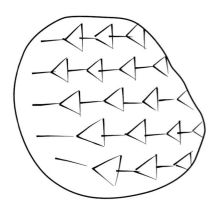

Figure 83. Scribal exercise.

which the pupils were taught to write. Several tablet groups, however, are to a certain extent indicative of how one might have dealt with the task. A first group consists of plainly shaped pieces of clay on which a number of lines or rows of impressions were incised with a stylus. These objects probably testify to the first lessons a scribal novice would have received (see fig. 83). Occasionally, such exercises were carried out on real writing tablets of the prevailing shape. Once a pupil reached this stage, he had probably acquired the ability to shape and prepare the script carrier. Some blank clay tablets might represent the results of such preparatory exercises (for example, W 9312,aa, unpublished).

Tablets or lumps of clay yielding various arrays of stylus impressions suggest that the next step was to become acquainted with the different sign elements, in order to acquire some competence before combining them to form real signs (fig. 84 and W 9123,d, published as *ATU* 1, no. 539). The result could be considered unsatisfactory, leading to the tablet being pressed together into a lump (fig. 85). Tablets that look like normal administrative texts except that they contain neither summations nor personal designations may be regarded as school exercises rather than authentic documents. From a group of texts compiled some 1300 years after the invention of writing which describe the adventures of a "son of the tablet house," we are told that the process of acquiring the command of the cuneiform script was a rather long and tedious affair (see the end of this chapter).

Another large tablet group should be placed within the context of the curriculum of advanced scribal students. These texts are usually referred to as lexical lists, since they consist of lists of words comparable to dictionary columns. Although the principles according to which the word sequences were compiled are not entirely clear, the entries do form semantic groups. One list, for

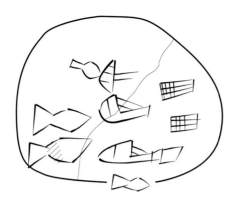

Figure 84. Scribal exercise.

example, contains signs and sign combinations representing exclusively different kinds of trees and shrubs and later in the text wooden objects, all qualified by the sign meaning "wood." Other lists are restricted to animals, divided into separate categories listing fish, birds, cattle, and so on. These lists may additionally discriminate between age and gender groups. Other lists enumerate different types of pottery vessels of various contents (fig. 86) and toponyms, but also other objects whose relationship is not always obvious.

One list in particular has contributed substantially to our understanding of society in archaic Mesopotamia. The entries of

Figure 85. Tablet "waster."

this list represent titles and professions, also known from contemporary economic texts (see chap. 14), in which such titles are mentioned in functional context. The special value of this list is also to be seen in the sequence in which the words occur. It begins with a sign composition which, according to an Akkadian "dictionary" of the second millennium B.C., is translated with the widely applied term for "king" (*šarrum*). This and the following ten entries are each combined with a sign that must have designated some sort of leader. Hence we find expressions such as "leader of justice," "leader of the city," "leader of the plow," and "leader of barley," each expression probably denoting the rank of those people in charge of the respective administrative fields.

The list continues with titles designating leading functions such as the head gardener or the head of the council of elders (?). Following titles which, according to later tradition, are to be placed within the cultic sphere, there are additional terms designating various fields of activity, within which hierarchical differentiations were made.

The sequences of the entries, beginning with the title that probably designates the highest dignitary, leads to the assumption that it was compiled according to the hierarchy of the persons represented by these titles.

These lists are different from all other texts in that they were continuously copied throughout the third millennium. Such copying not only occurred in great numbers within the same phase, as exemplified by the archaic texts from Uruk, among which the mentioned professions list is attested in not less than 165 copies, but this practice persisted into the subsequent periods.

This intensive copying activity and the continuous tradition of the texts over a period of 800 years and more most probably resulted from the texts being used in scribal training, as has already been postulated above. We will probably never be certain whether the texts served in the acquisition and practice of writing signs—the sequences seen could well have served as memory aids—and in achieving an elementary vocabulary for use in administrative texts, or whether they also served to categorize the human environment and therefore helped archaic society to understand itself. Beyond the function of the texts as transmitters of script, lexical lists must in any case have been highly valued, since the scribes painstakingly copied them in every detail throughout the entire third millennium, well into periods when language and script had evolved to such a degree that the old lists were to a large extent no longer understood.

The first detailed information concerning the profession and the social rank of the scribe is found in numbers of texts from the time of the Third Dynasty of Ur, dated to ca. 2000 B.C. This is underscored by the fact that the traditional goddess of fertility and

Figure 86. Part of a lexical list enumerating, among others objects, pottery vessels.

cereals, Nisaba, functioned as the deity of the scribes. Because of the lack of explicit early texts and assuming that the situation probably had not changed entirely, a more encompassing account of the context of scribal education of the time around 2000 may help to picture what education in the archaic period may have been like.

The designation for scribe, dub.šar, a word well attested from the middle of the third millennium on, appears in Ur III texts in connection with people of quite different social ranks. Not only did the ruler and other very high-ranking officials adorn themselves with the title, but lower-ranking and subordinate professionals were also called scribes. Such scribes could be further qualified, for example, "scribe of the palace," "scribe of the weaving mill," and so on. On the other hand, many titles that are known to us from the administrative complex are by no means instructive as to whether or not the people behind the titles had benefited from scribal education. We must, however, assume that virtually all the individuals in important positions in administration and economic management had some knowledge of the art of writing during this period.

The numerous economic documents of the Third Dynasty of Ur disclose more than any other source the fields of responsibility of the scribes. Extremely influential, for example, were the scribes at the royal court. They controlled the flow of information between the ruler and his kingdom. Comparable key positions were assumed by the personal secretaries of the various city governors in the country. In addition, a number of more common scribes were employed at the palace. An equally large group of administrative units were connected to the temple households. The temples could command extensive stretches of arable land, as we have seen in pre-Sargonic Lagash. Since agriculture was by far the largest economic sector in the country, most of the scribes worked in this sector. They were, for instance, charged with seeing after the maintenance of the irrigation canals, registering the rations of the labor force and the storage of the harvest, and controlling the supply of and guarding the agricultural tools. In animal husbandry, it was their job to control the receipt and conveyance of the animals at the points of transshipment. Uncounted numbers worked in the manufactory centers. They managed the bookkeeping of many small units attached to the temple or palace, but also those of the larger enterprises to which the so-called craft houses belonged. Such units comprised many professions, such as the smiths of precious metal, lapidaries, basket-weavers and ropemakers, and the like. The task of the scribe employed was to assure the supply of the raw materials and to control the distribution of rations as well as the output of the finished products. Other parts of the economy such as the textile industry, shipbuilding, pottery workshops, and the transport services had their own scribes. Finally, scribes fulfilled important tasks in the field of law. The great variational range of the positions occupied by the scribes discloses that they in fact spanned the entire upper echelons of the social ladder.

Numerous nondescript scribes usually received rations of barley, oil, and textiles and occasionally other produce. Some were also allotted fields, which they either cultivated themselves or leased out to tenant farmers. The scribal profession also presented opportunities for social climbing. Growing responsibility obviously led to better remuneration. Many texts document the rise of scribes to the level of high-ranking officials, such as to the office of an exchequer, prefect, land registrar, labor supervisor, chancellor, and even city governor. Scribal education itself, as said before, seems to have been a precondition for employment in an important position.

The determining factor for the professional career of a scribe was primarily his social background. Scribes from influential families stood a much better chance of success than those from more common homes. Well-situated individuals, of course, could choose between a greater number of training possibilities. Of great advantage, as well, was the circumstance of having been born into a family with ancestral tradition in the scribal arts, especially considering the fact that as early as the Ur III period clear tendencies of practice of hereditary right to office become visible, although the pursuit of a particular post was, of course, dependent on the acknowledgment of a superior institution or of the king.

An important element of the social position of the scribe is the seal he used. Every scribe required a seal to verify receipt of goods or otherwise authenticate documents. In many cases, the seal inscriptions not only disclose the name of the respective proprietor but also the name of his father and his father's profession. Career changes could cause the scribes to alter their seals. The seal types may also be significant, since many scribes used mass-produced seals, of which the stereotype seal design had been engraved in the stone before the seal was acquired. Only the seal inscription determined in such cases the individual character of the seal. Few high-ranking individuals could afford to buy a seal cut on special order—such seals were very expensive.

Enticing glimpses into the education of scribes at the end of the third and during the first half of the second millennium B.C. are provided particularly by the so-called edubba literature. These texts are in fact lessons which describe, partly in prose, partly in dialog, the school environment (Sumerian é.dub.ba = "tablet house," "school") of the time.

Some training centers were official institutions. Such is the case, for example, for the schools of the Ur III king Shulgi in Ur and Nippur. There may in fact be a connection between these institutions and the administrative reforms carried out about halfway through the the reign of that sovereign (2094–2047 B.C.),

which caused a sudden increase in the number of tablets. It may be, therefore, that the purpose of such foundations was to provide the necessary personnel in times of great demand of scribes, as was certainly the case during the latter part of the rule of Shulgi. Privately organized lessons, however, must have taken place too. When several families sent their children to a scribe for lessons, a private school would have developed, which, dependent on the success of the lessons, would have benefited from a good reputation. It is conceivable that the sector of scribal education formerly supported by private initiative increasingly came under state influence during the Ur III period. The more private character of the lessons seems preserved in the designation of the teacher as the ad.da é.dub.ba, meaning literally "father of the tablet house" or the šeš.gal, the "big/oldest brother." Accordingly, the pupil was called dumu é.dub.ba "child/son of the tablet house."

Regardless of such considerations, the archaeological loci of texts that pertain to the realm of the school and education demonstrate that our term "school" cannot be applied without reservation to comparable institutions in ancient Babylonia. In fact, such institutions were of a quite different nature. Tablets have been found inside such official buildings as palaces and temples, but also in normal private houses, for example, in Ur and Nippur. Educational ideals such as those encountered in royal eulogy hymns can hence not be regarded as the standard for the normal curriculum, but probably only applied to a small minority of the upper classes. Shulgi, for example, not only boasted of being in perfect command of the art of writing and an excellent musician but also claimed that he had learned how to gain profile in the assembly, to be wise in passing judgment and so on.

In contrast, the average training of a scribe had, of course, to be oriented to the requirements placed on a scribe in his later professional life. Besides learning to read and write, a crucial subject in his training was therefore mathematics. In order to establish the area of a field or the size of a labor force needed for a given task, a scribe needed to know the basic rules of calculation. Moreover, the prevailing forms of legal, administrative, and economic documents had to be learned by heart. Finally, it has to be assumed that the spread of specialization, which began at the latest during the Ur III period, also affected the education of the scribe. It seems that here, as well, the conjectured reforms under Shulgi would have had their impact.

A description of scribal education remains in many points conjectural, and again we depend on the texts of the early second millennium. School age began, as in other cultures, with earliest childhood, according to scanty textual references at the age of between five and seven years. According to the edubba literature, which describes everyday life at school, a pupil is not only called "my little one" by the teacher, but he is also, for example, washed by his mother. On account of the difficulty involved in learning cuneiform, an elementary course will have continued over several years. Advanced courses were probably aimed at the chosen employment. As a rule, education must have lasted until manhood, in a few cases even somewhat longer. There are reports dating to the time of the Third Dynasty of Ur on so-called junior scribes, who for certain periods of time received bread rations from the city governor and hence were included in the public rationing system. Although we are told nothing more about them, it seems apparent that they were advanced scribal students who were refining their skills by gathering practical experience in an economic enterprise or an administrative unit.

New challenges occurred when at the beginning of the old Babylonian period spoken Sumerian was increasingly replaced by the Semitic language Akkadian. The schools—at least some of them—soon become preoccupied with the written and oral legacy of Sumerian. A tradition thereby arose, which was to remain intact until, around the birth of Christ, cuneiform script went out of use.

For the beginners in the subject "Sumerian," there were simple exercises and easy hymns to the king as well as proverbs which the pupils could learn in order to become familiar with the language and its most important stylistic features. By means of lexical lists which had been used for generations, knowledge of script and vocabulary were extended. Bilingual editions now contained Akkadian translations and phonetic readings of signs. Paradigms, moreover, served as aids in the analysis of the Sumerian grammar.

Numerous exercise texts have been found at many sites. They are distinguished by several characteristics. During the early second millennium and even before, the tablets were often round. Usually, the texts reproduce only a short excerpt of a longer original, generally no longer than one or two sentences. Not only "prose" was learned, but also lexical exercises. Finally, we know of texts exhibiting both the handwriting of the teacher and the copy by the pupil. Advanced students of Sumerian probably copied longer text passages and excerpts from the lexical lists. A third stage in the education of a scribal student must have consisted of the reciting and copying of difficult literary texts.

In the edubba compositions, lessons in learning all the broad aspects of Sumerian is a popular topic. It remains, however, extremely difficult to assess how many of the scribes received comprehensive literary training as just outlined. But this erudite aspect of the edubba will not be discussed here. Instead, a few text passages will be presented from the composition "son of the tablet house," which convey a vivid impression of the everyday life at school of a young scribal pupil.

"Son of the tablet house, where have you been going since early childhood?"

"I have been going to the tablet house."

"What did you do in the tablet house?"

"I read my tablet, ate my breakfast, prepared my new tablet, wrote and finished the text. Then I was given a recitation and in the afternoon I was given writing exercises. After the tablet house had closed, I went home, came into the house, there my father was sitting . . . After I got up in the morning, my mother looked at me, and I said to her: 'make my breakfast, I should like to leave for the tablet house . . .'

"In the tablet house the supervisor asked me: 'Why are you so late?' I was frightened, my heart was beating. I stepped in front of my teacher and made a respectful bow."

But the day, which hadn't started well, was to become worse for the pupil. He was given a thrashing by various members of the school staff after he had spoken during a lesson, left the school grounds or written in an unsatisfactory manner. He therefore asks his father to invite his teacher over, to appease him with compliments and presents:

"The father paid attention to what the pupil said, and the teacher was called to their home. Upon setting foot inside the house, the teacher was given the seat of honor. The pupil was at his service, and everything he had learned of the art of writing he demonstrated in front of his father."

The teacher was then fed by the pupil's father, clothed in a new robe, given a present, a ring was put on his finger. The teacher does not remain unimpressed and now finds more friendly words for the pupil:

"Since you did not show disrespect for my words, did not ignore them, you will climb to the top of the scribal arts . . . May you be the leader among your brothers, and among your friends. May you be the first of all pupils . . . Well have you accomplished your duties as a pupil, you are now a cultured man."

H.N.

14. The Titles and Professions List

The titles and professions list from the group of compilations already discussed in the previous chapter consists of words and expressions of one semantic category. A very well preserved tablet from Fara, dating to the middle of the third millennium B.C. (fig. 89), is in fact a copy of a text known from the oldest phase of script development, Uruk IV (fig. 87), and contained on a large number of tablets from the following script phase III.

This list is of special interest for two reasons. The titles and professions list apparently was the most popular of the lexical treatises. Not only do we find copies within all text corpora covering a period of over one thousand years, beginning with the oldest phase of writing development and ending in the Old Babylonian period, but we also have a considerable quantity of copies from each period. The archaic script phase III is represented with approximately 165 texts and text fragments. In this case, it is more evident than in any other instance how meticulously the texts were copied, since despite this large number of witnesses practically no differences can be detected in the sign sequence registered.

This text was of particular interest in our efforts to decipher the archaic script, since even in the cases of problematic identification our reading of the signs was guided by their respective position in lists of the various historical periods (fig. 88). This list and some others were thus to a great extent responsible for a substantial increase in the number of sign identifications made in the past years.

In addition, the list proved extremely valuable for our understanding of social conditions in the earliest days of script development. Although we by no means understand every entry of the list,

Figure 87. Oldest version from Uruk of the titles and professions list dating to script phase Uruk IV.

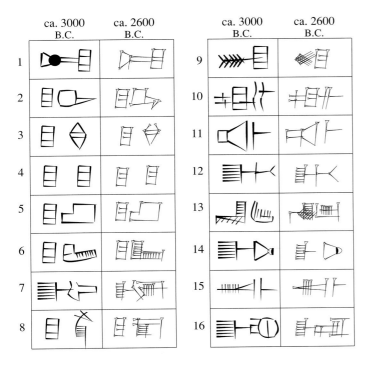

	ca. 3000 B.C.	ca. 2600 B.C.			ca. 3000 B.C.	ca. 2600 B.C.
1			9			
2			10			
3			11			
4			12			
5			13			
6			14			
7			15			
8			16			

Figure 88. Paleography of the signs occurring in text witnesses of the titles and professions list dating to the archaic script phase Uruk III and the Fara period, respectively.

it is clear that the titles, profession names and functional designations attested followed no random order, but rather formed units in a logically ordered sequence.

Formal aspects of the text led to the same conclusion, in that certain signs always appear in significant positions. The sign consisting of an upright narrow rectangle with two horizontal strokes (NAM$_2$), for example, only occurs in the first entries of the list. In later entries, a sign resembling a trident or a broom (GAL) appears very often. The interpretation of the first sign is not certain; it seems to denote "leader" or "commander," whereas the second is well known, since it clearly meant "great" or "great one" in later periods, and in combination with other signs it referred to something like "chief x."

Insofar as these determinations suggest that the titles were ordered in a sequence of rank, the first entry will be of particular importance, since it likely will have designated the individual of highest rank in the archaic administration. Unfortunately, the sign

NAMEŠDA (NAM$_2$+EŠDA) as well as a number of others no longer appears in the sign repertoire of the texts from periods after the archaic script phase III. However, the fact that it was copied and recopied over the course of many centuries seems to document a desire to preserve knowledge of the original meaning of this text. As a consequence, in a dictionary from the second millennium B.C., which probably served as an aid for learning the Sumerian language, the sign was translated into Semitic Akkadian with the word *šarrum*, meaning "king." This late translation tends to support our original suspicion that the first entry referred to the highest ranking of the titles listed. That the Sumerian word for king, lugal, was not used in the present context suggests that position and function of the highest dignitary had changed through time.

More sign combinations including the sign NAM$_2$ follow in the list. The sign placed either before or after this sign presumably refers to the field of responsibility of the particular "leaders." In the following lines these responsibilities are related to justice (DI), the city (URU), the plow (APIN) and barley (ŠE). Then follow a series of priests and wise men(?), the leader of the assembly(?) (KINGAL), and another high court official (GAL.TE), whose function is unknown. The remaining part of the text is dedicated to lower-ranking priests, to gardeners, cooks, and craftsmen, including the potter and baker.

The purpose of this text is therefore to be found not only in the mere desire of early scribes to compile a more or less complete list of the existing professions, but also to place each professional title in a context displaying its respective rank in society. Since this sequence was already well established in the earliest texts, it may be inferred that by the time of the archaic period, and probably even earlier, society was organized according to a strict hierarchical system. This, in fact, constitutes precious information, considering that nothing else, with the exception of a few scattered archaeological finds, offers anything comparable concerning the organization of society and social structure of this period.

That these entries reflect the real situation of the time is confirmed by the fact that some of the titles actually appear in connection with active individuals in the administrative documents. This, as a matter of interest, is particularly the case with the texts from the former Erlenmeyer collection, in which several of these titles are listed together as receivers of barley distributions (chap. 8). These attestations, however, do not as yet confirm our proposed interpretation of rank differences in the list, since in the examples shown in figure 90 the titles seem to assume equal positions.

H.N.

Figure 89. Example of the titles and professions list dating to the Fara period.

Photos of the texts illustrated in figure 90 (both sides of tablets depicted).

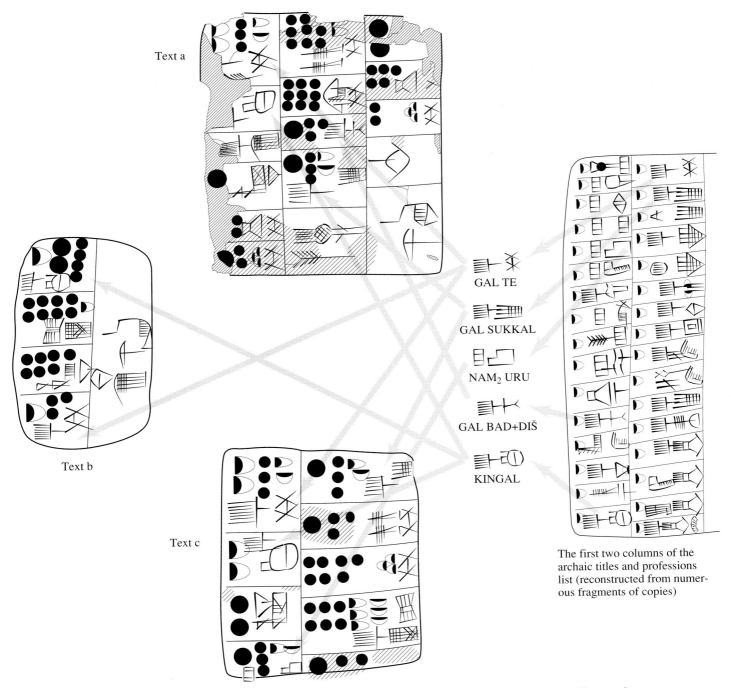

Text a

Text b

Text c

GAL TE

GAL SUKKAL

NAM$_2$ URU

GAL BAD+DIŠ

KINGAL

The first two columns of the archaic titles and professions list (reconstructed from numerous fragments of copies)

Figure 90. Occurrences of entries of the titles and professions list in contemporary administrative texts (tablet obverses illustrated).

15. The Development of Cuneiform Script

The earliest days of cuneiform can be traced back to the end of the fourth millennium B.C. It occurs for the first time in Uruk, a city which by that time was already a large metropolis. Impressive ruins of monumental architecture and fine arts have been unearthed in levels of the city which date to that age. Uruk's wealth was due in large part to the fact that the city was located in the middle of a rich agricultural belt and enjoyed the status of an important economic center.

Some 5000 inscribed archaic tablets and fragments were found almost without exception within the confines of the central precinct of Uruk, the temple complex of the city-goddess Inanna, called Eanna. Since the overwhelming majority of these texts were the accounts of a central administration controlling many different economic sectors, it is obvious that the Eanna precinct represented not only a cultic center, but also the economic heart of the city and region. The quantity as well as contents of these earliest written sources seem to prove that writing developed as a direct consequence of the compelling demands of an expanding economy, with its relentlessly growing administrative complex becoming increasingly dependent on memory aids in order to record and control transactions of all kinds.

However, such mnemonic devices as loose or enclosed clay tokens, "numerical tablets," and seals already existed before that time (see chap. 4), and may thus be considered at least the functional precursors of writing. The early script was no less than these early administrative aids, embedded in the economic life of early Babylonia.

The oldest members of the group of preliterate administrative aids, the clay tokens and the seals, made it possible to record relevant features of economic life, the amounts of goods or the individuals involved in a transaction. The purpose of such devices was, of course, to recall stored information at any moment in the future. The requirements of a complex economic system and the necessity of expanding administration generated the search for ways to record different types of information at the same time. Sealed clay bullae and sealed numerical tablets represent such a means, since they included both numerical data and person-related information.

With the clay tokens, the shapes of some of which seem explicitly to have referred to specific objects, and the flattened clay tablets in which round or oblong depressions stood for numerical values, the preconditions and techniques were available for the development of writing as we know it.

The attempts to find new possibilities of storing complex information suggest that the awareness of the problem was so well advanced that the option of writing seemed to all parties the most acceptable solution for meeting this multifaceted challenge. With the help of an established system, all necessary information could now be stored: not only numerical and personal data, but also information concerning goods, time, place, and even the category of the transaction, all of which could be subsequently consulted. It is hardly surprising that in a short period of time the knowledge of writing and related techniques of bookkeeping spread over the entire area of Babylonia.

The earliest written signs can be divided into four categories (fig. 91):

1. Partial or complete pictograms representing totally or *pars pro toto* the designated object (see, for example, the pictograms for "fish," "snake," or "ox")
2. Symbols, either natural or abstract, whose primary connotations are not recognizable and which therefore functioned presumably in a figurative sense (as in the case of the reed-bundle representing the goddess Inanna)
3. Abstract or arbitrarily shaped signs lacking any comprehensible association to the object depicted, for example, the circle and cross denoting "small cattle"
4. Numerical and metrological signs (discussed in chap. 6). It should be remembered, however, that during the period of the archaic texts from Uruk numbers were probably not conceived of as abstract values. Instead, scribes operated with a series of different numerical sign systems which varied considerably according to what was being counted or measured (e.g., grain, fields, animals).

Figure 91. Categories of archaic ideograms.

From the beginning of their existence, the basic signs were often qualified with additional graphic elements. Thus, in marking certain parts of a sign by means of hatched lines ("gunification") an accentuation of its meaning could be achieved. Made at the corresponding place of the sign for "head," for example, such etched lines could thus signify the "mouth."

In the earliest phase of writing, the signs usually designated concepts or nominal and perhaps also verbal roots, although lacking any apparent syntactic relation within the texts. Beyond simple signs, we also encounter sign combinations which were formed either by simply adding two basic elements (A+B) or by inscribing one sign in another (A×B). Sign combinations fulfilled different purposes. On the one hand, the single elements could be connected according to semantic criteria, as in the case of the combination of SAG ("head") + NINDA ("ration") = GU$_7$ ("disbursement"). Few and uncertain on the other hand are indications from the archaic period for the phonetic use of sign combinations, for example the combination of KA, "mouth," + ME with the phonetic value eme = "tongue," "language."

This latter example points to the problems connected with phonetic abstraction, which constitutes one of the elementary principles of writing itself. This principle was applied probably for the first time during writing phase Uruk III. Due to its phonetic value, a sign could, regardless of its original significance, represent a completely different word, provided, of course, both had an identical or at least similar pronunciation. In this way, as demonstrated from later evidence, the sign TI with Sumerian reading /ti/ for "arrow" could now be used to express the Sumerian word "life" pronounced /til/. If analyzed correctly, this would still be the only apparent indication of the spoken language behind the archaic script. Only in the case that the proto-cuneiform script actually constituted a reflection of spoken Sumerian would it be possible for a word written with the pictogram "arrow" to inherit the meaning "life" from a given context, since this homophony is known only in this language. In fact, a script only becomes bound to a language in the process of acquiring phonetic values. Basically, we should therefore consider neither the preliterate administrative aids nor the tablets from script phase IV bound to a particular language or linguistic group. The texts, in fact, could theoretically have been read in any of a number of languages, as long as its code system was known.

This situation underscores how difficult it is to ascribe the first written texts to a linguistic group. Most scholars familiar with the problem, however, are nonetheless inclined to link proto-cuneiform with the Sumerians. No doubts exist that Sumerians played a decisive role in the following development of cuneiform script. The completion of the phonetic abstraction, moreover, was facilitated by the fact that an overwhelming percentage of the Sumerian language consisted of one-syllable words. Phonetic use of the signs led to syllabic spelling, which later on would be felt necessary. Thus the verb bal ("to dig"), for example, could also be spelled with the syllabic signs ba + al. The archaic ideographic script thus progressively developed into a script of both ideograms and syllabograms during the third millennium B.C. With the introduction of syllabograms, names and words for which no signs had existed were suddenly accessible to written language. The same applied for grammatical relationships. Accordingly, the sign originally meaning "to beat" (ra) could be employed as a suffix to express a dative.

This process was apparently accelerated when, toward the middle of the third millennium at the latest, a differently structured language began to place new demands on the methods of writing. The Semitic language Akkadian inflected its verbs depending on tense and mode. In contrast to the agglutinating Sumerian system, according to which the verbal root always remained the same, the inflected, spoken form of an Akkadian verb could not be represented by the same sign, once differences in time and mode were supposed to be expressed. Akkadian could hence only be properly represented by phonetic signs which in the case of the cuneiform script were syllabic. It is consequently not surprising to see the first appearance of Semitic names at a time which coincides with the increased use of ideograms as phonetic indicators.

The fact that signs could be read differently is a major characteristic of the cuneiform script at every period until it fell into disuse. This circumstance, however, also constituted a major difficulty in the use of the script, for which early scribes sought solutions. The so-called determinative, for example, restricted the number of possible readings of a sign. As its name suggests, it was employed to determine the category of particular expressions using a set of either preceding or following signs. Such determinatives were used, for example, to qualify the names of deities, cities, pottery, animal types or wooden objects.

Another, albeit slight compensation for the confusing effect of the multivalence of the script was achieved through the circumstance that the number of signs gradually decreased through time. The corpus of texts from Uruk during the earliest script phase contained about 1200 different signs. With the transition from script phase IV to III, graphically similar signs converged, and rarely used signs were deleted from the sign repertoire, especially some sign ligatures that had probably been invented on an ad hoc basis. In the course of the centuries, the number of cuneiform signs was reduced by about half. Furthermore we have to assume that the sign repertoire of a scribe by no means included all theoretically possible signs. A scribe from the beginning of the

Figure 92. Administrative text from Uruk dating to script phase Uruk IV.

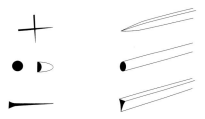

Figure 93. Stylus shapes and their respective impressions.

second millennium B.C., for example, could have managed with, on average, less than 200 signs, depending, of course, on where he was employed (see also chap. 13 concerning the education and profession of the scribe).

From the early third millennium B.C., script had factually the potential to faithfully represent spoken language. But since the practice of writing was generally restricted to procedures of recording economic transactions as well as to the compiling of word lists, both activities being rather undemanding insofar as the expression of syntactic relationships is concerned, pressure to take advantage of that potential did not arise. That process was to become a century-long affair which was not completed before the end of the third millennium, gradually replacing the mnemonic aids of archaic economic administration, the "écriture nucléaire," and the only facultative writing of grammatical elements with a fully developed language script.

Far-reaching changes similar to those concerning the internal features of cuneiform also occurred in the formal appearance of its signs. In this connection, we have already pointed to the unambiguous imagery of some of the earliest archaic signs which still clearly convey, even to the untrained eye, their pictographic message.

The earliest method of writing consisted of etching signs into the surface of a tablet by means of a pointed stylus. The consistency of the clay surface, however, proved inconvenient for etching rounded lines, due to the tendency of the clay to break away (fig. 92).

The relative inefficiency of the incising method was soon replaced by the more efficient technique of impressing straight strokes. That change went hand in hand with an alteration of the writing instrument from the early stylus with a pointed tip to the stylus with a triangular-sectioned tip of later tradition (fig. 93). This resulted in a significant change in the shape of the signs, since the technique of impressing signs by means of a straight stylus allowed only the marking of straight strokes. Round shapes from this point on had to be drawn by sequential impression of short straight strokes, as exemplified in the case of the sign KI ("place"). In but few instances, for example, the sign UDU denoting small cattle, were the original curves replaced by two curved lines, both being drawn out from the initial impressions (fig. 94). In addition, the new stylus was held at a sharper angle to the tablet surface than the former one. By pressing the tip of the stylus into the smooth clay surface and drawing it down, a short, straight wedge-shaped impression, deeper and wider at the "head" was made. For this reason, the script is conventionally referred to as "cuneiform" (Latin *cuneus* = wedge). The narrow side of the impression, often called its "tail," could be elongated to any desired length by keeping the stylus impressed while drawing it across the surface. Occasionally, curved lines were also drawn as seen in the example just mentioned. Finally, numerical signs were

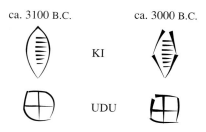

Figure 94. Early paleographic development of the signs KI and UDU.

shaped by impressing the tip of a round-sectioned stylus either vertically or obliquely into the tablet surface.

Although the triangular-sectioned stylus was already partly in use during script phase Uruk IV, it was not before phase III that it was to become the prevailing writing instrument (fig. 95). This transition from curvilinear to real cuneiform marks the first step in a process of increasing abstraction of the original signs. Whereas this development is still fully active during phase III at Uruk and Jemdet Nasr, it seems completed by the time of the archaic texts from Ur (see fig. 96). In the following phase, named after the southern Mesopotamian site of Fara, but including the texts from Abu Salabikh and Adab, the signs finally seem to have achieved a fully abstract appearance; in but few cases can the original pictograms be recognized (see fig. 97).

Having arrived at this point, one is confronted with the question of the direction in which the texts were written and read. The earliest texts were obviously read according to the natural

Figure 96. Administrative text from Uruk dating to script phase Ur archaic.

Figure 95. Administrative text from Uruk dating to script phase III.

Figure 97. Obverse of text from Fara.

119

orientation of the pictograms. That automatically meant that the columns were oriented horizontally and that the sequence of the cases accordingly ran from right to left. Inside the cases themselves, the signs were ordered in an array running generally from top to bottom. Later texts demonstrate that at some stage during the progress of graphic development the signs were rotated 90° counter-clockwise from their original orientation (fig. 98). When and exactly why this happened is a matter of speculation.

However, assuming that during the course of writing the tablet was originally held in the palm of the left hand at an angle of approximately 45° in relation to the scribe, we might propose one explanation of this development. So held, the tablet could also be turned slightly depending on its most convenient position for the relentlessly shifting direction of the stylus. The text was then read in its original position. Due to the advancing abstraction of the signs, this rotation back to original position became superfluous. The resulting effect was that the signs were read in their new orientation, a position which represented a 90° rotation (counter-clockwise) in relation to the original pictogram.

In the course of the second half of the third millennium, we notice that awkward wedge directions became increasingly obsolete. Apparently, we are here witnessing the first indications that the signs were being written horizontally. Current research, however, cannot define the exact chronology of this development. We neither know with certainty the reasons for this process, nor can we say when it was completed; convincing arguments have in any case been made that the texts were still being read according to the traditional writing direction as late as the early second millennium B.C.

The paleographic development during the centuries following the phase of Fara and Abu Salabikh is most characterized by the mentioned reduction of the number of wedge orientations as well as the continuing reduction of the number of signs as a whole (fig. 99). The so-called Winkelhaken, a deeply impressed oblique stroke consisting almost entirely of the "head," virtually unknown during the script phase of Fara, is now becoming more and more frequent.

A clear break then occurs in the Ur III period, when the traditional custom of impressing the circular and semicircular numerical signs with the round-sectioned end of the stylus was dropped. From now on, numerical signs were written like the other cuneiform signs (figs. 100–102).

But not only the script underwent important changes during the period in question. We also observe the appearance of a series of other substantial innovations, such as, for example, the structuring of the tablet surfaces. Since the beginning of archaic script phase IV, tablets had been divided into columns and smaller cases by

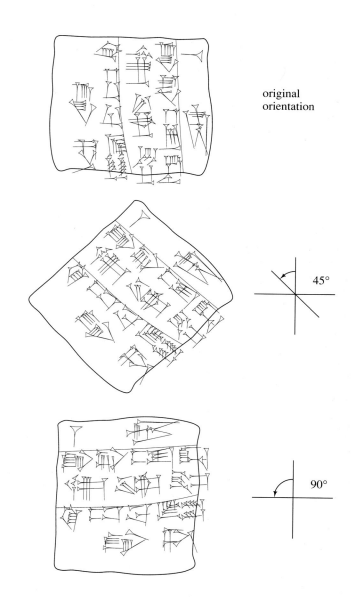

Figure 98. Rotation of script direction.

Figure 99. Administrative text from the Old Akkadian period.

Figure 101. Administrative text from the Ur III period.

Figure 100. Administrative text from the Ur III period.

Figure 102. Administrative text from the Ur III period.

Figure 103. Business letter from the Old Assyrian period.

Figure 105. Loan contract from the neo-Babylonian period.

Figure 104. Administrative text from the Middle Assyrian period.

means of horizontal and vertical lines. Every case contained one information unit. In the beginning, the order by which the signs were entered into each case followed no obvious rules. The situation changed with the increasing use of the signs as phonetic units, since these were only comprehensible if placed in an ordered sequence. After the time approximately coinciding with the reign of Eannatum of Lagash (ca. 2400 B.C.), spoken language determined the order of script.

From the period of the Fara and Abu Salabikh tablets, or the middle of the third millennium at the latest, moreover, columns on the obverse of a tablet were completed from the left to the right (I, II, III, IV), whereas on the reverse the sequence of the main text was continued on the right-hand side and continued to the left (VI, V). However, summarizing text sections such as totals, dates, administrative remarks, or signatures on the reverse side again followed the format rules observed on the obverse. In "turning the page" from the obverse to the reverse, a tablet was usually rotated around its upper edge. From the pre-Sargonic period onward the segment-structure of the tablets was slowly replaced by proper script lines. The traditional writing convention, however, did not disappear completely before the period of the Third Dynasty of Ur.

Until that time, literacy was chiefly restricted to the Babylonian region, so that we may state with confidence that the discussed alterations in literary practice followed linear developments. From the beginning of the second millennium, however, a second line of development evolved. The Assyrian region, that is, northern Mesopotamia, began at this time its own written tradition which, based on Babylonian models, produced a "northern" paleography.

One text (fig. 103) represents the script phase in the Old Assyrian period, the written material of which is best known from the intensive correspondence between Assur and its trading colonies in present-day Anatolia. Through the deletion of a whole set of signs and the further simplification of others, the Assyrian script acquired a relatively uniform appearance. This principle was also valid for the later development of script in the Assyrian region which, on the whole, became much more manageable than the Babylonian signary. The administrative text from Assur dating to the twelfth century B.C. shown in figure 104 serves as an example of that development.

In Babylonia during the period roughly coinciding with the old Assyrian phase in the north, the scribes wrote with a script which today is called Old Babylonian. On the formal level, both seem similar to the script of the Ur III period. A final example represented in figure 105 dates from a period more than a thousand years later and, as expected, again reveals radical simplifications of the script in comparison with that of the Ur III

period. A strong tendency toward much smaller tablet formats, insofar as letters and administrative and economic documents are concerned, is also apparent. Such reduction was implemented through the miniaturization of script, a compact writing of signs, and a general tendency toward writing in a cursive manner, with signs pressed together one into the other.

Sumerian was only one, but probably the oldest of a whole series of middle eastern languages which were written in cuneiform script. As already stated, the first evidence for the use of cuneiform as a representation of the Semitic Akkadian language falls in the middle of the third millennium. The written manifestation of this language required an expansion of the syllabic repertoire, although the principle of the logo-syllabic script remained in use. Whereas this phenomenon testified to the great flexibility of the script system, which most notably accounted for its convenience in the representation of other languages, thereby proving to be one of the most successful writing systems of the pre-classical world, it did not manage to eliminate other difficulties. In this respect the Sumerian-oriented phonetic values seemed unable to reproduce the considerable stock of Semitic consonants adequately, the result of which was a renewed increase of sign multivalence.

Cuneiform script spread early on into other regions of western Asia bordering Babylonia. Most prominent in this context are the recent text discoveries in the palace archives of the ancient Syrian city of Ebla. The texts written in Eblaite, a northwestern Semitic language, were compiled at a time when script in Babylonia was employed for the first time to represent Semitic names. In Elam, located to the east of Babylonia, we observe that cuneiform was used to write the Elamite language, which was related neither to Akkadian nor to Sumerian. In the second millennium, the cuneiform script enjoyed further expansion. After the Hurrians, who inhabited northern Mesopotamian regions at the time, acquired the script, it was transmitted to Indo-European-speaking groups that had settled in Anatolia, of which the most prominent were the Hittites.

The numerous Akkadian letters found in the archive of the royal court at Egyptian el-Amarna, moreover, demonstrate convincingly the success of the Akkadian language, advancing to become the diplomatic language of the entire Near East in the second millennium. Finally, the Urartians, who were related to the Hurrians, employed the script in the ninth and eighth centuries B.C. in the Armenian highlands.

The script employed at Ugarit, a port city located on the Mediterranean coast of Syria (fourteenth and thirteenth centuries B.C.) and the old Persian script of the Achaemenians have only a formal resemblance to cuneiform. Both scripts only numbered about thirty signs, each of which functioned more or less like proper letters of an alphabet.

Although the cuneiform script outlived the great empires of the Assyrians and Babylonians, both collapsing under the pressure of the Medes and the Persians, its decline could no longer be halted.

By this time the Aramaean dialects had replaced Akkadian as the main spoken language in Mesopotamia and, with the adoption of the Aramaean alphabet containing only 22 letters, cuneiform lost all meaning. The latest text compiled in this script dates to the year 74/75 A.D.

H.N.

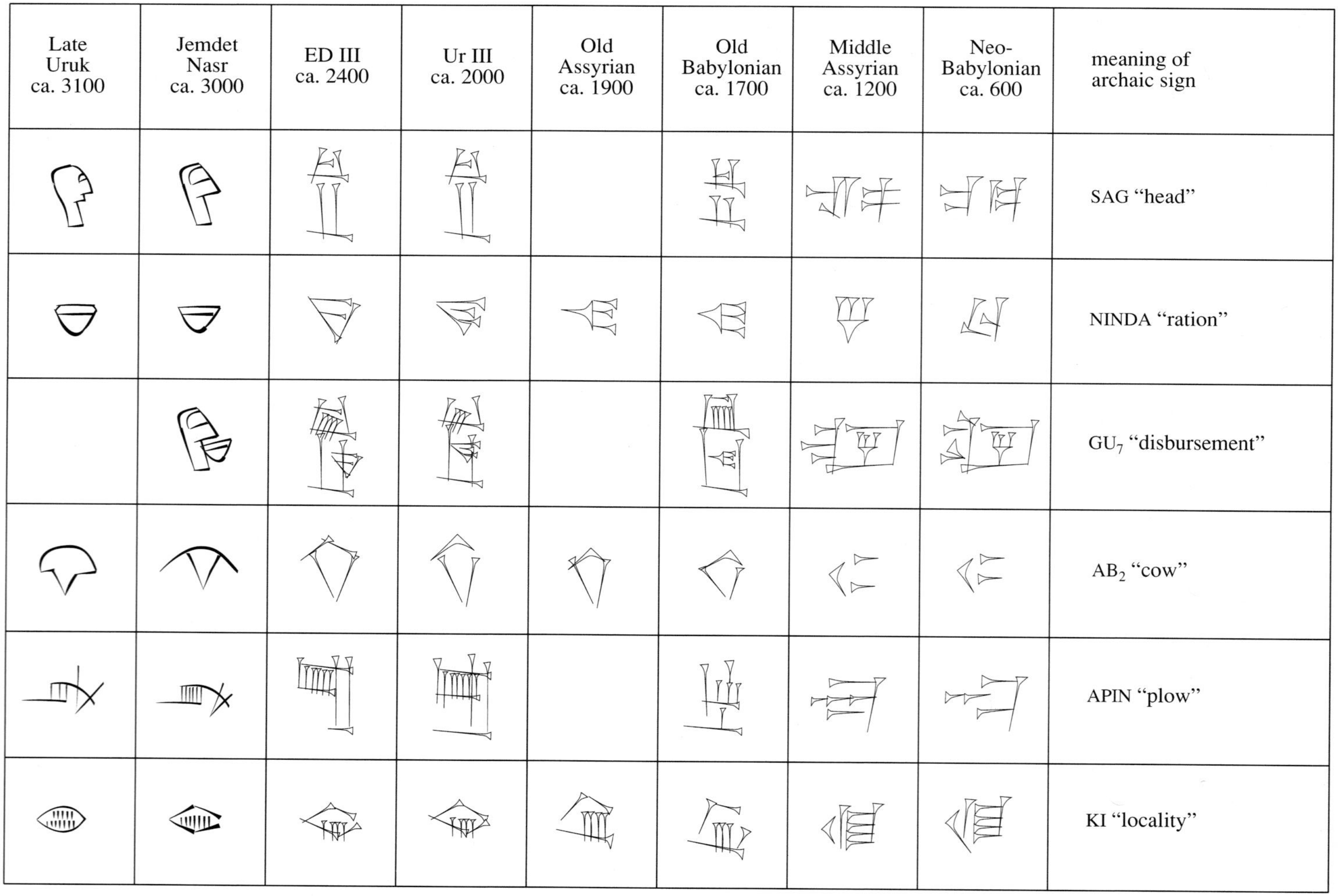

Late Uruk ca. 3100	Jemdet Nasr ca. 3000	ED III ca. 2400	Ur III ca. 2000	Old Assyrian ca. 1900	Old Babylonian ca. 1700	Middle Assyrian ca. 1200	Neo-Babylonian ca. 600	meaning of archaic sign
								SAG "head"
								NINDA "ration"
								GU7 "disbursement"
								AB2 "cow"
								APIN "plow"
								KI "locality"

Figure 106. Paleographic development of selected cuneiform signs.

124

16. The Development of Arithmetic

The period from the late fourth to the early second millennium B.C. is marked by the creation and early development of the cuneiform script. During this period, the early mnemonic symbols, which had originally been introduced by archaic period administrators to register palace and temple stocks, gradually evolved into a universal and durable means of representing articulated language. This same period is, however, also noted for another important cultural achievement, namely, the development and propagation of powerful arithmetic.

The point of departure for that development is a phase in which predominantly elementary, so-called proto-arithmetical techniques prevailed. It seems that such techniques did not differ significantly from comparable techniques used in modern preliterate societies. However, hand in hand with the progress of writing and regularly conditioned by its expanding functions as a means of storing information and controlling economic transactions, the methods of representing and processing quantitative information were also subject to change and improvement. The culmination and conclusion of that development toward the end of the period in question resulted in the invention of a sexagesimal positional system, a system structured according to simple and coherent rules of numerical representation by aid of abstract, context-independent numerical signs.

The Proto-Arithmetical Techniques in the Preliterate Period

There is a fundamental difference between modern numerical signs on the one hand, for example, the sign "5," and symbolic counting aids on the other, as in the case of fingers used in counting. The ability to use the sign "5" requires the understanding of its meaning, namely, an understanding of what a number is and the knowledge of the specific number "5" represented by the sign. With finger-aided calculations, the situation is clearly different. In this case, fingers do not represent numbers but rather represent merely the counted objects or higher counting units such as counting groups. This use of symbols, which stand for discrete, concrete objects and so function only as an indirect means of carrying information about their number, assumes no developed forms of arithmetic thought and no concept of number, but rather only the ability to establish correspondences between the number symbols and the counted objects. Since these aids and their related techniques precede the developmental stages of proper arithmetic, such techniques are called "proto-arithmetical."

Proto-arithmetical aids are known from virtually all studied primitive cultures. They also occur in modern society, since they are of great assistance in conveying our notion of abstract numbers to small children. In every culture, the proto-arithmetical aids form the foundation and necessary precondition for the development of an explicit concept of number.

Three groups of archaeological artifacts offer valuable information concerning the proto-arithmetical techniques used in the Near East during the age before the invention of writing (see chap. 4 for more on preliterate administrative aids). The first group is formed by the clay tokens, of which at least some assumed proto-arithmetical functions. These tokens with proto-arithmetical functions are hereafter referred to as "counters." The so-called "numerical tablets" constitute the second group, consisting of small, mostly sealed clay tablets containing rows of impressed signs which apparently correspond to a number of registered products. The third group, finally, consists of "sealed clay bullae." The last group forms a functional link between the counters and the numerical tablets. Accordingly, counters were enclosed in the bullae and kept permanently together, thus preserving specific qualitative and quantitative information in the same way as the signs impressed on the numerical tablets. The position of the sealed clay bullae between counters and numerical tablets is also underscored by the fact that some of them bear impressions on their surface largely corresponding to the signs on the numerical tablets. The impressions on the clay bullae may therefore constitute the precursors of the signs on numerical tablets. This chronological sequence, however, cannot be proven with hard archaeological evidence.

Counters probably came into use at a much earlier stage than numerical tablets and sealed clay bullae. Comparable artifacts have in fact been found in archaeological levels dating back to the eighth millennium B.C., and from about the fifth millennium onwards, the frequency of such artifacts increases. As yet, however, their role as functional precursors of the later counters cannot be confirmed. Some of the archaeological record even seems to contradict this hypothesis.

The archaeological evidence does, however, confirm that with increasing urbanization in the second half of the fourth millennium B.C. the use of clay tokens intensified considerably and probably even underwent functional change. The oldest numerical tablets and sealed clay bullae also date to the same period. The tokens contained inside the bullae, therefore, provide the earliest clear evidence that they were, in fact, counters.

Figure 107 displays a sealed clay bulla next to the counters which had probably been enclosed within it. The bulla originates from Uruk, where it was found together with 23 other bullae. Some of the clay envelopes remain as yet unopened; it is hoped that in the future more detailed information can be extracted from

Figure 107. Sealed clay bulla from Uruk with counters of unknown meaning.

their contents. In those cases where the bullae were opened, we are, unfortunately, unable to ascribe with confidence the tokens to their original envelopes. In fact, the tokens were stored separately since their function had not been understood at the time of their excavation. Because of these unlucky archaeological find records, we are not even able to establish whether they date to the pre-literate period or the period of the earliest written tablets. Finds from other sites, however, prove that the practice of keeping counters inside clay balls was characteristic of the period immediately preceding the invention of writing.

The counters, which were probably all originally enclosed in bullae, are differently shaped. Because of the similarity between the tokens shown in figure 108 and an ideogram of the archaic script that has been translated "oil," the sign ◁▷ (NI), the token of the illustrated form has been regarded as the precursor of the corresponding ideogram allegedly depicting an oil vessel. Some scholars have gone so far as to consider all tokens forerunners of later ideograms.

At present it is, however, advisable to differentiate between tokens in general and those that have actually been extracted from bullae, since the latter are the only objects whose function as "counters" is obvious.

Although many clay tokens in fact bear a striking resemblance to some of the archaic ideograms, of those found in context with bullae only the "oil" token is attested. In view of the relatively small number of different shapes exhibited by counters, it seems unlikely that they could have been ascribed meanings so specific as proto-cuneiform signs. Should the similarity between the "oil" token and the pottery jar prove not to be merely coincidental and the token have an ideographic value, then it seems more likely that it was used on a more general level to designate a pottery vessel, not its particular contents.

Most of the sealed bullae contain, the same as in the case of the bulla depicted in figure 107, counters of abstract and geometrical

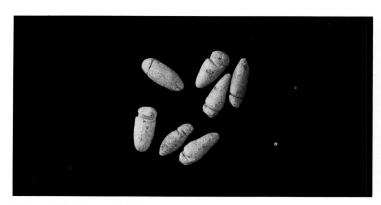

Figure 108. Ideographoid counters.

126

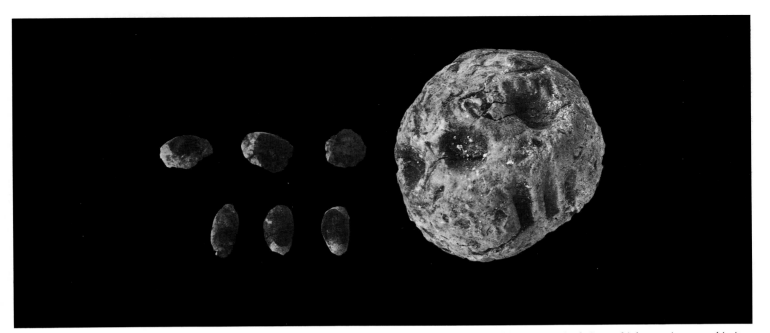

Figure 109. Example of a numerical match between the contents of a clay bulla and the precursors of later numerical signs which were impressed in its surface, partly with a stylus and partly with fingers.

shapes of no apparent pictographic meaning. The shapes are virtually the same as those of tokens occurring in older levels, namely, tokens mostly in the form of simple pegs, spheres, cones, tetrahedrons, and cylinders.

Unfortunately, the true meaning of the shapes of the counters remains unclear. The fact that most clay bullae contained differently shaped objects suggests only that each had its distinct meaning and consequently that the clay bullae served to assemble symbols with different meanings in order to represent a more complex piece of information. Even if the counters seem less articulate than ideograms, the use of differentiated shapes constituted a mnemonic means of transmitting specific information concerning the nature of the represented objects, for example, the product type, the units they were measured or counted in, and so on.

More detailed indications of the function of the counters are provided by those bullae whose surfaces in addition to seal impressions bear marks like those preserved on the bulla from Susa shown in figure 109. Relatively few specimens of that type are known to date, and the contents of those known were as a rule either partially or totally lost during excavations or perhaps even in antiquity. In the majority of those impressed bullae whose

contents were preserved, however, we observe a striking correspondence between type and number of counters and the signs impressed in the surface of the clay balls.

This is, in fact, far and away the strongest evidence for the proposed function of the tokens contained inside the bullae as counters, because the exact number was obviously important. In addition, the impressed signs on the surface of the bullae are very similar to those observed on numerical tablets, and the circumstances under which some of the artifacts have been found point unambiguously to a similar function of both symbol types. As far as the latter are concerned, it is clear that the numerical signs on archaic tablets developed from such signs. Hence, from the correspondence between the counters inside the sealed bullae and the signs on their surface we may conclude that the tokens, the signs on the numerical tablets as well as the numerical signs from later periods represent different metrological and counting units. The numerical tablets from the preliterate period such as the two gypsum tablets from Uruk seen in figure 110 are as a rule, however, singularly uninvolved, with but very seldom a more complex form.

In the few cases of more complex numerical tablets and to a lesser degree the surface impressions on the sealed clay bullae, the

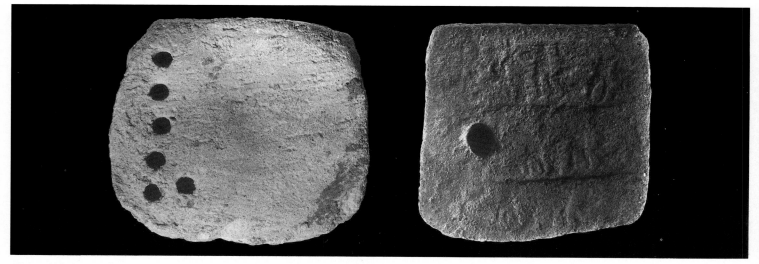

Figure 110. Simple "numerical tablets" of gypsum originating from Uruk and probably dating to the preliterate period.

similarity of their notations with later numerical signs suggests that some of the signs must have represented high ranking units, provided, of course, the interpretation of the signs as numerical and metrological units is correct. One example is given by the numerical tablet from Susa in figure 111. Here, the large signs impressed into the clay represent the highest units. However, its

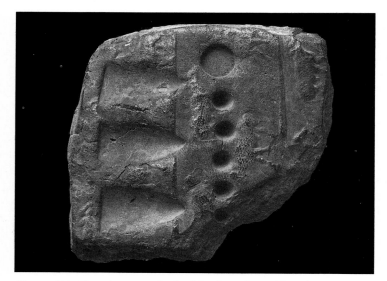

Figure 111. Complex numerical tablet from Susa. The sign sequence seems to indicate the rank of the numerical signs.

postulated dating to the preliterate period is not proven, as is the case with many of the other counters, numerical tablets, and clay bullae.

In addition to the similarities between the impressions on preliterate clay bullae and numerical tablets and later numerical notations, there are also a number of significant differences. A comparison of the evidence from various sites dated with confidence to the preliterate period demonstrates that neither the signs' shape nor the way or even the sequence in which they were written followed a common, interregional convention. Thus, apart from the structural similarity to later numerical signs, there is hardly a discernible link to proto-cuneiform numerical signs that could lead to inferences concerning the numerical meaning of the earliest signs. Even notations originating from a single find context often exhibit such internal differences that one is tempted to reject the notion of the existence of even local conventions for sign forms during that period.

The clay bulla from Susa in figure 109 bears impressions, some of which were made with a stylus, some with fingers. The marks on the clay bulla in figure 8, also found in Susa, were, on the other hand, impressed with counters. The clay bulla in figure 112 reveals grooves that were scratched into the already hardened surface with a sharp object. These marks bear no resemblance whatsoever to any other known signs of this period. All the same, X rays of the contents of this bulla show that even this entirely atypical example notation on the bulla surface exhibits a connection with its contents.

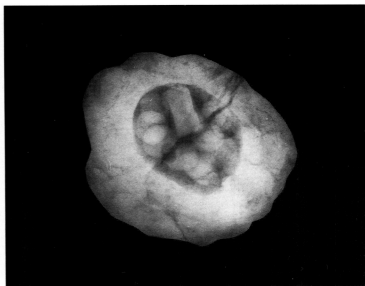

Figure 112. Sealed clay bulla containing an atypical "numerical notation" from Susa. To the right an X ray of its contents.

Comparable differences are also evident concerning the numerical tablets. Whereas in such texts the phenomenon can be observed that signs exhibited interregional similarities in the way they were written, no obvious correspondence between these and proto-cuneiform notations can be posited. Tablets similar to the square tablet from Uruk seen in figure 113a, for example, are also known from the distant sites of Habuba Kabira and Choga Mish, but no parallel notations from later text material have been helpful in trying to grasp the meaning of the pattern in which the signs were impressed on the tablets.

The second numerical tablet shown in figure 113b originates from the same archaeological context as the first tablet of that figure. According to their shapes and pattern, there seems to be a clear connection between the signs impressed on this tablet and the signs ▷, •, and ▷ with the values "60," "10," "1," respectively, of the later sexagesimal system. The tablet contains, however, a peculiar combination of two rows of signs including at least ten repetitions of the sign ▷, which never occurs in an archaic numerical notation written in the sexagesimal system. In the archaic period, the rows would at least have been clearly marked as belonging to two separate notations.

The lack of apparent conventions pertaining to formal criteria of numerical notations during the period immediately before the invention of writing stands in contrast to the relatively strict rules already obeyed at the time of the Uruk IVa period texts, as well as

to the conspicuous uniformity of the shapes of those tokens which belong to the group of symbols with proto-arithmetical functions, called "counters" here. In fact, the same simple geometric shapes of tokens are found over several millennia in a large number of sites. The conclusion thus seems justified that the period just prior to the invention of writing formed a transitional phase in regard to arithmetic. Although numerical notations similar to those from later periods already existed during this transitional phase, together they seem to document the very flexible use of proto-arithmetical devices rather than a symbolic system with binding conventions.

The question of whether in this period characterized by the use of only partially conventionalized symbols only a particular representational form of quantitative information developed or whether the notion of quantity itself changed remains difficult to answer. The comprehensive systems of quantitative structuring that can be identified in the archaic tablets encountered in immediately following archaeological levels did not yet seem to exist during this phase. Contrary to the situation known from the preliterate period, these later comprehensive systems were structured counting systems applying even to very high values. They constitute numerical relations transcending any immediate intuition between metrological units, which were originally based on natural measures with evident meanings.

Some of the evidence points to a shift in the concept of quantity itself. Instructive in this respect is a well-stratified discovery in

Figure 113. Numerical tablets from Uruk, the notations of which do not yet conform to rules observed in the archaic tablets.

metrological and numerical systems of this region, however, never exceeded ten before changing to the next higher unit. It can therefore be inferred from this evidence that there was a close connection between the invention of writing and the formation of standardized systems of measures and numbers. Genuine numerical sign systems comparable to the ones known from the archaic texts have so far not been discerned in preliterate numerical tablets. These tablets may document the phase of their formation.

In summary one can make the following observation: before the appearance of the first true ideograms, numerical notations were already known. In other words the first written signs were therefore exclusively "numerical." During this phase, their shapes most probably did not follow strict conventions. They certainly were not numerals in the modern sense. In fact they were signs used for counting units with qualitative connotations and by no means signs for abstract numbers.

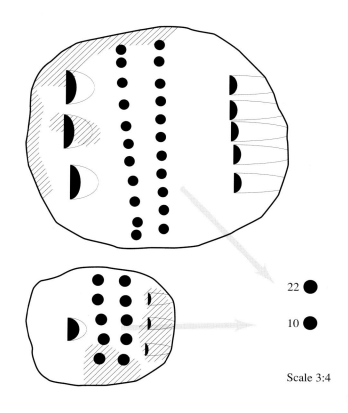

Figure 114. Two preliterate numerical tablets from Jebel Aruda documenting sign repetitions exceeding the decimal limit of later numerical notations.

Jebel Aruda, a site near the Syrian Euphrates. A number of tablets were found here which may be reckoned as one of the few finds of this kind to be dated with confidence to a preliterate cultural surrounding. Despite the fact that the tablets contained sign combinations closely resembling later numerical notations, not only were the signs not standardized, but they also exhibited structural differences from all known later numerical and metrological systems. The example illustrated in figure 114 demonstrates that within complex notations signs were repeated here ten times and more. The repetition of signs of all developed

Archaic Arithmetic

Despite the fundamental change the practice of noting quantities underwent between the preliterate period and the time of the first archaic texts, this development still did not seem to lead to a modern kind of numerical notation, but rather to a peculiar symbol system for the codification of quantitative information unparalleled in the later history of arithmetic. This is in part the reason why only recently, especially as a result of the work in Berlin on the decipherment of the archaic texts, the structure of these numerical systems could be completely reconstructed.

The special features of the numerical signs in the archaic texts are the following:

1. The graphic form of the numerical signs is, from the archaic age on, subject to universally valid rules, leaving aside a certain carelessness in writing, which points more to the effects of dull routine than to a lack of conventions. Once the meaning of a sign is known, which was the case until recently only to a limited degree, no difficulties are encountered in recognizing which sign the scribe meant in each particular case.

2. The number of different signs was increased considerably through graphic differentiation. In the known corpus of archaic texts, some 60 different signs strictly discernible as numerical signs have been isolated. The reason for this rather remarkable differentiation was to include in a given numerical notation qualitative aspects about the counted product, in other words, to make clear with the numerical signs the type of product meant. The high differentiation of the numerical signs thus tended to blur their differences to ideograms.

3. In the same way some ideograms carried quantitative information. Some pictograms denoting domestic animals, for example, combine with number-like signs to express the age of those animals (see the examples in chap. 12).

4. Rigid numerical relationships exist between the signs. Depending on the context, a certain number of each sign is always replaced by a higher unit. This "replacement rule" causes numerical relations to arise which bind the numerical signs to one another.

5. Together, such numerical relations, however, do not form a single system of numerical signs but rather they form many different systems, each of which applied to specific groups of objects (see the presentation of the numerical systems in chap. 6). Some of these systems are very similar. However, strict rules govern their application in context with specific objects. For example, two of these systems, the sexagesimal and the bisexagesimal systems, both include the signs ▷ , •, and ▶, with the respective values "1," "10," and "60." They differ, however, for higher-valued numbers. Whether two of the signs ▶, each representing a value of "60," were replaced by one sign ⋊ with the value "120," or whether ten of these signs were replaced by the sign ▶• to express the value "600," was entirely dependent on the nature of the counted product. Therefore it could never happen that, for example, five of the signs ⋊ (each signifying "120"), usually employed to express numbers of grain products, were replaced by the sign ▶• for "600," which itself was restricted to use with other measures, for example, for jars of beer. Although we today consider the signs to represent the numbers "120" and "600" respectively, they apparently had more concrete meaning for the archaic scribe, which made it impossible to imagine the one sign being simply five times the other.

6. The aspect of the archaic numerical signs which contradicts the modern understanding of number most is their arithmetical ambiguity. Some numerical signs, especially those relating to cereals, are so specialized and thus so closely related to counted products that each had but one numerical value. All signs that are used in various contexts, that is, the more "abstract" signs, however, tend to alter their arithmetical value according to the field of application they are used in. For example, the frequently occurring sign • represents 10 of the units ▷ when applied to discrete objects. In connection with dry measures of cereals, it represents 6 units, whereas with surfaces measures 18; thus, for example,

Figure 115. Simple proto-arithmetical summation by sign repetition.

131

1 •	=	10 ▷	in context with sheep
1 •	=	6 ▷	in context with barley
1 •	=	18 ▷	in context with fields

Apart from the creation of numerical signs with these unusual characteristics, the invention of writing had yet another consequence for arithmetic: archaic texts document for the first time symbolic operations which may be labeled "calculations." "Additions" in a certain sense form the most frequent type of operation. At the same time this operation seems to be the only one which was universally applicable independent of context.

Figure 115 displays a tablet representing the most simple case of such an "addition." The entries on the obverse contain the sign ▷ a total of seven times, each sign representing a jar filled with beer. On the reverse side of the tablet, the seven signs reappear, forming together with the sign for "jar" the "total" of the registered jars. Obviously, this procedure of addition by sign repetition hardly differs from the proto-arithmetical method of totaling counters by placing them next to each other. Originally, therefore, addition was not an arithmetical operation in the proper sense of the word at all. It was much the same as the manipulation of the registered goods themselves. The essential innovation brought about by the invention of writing may be seen in the first place in the fact that the summanda did not disappear through the totaling, but were retained simultaneously next to the total as separate units of information, whereas in the totaling of tokens the same objects that first represent the summanda also form the sum. This structural difference between the symbolic operation of the addition and the represented real process of summarizing probably formed the point of departure for later abstraction of object quantities, finally leading to an abstract concept of number.

Even if the additions documented by the archaic texts are all in principle identical with the simple example just seen, they become considerably more complex through the replacement of repeated signs with larger units and through the use of different numerical sign systems. A typical example is offered by the tablet in figure 116.

The obverse of the tablet contains several entries relating to various cereal products. The entries were written in three different numerical sign systems; the structure of all three systems was identical, but each was applied to a different, specific product. The first of these systems was apparently used for normal barley (signs ▷ and •), the second for cracked barley or groats (signs ◁ and ∴•), and finally the third for malt (sign ◣). Together, the entries contain 10 signs of the form ▷, 3 of the form ◁, 3 of the form ◣, 7 signs of the form •, and one of the form ∴•. In forming the total of the three products, 12 of the 16 signs of the form ▷, ◁ and ◣

were represented by 2 signs of the form •. The remaining 4 signs reappear in the total as 4 signs of the form ▷. Then the 9 signs of the form • together with one sign of the form ∴• were represented by one sign of the form ●, also included in the final sum. This tablet therefore still does not exemplify a true case of an addition in the strict sense of the word, since the signs continued to represent "units," not "numbers," the sum being nothing more than a simple combination of these units. Basically, only one other operation needs mentioning next to that of combining units: the replacement of a certain number of a specific sign, in the present instance representing a certain capacity measure, with the sign representing the next larger capacity unit.

Usually, the numerical notations in archaic texts represent not only the quantity of a product but also the type of the measures employed and often even the nature of the product itself. This led to the complex differentiation of the numerical signs evident in the large number of various signs. In certain contexts, signs used to denote amounts of different goods had to be varied graphically even when they represented exactly the same quantities.

An inchoate stage of differentiation between the representation of quantity on the one hand and the representation of the product type and metrological units on the other is, just the same, evident in the archaic texts. A good example of this development is offered by the text W 21682 (published in *ATU* 2, pl. 54); its reverse is illustrated in figure 117. Two times five units of two different dairy products, represented by the signs ▥▷ and ▦▷ and measured in SILA$_3$ (sign ≻), are here combined in a total represented by one unit of a jar (sign ⊂▷). These notations record the nature of the dairy products, their quantities and the units they were measured in with distinct signs.

Another way of rendering the increasingly large number of apparent metrological systems is demonstrated by the text in figure 118; the reconstruction is based on comparison with parallel texts. Here, entries recording amounts of an unidentified product, apparently measured in capacity units, were divided into a maximum number of three subcases according to the three measuring units employed. Each subcase designates a unit, the numerical signs inside of which stand for its amount. The total of all entries is based on the following numerical relations between the three metrological units:

the smallest unit is 1 ⊨			(recorded in the third subcase)
5 ⊨	=	1 ◥	(recorded in the second subcase)
2 ◥	=	1 ▷	(recorded in the first subcase)

Although addition in the archaic texts was always performed based on two operations, namely, on the repetition of signs repre-

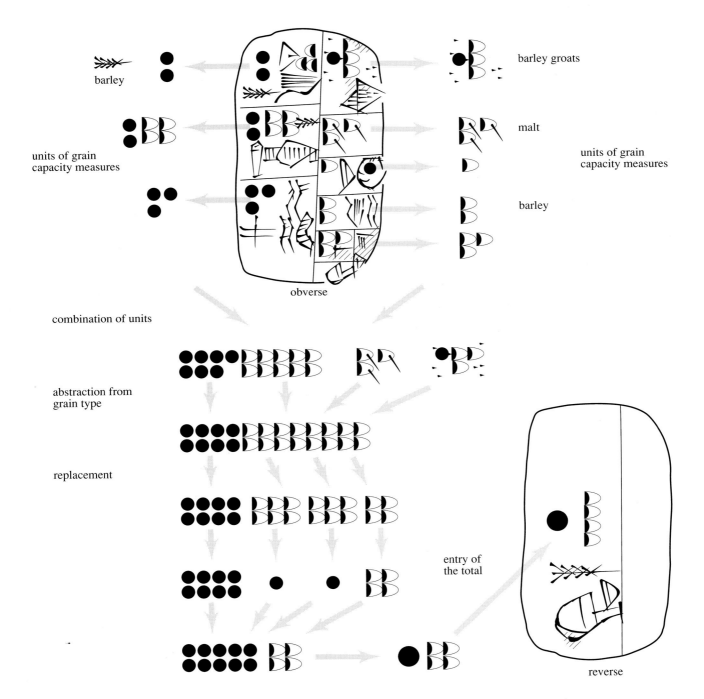

barley

barley groats

units of grain
capacity measures

malt

units of grain
capacity measures

barley

obverse

combination of units

abstraction from
grain type

replacement

entry of
the total

reverse

Figure 116. Complex proto-arithmetical summation involving replacement rules for symbols representing concrete units.

senting units and the subsequent replacement of a certain number of smaller units by larger ones, it could nevertheless assume a variety of forms. Because of the context-dependent meaning of archaic numerical signs, the scribes, in order to make correct additions, had to know which objects were represented by the numerical signs.

Relatively simple calculations could in this way become quite complex. In particular, a whole array of specific methods which could not be used for other operations were applied if the simpler adding techniques did not suffice. Although, for instance, multiplication as such did not exist as a generally applicable method, various specific techniques were available to solve problems for which we would apply multiplication. Examples illustrating the most complicated of such operations, for example, the calculation of field surface or of proportional relations between ingredients like barley groats and malt for the production of certain cereal products, have already been presented in previous chapters (see chaps. 10 and 8).

How such calculations were performed is not understood in detail. Instruments that could have served as calculation aids are as yet not attested in archaeological finds, or have not been identified as such. Lexical lists from later periods, however, suggest that the

Sumerians used tallying boards made of wood, which being perishable would not have been unearthed in excavations. There is also some evidence that the sign SANGA (▤), designating the chancellor of an economic unit, derives from a pictogram depicting such a tallying board. This, in fact, is supported by the cuneiform sign ŠID which, also having developed from this sign, was employed as an ideogram with the meaning "account."

Even if we do not know every detail of the methods of calculation in the archaic texts, at least we are able to see that the management of measured economic goods had, as a result of the development of writing and despite the lack of an abstract concept of number and of generalized methods of calculation, reached such an advanced level of efficiency during that period that those methods can no longer be put on the level of proto-arithmetic. We believe that a new term for these operations is required: "archaic arithmetic."

The Development of Arithmetic during the Third Millennium B.C.
The texts from the Fara period, the first period after the age of the archaic texts with inscribed tablets, already reveal fundamental changes in the attitude of the scribe toward arithmetical problems. Attempts to find new and specific numerical signs to represent the

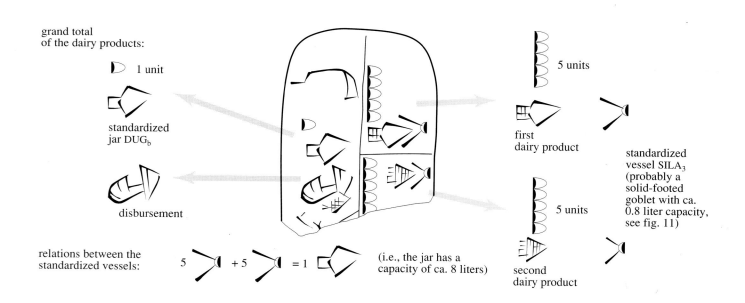

Figure 117. Incipient differentiation between "quantity" and "measurement unit" based on content-independent standardized vessels.

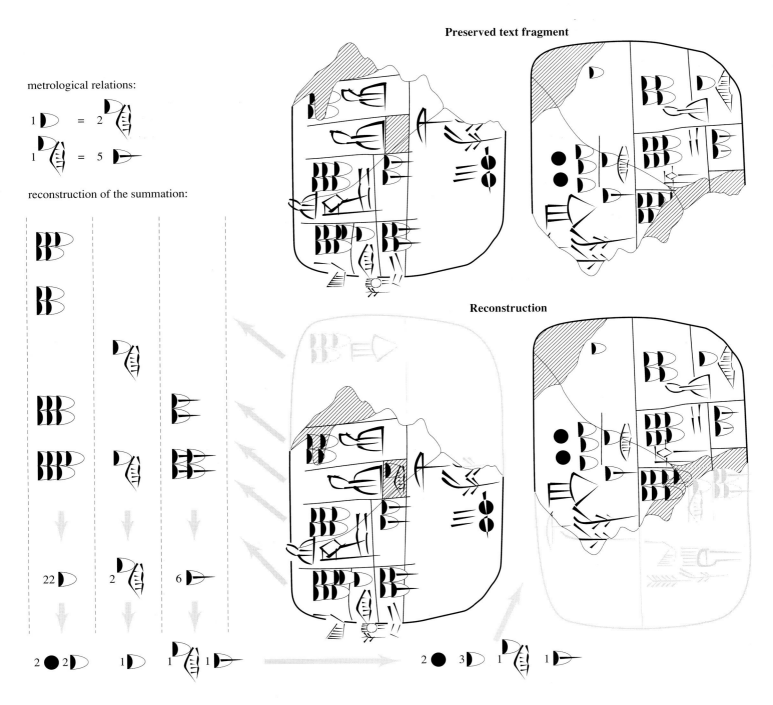

Figure 118. Example of the representation of metrological relations by tablet format.

Figure 119. Scribal exercise dating to the Fara period; the text is the oldest document testifying to the systematic study of arithmetical operations.

137

growing numbers of different goods seem to have failed and were eventually abandoned. From that point on scribes were becoming increasingly preoccupied with finding better ways of differentiating between numerical signs, metrological signs, and signs for the measured or counted goods. The majority of the archaic signs were falling into disuse. Discrete goods were, with few exceptions, counted in the sexagesimal system. The variety of different metrological systems, though, persisted and as a result a limited number of numerical signs which were still used in more than one system had still varying values which depended on the context. Furthermore, the method of adapting the numerical relations between numerical signs to the relations between the corresponding measuring units continued, so that in the case of a change in the measures the values of the respective signs were changed correspondingly. This assimilation of numerical notations to measures proved convenient for the scribes, but it obstructed the formation of unique numerical signs for all areas of application and delayed a radical break with the procedures of archaic arithmetic.

The oldest documents relating to a systematic study of the arithmetical techniques which originated in the archaic period date as well to the Fara period. The most important document of this type is the systematically structured table of square field areas shown in figure 119.

Measuring units and the numerical signs that represented them were in the case of length measures still the same as those of the archaic period. Insofar as area measures are concerned, a few unessential differences can be observed; most noteworthy is the

Figure 120. Late Old Akkadian annual account of the catch results of fishermen.

difference in the signs for the area unit bur'u (see chap. 10 for the structure of area measures). The explicit terminology in the first, slightly damaged line of the tablet is, however, partly new and already corresponds to later tradition. The first length is qualified with the word "sag," meaning "head," therefore signifying the "head side" of the field. The length unit used is ^{ninda}ninda$_x$ (the sign DU with the phonetic indicator NINDA), a term which in later periods is shortened to ninda. The second side of the field is qualified sá, meaning "to be equal," hence expressing its identity

obverse, column II, lines 1-2:
typical entry of the deliveries of fishermen

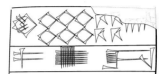

60,180 (?) fish,

foreman: Ú-da

reverse, column I (right column), line 9:
notation of capacity measures with
archaic numerical signs

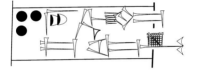

30 minus 2 (gur)
smoked fish

gur sag+gál

reverse, column II (left column), line 10:
summation of the deliveries of marine fish

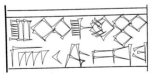

Altogether: 478,800

minus 250 marine fish

(i.e., 478,550 fish)

Old Akkadian numerical signs:

$\vee$	= 1	$\diamond$	= 3,600	$\mathbb{D}$	= 1 gur sag+gál
$\langle$	= 10	⬙	= 36,000	●	= 10 gur sag+gál
$\vee$	= 60				
$\mathbb{K}$	= 600	⬙—	= 216,000		

Figure 121. Numerical notations from the text illustrated in figure 120.

with the first side. Finally, the area is given, preceded by the sign GÁN for "(area of a) field," a custom which was retained in almost all periods.

The sequence of the areas in the list is ordered according to decreasing size. The following areas are recorded:

Length		Width		Area	
10 × 60	^{ninda}ninda$_x$ sag	10 × 60	sá	3 (šár) 2 (bur'u)	GÁN
9 × 60		9 × 60	sá	2 (šár) 4 (bur'u) 2 (bùr)	
8 × 60		8 × 60	sá	2 (šár) 8 (bùr)	
7 × 60		7 × 60	sá	1 (šár) 3 (bur'u) 8 (bùr)	
6 × 60		6 × 60	sá	1 (šár) 1 (bur'u) 2 (bùr)	
5 × 60		5 × 60	sá	5 (bur'u)	
4 × 60		4 × 60	sá	3 (bur'u) 2 (bùr)	
3 × 60		3 × 60	sá	1 (bur'u) 8 (bùr)	
2 × 60		2 × 60	sá	8 (bùr)	
1 × 60		1 × 60	sá	2 (bùr)	
5 × 10		5 × 10	sá	1 (bùr) 1 (èše) 1 (iku)	
4 × 10		4 × 10	sá	2 (èše) 4 (iku)	
3 × 10		3 × 10	sá	1 (èše) 3 (iku)	
2 × 10		2 × 10	sá	4 (iku)	
1 × 10		1 × 10	sá	1 (iku)	
5 × 1		5 × 1	sá	1/4 (iku)	

The exact purpose of this table of areas of square fields is not known. We may exclude the possibility that it served as some sort of table of calculations used to consult particular values. The list was more likely to have been written as an exercise containing easily determinable field surfaces every land-surveyor was required to know which could be added together in calculating complicated surfaces.

The arithmetic represented by this field area tablet from the Fara period remained in use during the entire third millennium. The number of the basic numerical sign systems had been reduced to the two applied in this list, namely, the sexagesimal system and the area measure system. Both systems were expanded considerably, now including very large numerical values. Furthermore, numerous new metrological systems came into being, often with specific forms of numerical notations and of a restricted local character. These systems were partially subject to change, mainly caused by changes in the sizes of their metrological units. The arithmetical relations of grain capacity measures especially changed during the third millennium, often revealing local variations. In the texts of the Fara period, a more or less uniform capacity system for grain and other dry measure goods replaced the archaic system for the notation of cereals. In the course of the millennium the system, however, changed several times again.

Accordingly, the signs which were used in the texts to denote amounts of grain are attested with different numerical values in different periods, but occasionally even in the same period, although in different locations.

Although the core of third millennium arithmetic remained much the same, its appearance exhibits considerable changes. In a long process which only concluded in the Ur III period at the end of the millennium, numerical signs, traditionally impressed into the clay with a round stylus, were increasingly replaced by cuneiform signs which imitated their form, but which were impressed with the same stylus as that used for ideograms.

   →   (e.g., as a sign of the sexagesimal system)
   →   (e.g., as a surface or capacity measure unit)
   →
   →
   →
   →
   →   (as a sign of the sexagesimal system)
   →   (as a surface measurement)
   →

For an extended period, both curvilinear and cuneiform numerical signs did appear together in a number of tablets, exploiting the apparent differences in graphic form to indicate specific entries, for example, those to be included in a subsequent summation.

The text shown in figure 120, either dating to the Old Akkadian period or the period of Gudea, belongs to this group of texts. It contains an accounting of fish that had been delivered to the authorities by the foremen of numerous gangs of fishermen in the course of one year. Fish was very widely consumed, since the rivers and canals of lower Mesopotamia as well as the Persian Gulf were extremely rich fishing grounds. The quantities of fish recorded in the text are accordingly large. The first two lines of the second column on the obverse of the tablet are shown in figure 121 and serve together as a typical entry in the account. The total amount of fish delivered by the foremen of the marine fishermen alone is given as 478,550 fish at the end of the preserved part of the left column on the reverse (see also fig. 121).

The only figure in this text written by means of the traditional rounded stylus is found in the second column of the reverse. The reason for this deviating notation is evident: it relates to a stock of "smoked" fish. Smoked fish was in fact measured in capacity units

Figure 122. Tablet from the Ur III period balancing a theoretical calculation of the harvest yield of the province of Lagash against the actual harvest during three different years.

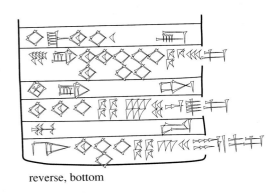

reverse, bottom

Theoretical calculation of a harvest

A yield was assumed of 30 gur per bùr, i.e., ca. 9,000 liters or 5.4 tons of grain per area unit of 15.6 acres.

Arithmetical operations in calculating the harvest:

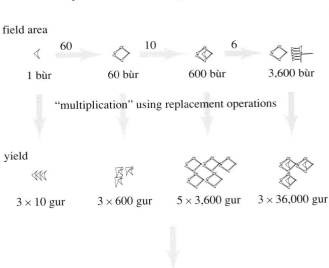

Translation

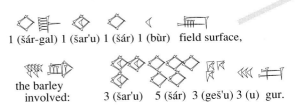

1 (šár-gal) 1 (šar'u) 1 (šár) 1 (bùr) field surface,

the barley involved: 3 (šar'u) 5 (šár) 3 (geš'u) 3 (u) gur.

Therefrom

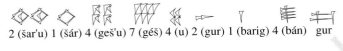

2 (šar'u) 1 (šár) 4 (geš'u) 7 (géš) 4 (u) 2 (gur) 1 (barig) 4 (bán) gur

delivered.

Deficit:

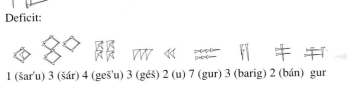

1 (šar'u) 3 (šár) 4 (geš'u) 3 (géš) 2 (u) 7 (gur) 3 (barig) 2 (bán) gur

Calculation of the debit

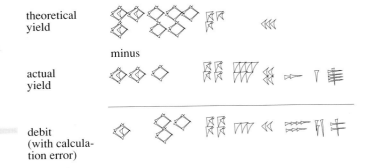

Figure 123. The calculation of the harvest yield of the province of Lagash for the third year recorded in the text illustrated in figure 122.

141

and hence not counted piece by piece. The use of the archaic form of numerical signs prevents the accidental inclusion of the notation in the total of the counted fish.

The tablet represented in figure 122, dating to the Ur III period, exemplifies the culmination of the development of arithmetic during the third millennium B.C. The text contains the theoretical calculation of the expected harvest yields for three different years in the entire province of Lagash and the comparison of these expectations with the yields actually delivered to the administration during these years.

In figure 123, the well-preserved record concerning the third year is depicted. Each of these records contains first the total area of the fields cultivated in the respective year, averaging around 270 square kilometers. The areas were noted with the cuneiform signs compiled in the following list:

⊢	=	1	iku	≈	3,600	m²
⋈	=	1	èše	=	6	iku
⟨	=	1	bùr	=	3	èše
⌀	=	1	bur'u	=	10	bùr
◇	=	1	šár	=	6	bur'u
◈	=	1	šar'u	=	10	šár
◇▤⊢	=	1	šár.gal	=	6	šar'u

Following the area notation of the fields, the expected harvest yield is given. The calculation is based on the assumption that each bùr of field yields 30 gur of grain. The grain quantities are expressed in the simplified capacity measure system of the Ur III period, consisting of the following units:

	=	1	sìla	≈	1	liter
	=	1	bán	=	10	sìla
	=	2	bán			
	=	3	bán			
	=	4	bán			
	=	5	bán			
	=	1	barig	=	6	bán
	=	1	gur	=	5	barig
	=	10	gur			
	=	60	gur			
	=	600	gur			
	=	3,600	gur			
	=	36,000	gur			

The actual yield is then given in the third and fourth cases, followed by the calculated difference; in the case of the third year depicted it represents a considerable deficit, indicated by the sign

combination LÁ+NI. Only in the case of the first year recorded did the actual harvest exceed the expected yield.

The Invention of Sexagesimal Place Value System

The greatest impact on the development of Babylonian arithmetic was the invention of the sexagesimal place value system toward the end of the third millennium B.C. Nothing, however, is known about the exact circumstances of this invention. The assumption by a number of scientists that it occurred in the Ur III period is based primarily on the alleged dating to this period of several numerical tables containing notations in this system. Since this dating rests on paleographic criteria and since the tablets consist almost exclusively of numbers, the paleographic utility of which is at best limited, the real date of this text group is not absolutely certain. What is certain is that by the time of the Old Babylonian period the sexagesimal place value system was fully developed. In fact, most of the evidence relating to the use of this new notation system dates to that period. Part of that evidence is to be found in a particularly interesting group of some one hundred tablets and tablet fragments containing tables of numbers. These tables illustrate how scribes systematically practiced with the new notational system, which offered virtually unlimited possibilities of calculating according to uniform rules with arbitrarily large or small numbers.

What was the innovation? The new principle of numerical representation may be illustrated using the number represented in the second line of the tablet shown in figure 128. The value of 100^3 is represented in this notation, equivalent to 1,000,000. According to the traditional notational system, this number would have been written

$$◇◇◇▤⊢ \quad ◈◇◇ \quad ◇◇◇◇◇◇ \quad ⟨⟨⟨⟨ \quad 𝍦 \quad ⟪$$

However, the tablet contains only the short notation

$$𝍦 \quad ⟨⟨⟨ \quad 𝍦 \quad ⟪ \quad 𝍦 \quad ⟪$$

In modern numerals this would be

$$4 \ 37 \ 46 \ 40$$

This transcription stands for the following number:

$$(4 \times 60^4) + (37 \times 60^3) + (46 \times 60) + 40 = 1,000,000$$

Apart from the altered graphic form of some of the signs, the main simplification of the notation consisted of the use of the same two signs for all levels of the counting hierarchy, namely, the signs which had originally only the values "1" and "10." Now, all powers of the basic number 60 were represented by the same sign as for 1, the tenfold numbers of these by the same sign as that for 10. For this reason and because a "sexagesimal point" did not exist, there was no way to express the absolute value of a number. The sign ⌐, for example, could assume the values 1, 60, 3,600, and so on but also $1/60$ and $1/3,600$.

This new numerical representation afforded Babylonian scribes the means to develop general methods of computation similar to those we use today. That they well knew how to take advantage of this possibility is proven by the existence of numerous so-called combined multiplication tables.

One such table is shown in figure 124. Tables of this type probably represent simple arithmetical exercises, although they could as well have been used as reference tables for multiplication. Basically, they represent the sexagesimal version of our multiplication table. One peculiarity of such tablets is that they not only offer the multiples of numbers from 1 to 10, 20, 30, 40, and 50, but also state the reciprocal values of the numbers from 1 to 10, as well as the multiples of most of the important reciprocal values and other common factors. Accordingly, they proved useful for swift multiplications with the most important fractions.

After having noted the sexagesimal representations of the fractions (= $2/3$) and šu.ri.a (= $1/2$), the depicted tablet begins with a list of the reciprocal values of important numbers ranging from ⫶ to ⌐⫶⌐ (2 to 1 21; in decimal numbers 2 to 81). A multiplication table follows, listing the multiples of the numbers:

The multiples of numbers below 9 are missing, probably for reasons of space. Instead, a very interesting tabulated list was squeezed into the remaining free area. The table begins by listing the reciprocal value of ⫶⫵ (2 5; in decimal figures 125), corresponding to ⟨⫵⟨⫵. The next entry is a pair of numbers which was formed through doubling the initial value ⫶⫵ and dividing the reciprocal value ⟨⫵⟨⫵ by two. Eleven more reciprocal values are calculated according to the same principle, the last lines of which, having been written along the margin, are nearly illegible. This calculation exercise at the end of the tablet provides a very good impression of the method by which the Babylonians probably determined reciprocal values for a compilation of reciprocal tables used in division problems.

In order to use the new calculation techniques in the scribal profession, the traditional numerical notations had to be translated into the new notations. Scribes really did perform such exercises, as is evidenced by the fragments of the tablets shown in figures 125–126.

In the first of the tablets, the new numerical notations for length units between 1 "finger" (šu.si) and 6 "cubits" (kùš) are given. One Babylonian "cubit" was the equivalent of 30 "fingers." The structure of this table follows the arrangement of the traditional measures and not the simpler arithmetical progression, offered by the new numerical notation system. The original table could in any case be reconstructed entirely from the structure of the present fragment. It contained the following values:

	(= 50)
	(= 45)
	(= 44 26 40)
	(= 40)
	(= 36)
	(= 30)
	(= 25)
	(= 24)
	(= 22 30)
	(= 20)
	(= 18)
	(= 16 40)
	(= 16)
	(= 15)
	(= 12 30)
	(= 12)
	(= 10)
	(= 9)

Col.	I		II	Translation		
Obverse:						
		šu.si		1 finger =	2	
		šu.si		2 fingers =	4	
		šu.si		3 fingers =	6	
		šu.si		4 fingers =	8	
		šu.si		5 fingers =	10	
		šu.si		6 fingers =	12	
		šu.si		7 fingers =	14	
		šu.si		8 fingers =	16	
		šu.si		9 fingers =	18	
		kùš		$1/3$ cubit =	20	
		kùš		$1/2$ cubit =	30	
		kùš		$2/3$ cubit =	40	
		kùš		1 cubit =	1	
		kùš		1 $1/3$ cubits =	1	20
		kùš		1 $1/2$ cubits =	1	30
		kùš		1 $2/3$ cubits =	1	40
		kùš		2 cubits =	2	

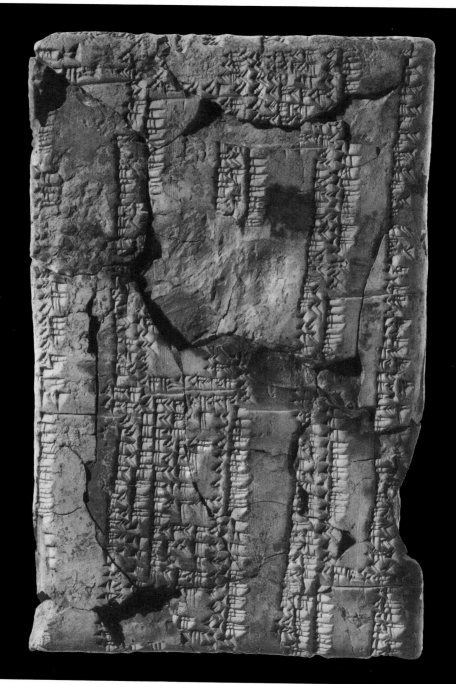

Figure 124. Old Babylonian standard combined multiplication table.

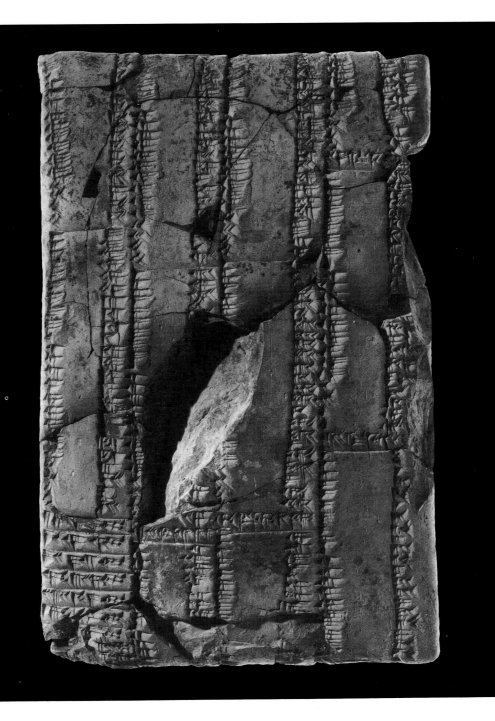

Reverse:

𒈫 𒑚 kùš	𒈫𒎙	2 1/3 cubits =	2 20
𒈫 𒈦 kùš	𒈫𒌍	2 1/2 cubits =	2 30
𒈫 𒑛 kùš	𒈫𒐏	2 2/3 cubits =	2 40
𒐈 kùš	𒐈	3 cubits =	3
𒐈 𒑚 kùš	𒐈𒎙	3 1/3 cubits =	3 20
𒐈 𒈦 kùš	𒐈𒌍	3 1/2 cubits =	3 30
𒐈 𒑛 kùš	𒐈𒐏	3 2/3 cubits =	3 40
𒐉 kùš	𒐉	4 cubits =	4
𒐉 𒑚 kùš	𒐉𒎙	4 1/3 cubits =	4 20
𒐉 𒈦 kùš	𒐉𒌍	4 1/2 cubits =	4 30
𒐉 𒑛 kùš	𒐉𒐏	4 2/3 cubits =	4 40
𒐊 kùš	𒐊	5 cubits =	5
𒐊 𒑚 kùš	𒐊𒎙	5 1/3 cubits =	5 20
𒐊 𒈦 kùš	𒐊𒌍	5 1/2 cubits =	5 30
𒐊 𒑛 kùš	𒐊𒐏	5 2/3 cubits =	5 40
𒐋 kùš	𒐋	6 cubits =	6

The second tablet displays the same basic structure, although this text pertains to weights between 1 "barleycorn" (še) and 1 1/2 gín (1 gín = 180 še; about 8 1/3 grams). In this instance as well, at least the beginning of the table with values between 1 and 10 še can be reconstructed:

Col. *I*	*II*	*Translation*	
𒁹 še	𒎙	1 še (barleycorn) =	20
𒈫 še	𒐏	2 še =	40
𒐈 še	𒁹	3 še =	1
𒐉 še	𒁹𒎙	4 še =	1 20
𒐊 še	𒁹𒐏	5 še =	1 40
𒐋 še	𒈫	6 še =	2
𒐌 še	𒈫𒎙	7 še =	2 20
𒐍 še	𒈫𒐏	8 še =	2 40
𒐎 še	𒐈	9 še =	3
𒌋 še	𒐈𒎙	10 še =	3 20

In the middle, damaged part of the table (end of the obverse and beginning of the reverse), the figures for weights between 11 and 30 še were listed. The end of the tablet is, again, nearly completely preserved. It contained following values:

Col. I	II	Translation	
igi.𒐋.gál 𒌋 še	𒌋𒐈𒎙	1/6 gín and 10 še =	13 20
igi.𒐉.gál	𒌋𒐊	1/4 gín =	15
igi.𒐉.gál 𒐊 še	𒌋𒐋𒐏	1/4 gín and 5 še =	16 40
𒑚 gín	𒎙	1/3 gín =	20
𒈦 gín	𒌍	1/2 gín =	30
𒑛 gín	𒐏	2/3 gín =	40
𒑛 gín 𒐊 še	𒐏𒐊	2/3 gín and 5 še =	45
𒑜 gín	𒐐	5/6 gín =	50
𒁹 gín	𒁹	1 gín =	1
𒁹 gín igi.𒐋.gál	𒁹𒌋	1 1/6 gín =	1 10
𒁹 gín igi.𒐋.gál 𒌋 še	𒁹𒌋𒐈𒎙	1 1/6 gín and 10 še =	1 13 20
𒁹 gín igi.𒐉.gál	𒁹𒌋𒐊	1 1/4 gín =	1 15

In this part of the table, in addition to specific signs for the standard fractions 1/3 (𒑚), 1/2 (𒈦), 2/3 (𒑛) and 5/6 (𒑜), a special form for the notation of reciprocal values was used. It probably originated as a method of noting those fractions of weights which could not be represented by traditional fractions. According to this form of notation, 1/6 gín was written igi.6.gál and 1/4 gín igi.4.gál, a method which could easily be generalized to represent reciprocal values of any other number. After the invention of the sexagesimal place value system, this way of writing fractions thus became the standard terminology in tables of reciprocals used for division operations in Old Babylonian calculation procedures.

Despite the obvious efficiency of this new notational system, it could not displace in daily administrative life the traditional way of recording measures. Even in the case of recording normal numbers, the traditional method with its specific signs for noting

Figure 125. A tablet listing the conversions of traditional length units into the "abstract" sexagesimal system.

each new power of 60 was preferred. Although this traditional way of writing numbers was less elegant than place value notation, it did allow a rapid identification of the relative size of any noted value. Therefore, Old Babylonian scribes not only had to acquaint themselves with the new technique of operating with numbers, but also had to continue to learn the traditional numerical notations. Tablets containing metrological notations listed according to size most probably served this purpose. The tablet in figure 127 displays an unusually detailed example of such lists.

This poorly preserved tablet enumerates according to size the traditional surface measures of the third millennium B.C. The list begins with the unit "1 gín." The unit gín, originally used exclusively in connection with weights for $1/60$ of a mana, later became a generalized designation of $1/60$. In the present context it designates a surface of $1/60$ šar, corresponding to about 0.6 m². The list ends in the badly damaged part of the reverse with a surface represented by the sign combination šár.gal, corresponding to approximately 235 km².

The Old Babylonian scribes thus continued to learn and use the traditional numerical and metrological systems in writing administrative texts. What they were able to accomplish using the new system of numerical notation is demonstrated by a special category of texts which are today referred to as "mathematical cuneiform texts." These texts contain solutions to problems which were, for daily administration, entirely useless, but which were at the same time extremely difficult, for example, calculating the length and width of a field knowing only its area and circumference.

Figure 126. A tablet listing the conversions of traditional weight units into the "abstract" sexagesimal system.

Figure 128 shows a strikingly simple yet very impressive example of the application of the new system of number representation for such leisurely objectives. One of the sides (obverse?) of the tablet contains, following a plausible reconstruction of the damaged area of the tablet, the following scheme of figures:

```
[1 40 a.]rá 1 40    2   46   40
a.rá  1 40          4   37   46   40
a.rá  1 40          7   42   57   46   [40]
a.rá  1 40         12   51   36   17   46   [40]
a.rá  1 40         21   26   29   37   46   40
a.rá  1 40         35   44    9   22   57   46   [40]
a.rá  1 40         59   33   35   38   16   17   [ ]
a.rá  1 40          1   39   15  [ ]            37   [ ]
a.rá  1 40          2   48   26?  39   X?  [ ]
```

The initial sexagesimal number 1 40 (= 1 × 60 + 40) represents, in modern notation, the number 100. The following Sumerian word a.rá means "times." After the invention of the sexagesimal place value notation system, this term became the standard technical term for the multiplication technique. In the first line we thus read 100 × 100, which is followed by the product 2 46 40 (= 2 × 3,600 + 46 × 60 + 40 = 10,000). In the following line, the preceding product is again multiplied by 100 and so on, concluding in the bottom line with a final figure of 100^{10}, which according to modern notation corresponds to the rather imposing number 100,000,000,000,000,000,000.

The performance of the Old Babylonian scribe who carried out this calculation is not faulted by drawing attention to an error he committed in the sixth line which, despite the damaged condition of the tablet in this area, is easily recognized. The consequence of that mistake is that the following numbers in the chart are all incorrect.

As a matter of fact, the scribe's mistake is rather interesting and deserves our attention. At the time of the compilation of this text, the sexagesimal system of the Babylonians did not include the zero, which represented a major deficit. The zero was only invented some thousand years later. Apparently, the scribes were compelled to keep in mind and in subsequent calculations account for the fact that a place which we would indicate by a zero was not occupied. Obviously, the scribes did not mark this space, as can be clearly observed in the present text, although as a rule they did not commit errors related to this problem. This suggests that such tablets contain, as a rule, only results of calculations which were performed earlier by means of a tallying board or some other calculation aid. It is, for example, possible that on such a tallying

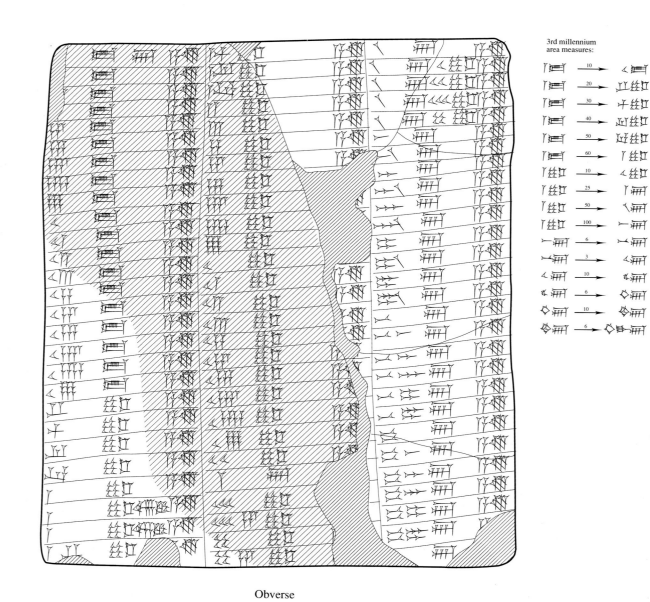

Obverse

Figure 127. Old Babylonian school text listing area measures from 1 gín (ca. 0.6 m²) to 1 šár.gal (ca. 235 km²).

approximate absolute values
of the area measures:

		1 gín 0.6 m²
		1 šar 36 m²
		1(iku) GÁN 3600 m²
		1(èše) GÁN 21,600 m²
		1(bùr) GÁN 64,800 m²
		1(bur'u) GÁN 648,000 m²
		1(šár) GÁN 3.9 km²
		1(šar'u) GÁN 39 km²
		1(šár.gal) GÁN 233 km²

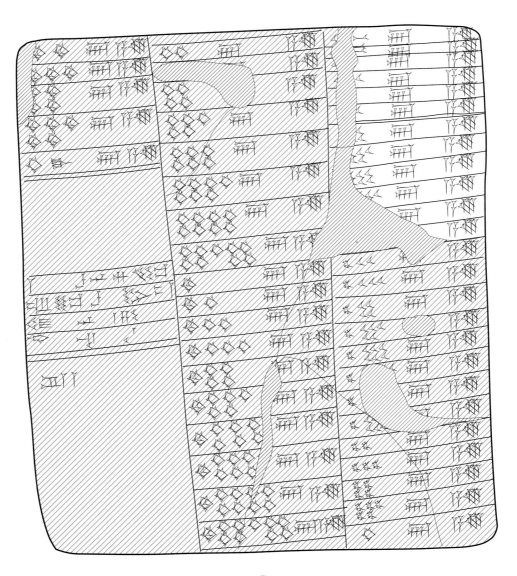

Reverse

149

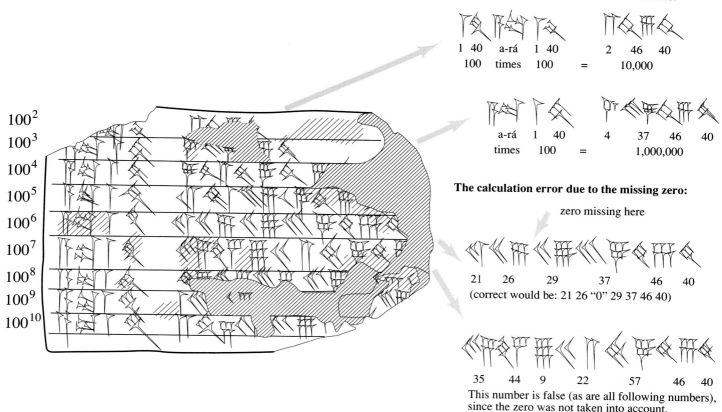

Reconstruction and translation of the first two lines:

1 40   a-rá   1 40   2   46   40
100   times   100   =   10,000

a-rá   1   40   4   37   46   40
times   100   =   1,000,000

The calculation error due to the missing zero:

zero missing here

21   26   29   37   46   40
(correct would be: 21 26 "0" 29 37 46 40)

35   44   9   22   57   46   40
This number is false (as are all following numbers), since the zero was not taken into account.

100^2
100^3
100^4
100^5
100^6
100^7
100^8
100^9
100^{10}

Figure 128. Obverse(?) of an Old Babylonian school text demonstrating a repeated multiplication with the sexagesimal number 1 40 (equivalent to the decimal number 100).

board the space for the zero would simply have been left free and thus the zero automatically accounted for. The author of the present tablet was, however, unlucky. In the sixth line the zero should have been noted for the first time. The scribe, however, wrote as usual

instead of   21 26 29 37 46 40
              21 26 "0" 29 37 46 40

and promptly used that figure to calculate the number of the next line

               33 44 9 22 57 46 40
instead of correctly   35 43 20 49 22 57 46 40

The calculations on the opposite side of the tablet listing the powers of the number 5 are, in comparison, simple. The largest number which was in fact calculated correctly is "only" 5^{10}, that is the number 9,765,625, the sexagesimal representation of which is 45 12 40 25. The text reads:

5 a.rá 5	25			
a.rá 5	2	5		
a.rá 5	10	25		
a.rá 5	52	5		
a.rá 5	4	20	25	
a.rá 5	21	42	5?	
a.rá 5	1	48?	30	26
a.rá 5	9	2	32	5
[a.]rá 5	45	12	40	25

The use of the sexagesimal place value notation system was to remain limited to these "mathematical texts" for some time to come. It would probably even have fallen into oblivion, had it not become the most important instrument of a surging discipline approximately fifteen hundred years after its invention, today referred to as "Babylonian astronomy," being the oldest applied science of the world to be based on empirical observation.

P.D./R.E.

151

17. Computer-Assisted Decipherment and Editing of Archaic Texts

In this last chapter, some methods of electronic data processing which have been applied to the editing and interpretation of the archaic texts are described. Technological progress, especially in the development of advanced programming languages for the processing of nonnumerical data and of powerful programs for processing graphic information, has opened for us the possibility of creating new procedures and developing, step by step, computer-assisted methods for ever more complex tasks.

The point of departure for our use of electronic data processing was the problem of cataloguing the large numbers of archaic text fragments and of determining inherent connections among them. To date, approximately 5000 archaic tablets and tablet fragments have been inventoried from the main site of Uruk, of which about 4400 are either insufficiently published or not published at all. In view of those large figures and the severe fragmentation of most texts, it seemed necessary even for the simple edition of these texts to make use of electronic data-processing methods. Before 1980, catalogue information and text transliterations were already put on a machine-readable storage medium. It soon became evident, however, that effective data processing of this material surpassed the limited possibilities of the field-specific oriented project, especially since there had been no precedents for the application of electronic data processing in solving similar problems within Assyriology. Therefore, processing of the stored data and extensive use of methods offered by the new technologies only began in 1984 with the commencement of an interdisciplinary cooperation between the research project Archaische Texte aus Uruk of the Freie Universität Berlin and a project entitled Cultural Development and Cognition at the Max-Planck-Institut für Bildungsforschung.

During the first phase of this cooperation, our efforts were concentrated on applying to the stored transliterations of the archaic texts standard methods of the processing of qualitative data which have been used for some time in the social sciences. A computer-generated glossary of all texts registered to that date, for example, was compiled using such methods.

Essential for the further planning of the cooperative project was the success we had when we tried, by means of computer-assisted processing, in particular statistical methods, to clarify the structures of the various numerical sign systems used by scribes of the archaic texts. The results of those efforts are given in chapter 8. Persistent widespread skepticism concerning the applicability of advanced techniques of electronic data processing in the soft sciences, especially in the "exotic" disciplines, is largely based on the belief that for these fields the cost involved is too high and the necessary technological know-how lacking. However, the thorough clarification of the structure of the archaic numerical sign systems within a relatively short time demonstrated that through interdisciplinary cooperation a cost-effective balance between expenditure and revenue in the introduction and application of new electronic methods could be found.

This early success encouraged our decision in the following phases of the project to use enhanced procedures and to develop completely new methods for the computer-assisted edition of the texts. The first step was to compile a reliable and complete database of all known archaic texts from Mesopotamia. Second, a project-specific programming environment was implemented using an artificial intelligence programming language, in which all occurring problems concerning edition, transcription, and discernment of semantic relationships within the text corpora are solved interactively before the monitor. The third and final step involved the replacement of traditional techniques of copying tablet originals by hand with methods of computer graphics.

The Database of the Project

Electronic processing had particularly proven useful in deciphering the numerical sign systems, since it enabled us to check the general validity of any hypothesis used ad hoc to interpret particular texts by rapidly examining a large number of texts. Using such methods, initially highly speculative ideas about the contents of individual texts can thus be developed to become reliable interpretations of global structures of the the entire text corpus. Such methods, requiring a reliable database of all texts to be examined, may in principle have been possible without the technology provided by electronic data processing—but only at an irresponsibly high labor cost.

To insure the necessary completeness of our database, the Uruk Project in Berlin was extended in the years 1986 and 1987 to include all proto-cuneiform texts known from Mesopotamia. Today, our database contains all known texts from the earliest phases of literacy in the Near East. All in all, this amounts to about 5,600 text transliterations. Both the Seminar für Vorderasiatische Altertumskunde of the Freie Universität Berlin as well as the Max-Planck-Institut für Bildungsforschung are connected via terminals to the mainframe computer of the university, where the work on the database is done.

The database not only includes complete transliterations and catalogue entries but also increasingly the results obtained from work on the texts. More than half of the stored transliterations have been collated with the originals. The data bank therefore provides easy access to all unpublished texts and its dependability even surpasses that of the published texts. It therefore opens unparalleled possibilities for studying the period characterized by the creation of writing and at the same time forms the basis of all future work related to the publication of the archaic texts.

The Methods of Computer-Assisted Processing

The scientific value of this database is, however, not justified solely by its comprehensiveness, but even more so by its organizational form. After having carefully studied the technical options available in the early 1980s for processing nonnumerical information, it became evident that the programming systems based on artificial intelligence were best qualified to reproduce the routine steps of philological work in the computer, insofar as this routine retained its basic mechanical nature, for example, in compiling sign lists and glossaries.

A particular advantage of using such programming systems lies in the fact that most tasks that crop up during transcription work can be carried out interactively and without great programming effort in dialogue mode. Many tasks are in fact required only once. To assign such tasks to the computer would represent an intolerable waste of time and money, considering that qualified specialists would have to write individual programs for each task. The specificity and diversity of these tasks are, moreover, so great that practically none of them could be executed using standardized data bank functionalities. Yet despite this diversity the work remains relatively simple and logical, as long as it concentrates on the interpretation of the texts and the subsequent control of these interpretations using the entire text corpus. The operationalization of the tasks is easy, provided commands for a translation into machine-driven processes are available which correspond to normal thinking during conceptual structuring of problems.

Precisely this condition is met by higher programming languages that have been developed for the implementation of artificial intelligence. We use INTERLISP, a dialect of LISP (*list processing*), the oldest artificial intelligence programming language. This dialect was specifically developed for interactive work in dialogue mode. The version we are using is implemented on a Siemens 7.580 E mainframe computer. The basic data structures this "language" refers to are "lists" of "words" comparable to those employed in philological research.

Each accomplished task related to the stored transliterations and catalogue data may be defined as a new concept in the programming language. The computer therefore constantly "learns" new concepts, all related to the processing of archaic texts. The dialogue with the computer hence slowly changes as the number of accomplished tasks increases; today, this dialogue takes place in a conceptual field closely related to our specific analyses: with each occurring problem and its subsequent solution this field is extended by several concepts. The extraordinary labor-effectiveness of this procedure is to be found in the fact that the methods of philological work are to a lesser degree determined by the possibilities of the computer than the other way round. In this manner sign lists, glossaries and concordances are compiled in an increasingly simple way. In addition, sign combinations are identified, text scores automatically written, catalogue information reorganized, special inventories for museum work compiled and final publication layouts with transliterations, glossaries, and the like established before the texts go to print.

The Application of Electronic Layout Programs and Computer Graphics

In the years since 1985, the edition of archaic texts has increasingly been supported by an entirely different method of computer application. Beyond the dramatic developments in layout and graphic programs of recent years, great progress has recently been achieved in integrating personal computers into mainframe networks. Two achievements of the project result from these developments. First, preparing a manuscript for publication on the mainframe is supplemented by an extra layout phase on a personal computer with a powerful graphic environment; second, mature text copies are now produced using methods of modern computer graphics.

Most of the layout work itself is carried out on Apple Macintosh computers, chosen because of the sophisticated graphics software developed for these computer systems. Through a commercially available hardware extension, the Macintosh functions as a terminal of the Siemens mainframe, enabling the direct transfer of data between the Macintosh and the mainframe. Large manuscripts such as glossaries for publications are usually compiled and partially formatted on the mainframe before the file is transferred to the Macintosh. Here, publication-specific characters from special fonts replace coded signs within the text. The final version is eventually printed on a simple 300dpi laser printer to serve as proof sheets before the manuscript is done up with electronic photosetting on film, the exposure ranging in resolution from 1200 to 2500dpi. These films serve as offset pages. The manuscript of the present book was produced in the same way; only the photographs were reproduced in the traditional manner before they were mounted into the computer-generated print text.

Possibly the most interesting application of electronic data processing in the editing procedures of the archaic texts is the use of computer graphics to produce text copies rather than the tradi-

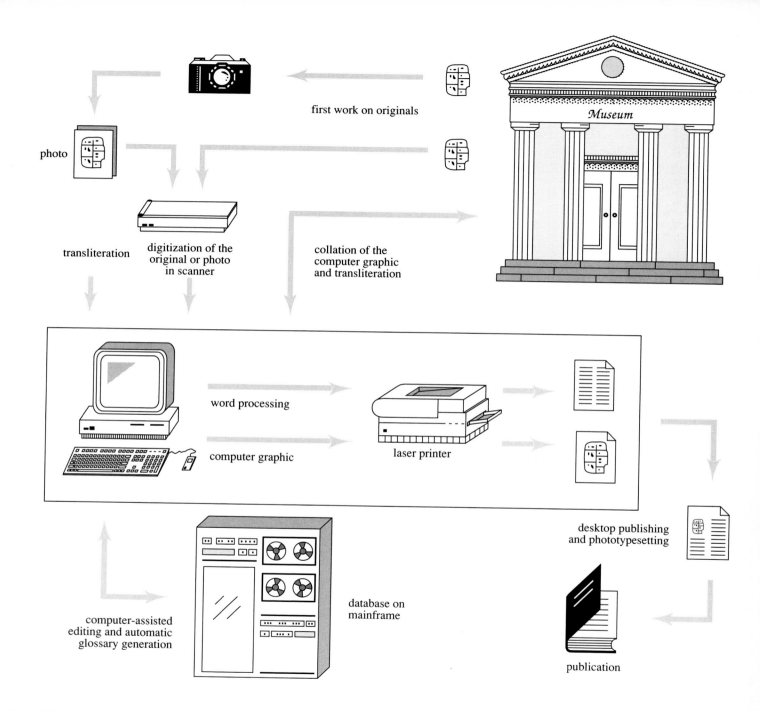

first work on originals

photo

Museum

transliteration

digitization of the
original or photo
in scanner

collation of the
computer graphic
and transliteration

word processing

computer graphic

laser printer

desktop publishing
and phototypesetting

computer-assisted
editing and automatic
glossary generation

database on
mainframe

publication

Figure 129. Overview of computer-assisted editorial work.

154

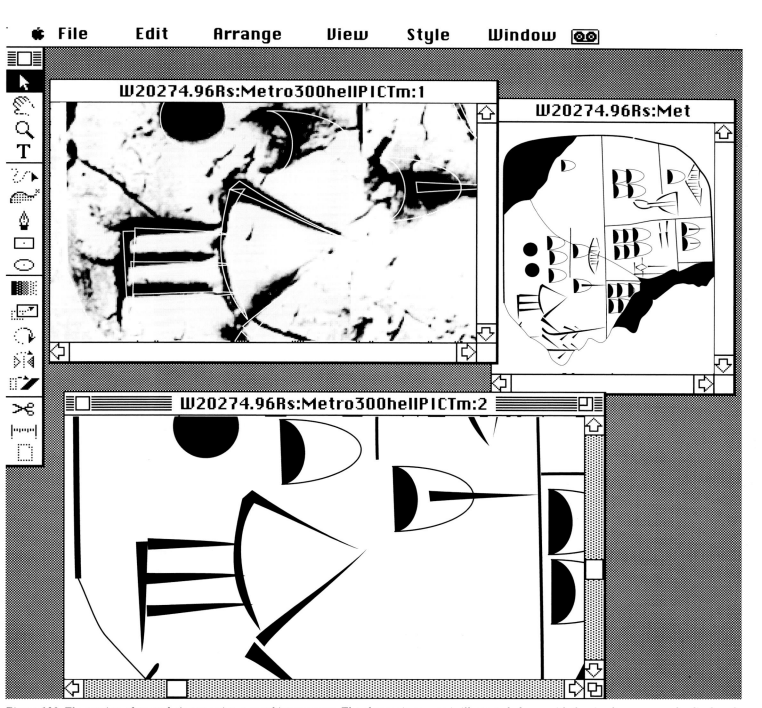

Figure 130. The tracing of an archaic text using a graphics program. The electronic canvas is illustrated above, with the simultaneous results displayed in a window below (see also fig. 118).

155

tional copying of the texts by hand. A method was developed by which expensive trips to cities with large state museums are reduced substantially (see fig. 129). This method consists of the following steps:

1. A photograph of the tablet to be copied is made or ordered from the respective institution. The photograph is then digitized with a scanner, an apparatus which scans the image of the tablet with a laser beam, thus breaking it down into individual pixels which are processed in the computer.
2. With an appropriate design program, the digitized photograph is placed as a drawing template under an empty electronic canvas, so that the tablet's shape, division lines, and discernible signs can be traced on the screen (fig. 130). The result is a preliminary copy of the text with correct proportions which in the end is printed on drawing paper with a laser printer.
3. This preliminary copy is then compared with the original tablet in the museum and corrected and completed by hand.
4. The improved copy is then again fed into the computer with the scanner; it serves in the same manner as the original photograph as a template to correct the preliminary copy of the tablet.
5. Finally, using a layout program the copy is placed in the manuscript and the final layout for publication is prepared.

Of course the ordering and use of museum photos has its drawbacks, the most obvious being work delays and the costs of having tablets photographed which often due to their poor state of preservation were heretofore considered unworthy of such attention by museum personnel. The photographic results will reflect these facts. In preparing for publication the first volume of the archaic administrative texts excavated at Uruk (*ATU* 5; Berlin, forthcoming), one of us (Englund) has, with the kind permission of the Vorderasiatisches Museum, Berlin, had the opportunity to use the project's flat-bed scanner with the tablet originals in the museum.

The digitized originals result in gray-scale images of very high quality; attributes of these images such as contrast and brightness may be appropriately adjusted both to serve as templates in graphics programs—thus eliminating the preliminary drawing work described above—and to be read into the project's database as tablet photo reproductions. We are currently experimenting with the feasibility of using compressed high-resolution image files to replace traditionally pasted photographs in text editions. It may be hoped that state-owned museums will in due course make possible the general use of such electronic aids in their study rooms.

In work on the archaic tablets this procedure has proven more effective than the hand-copying method still broadly employed in Assyriology which generally involves a first stage of pencil copy, followed by the inking up of the copy for printing and finally inserting this copy into the text by means of the traditional method of composing the layout. This traditional method results in higher production costs for the publication, both in terms of initial pasting and in terms of anticipated mistakes by printers and subsequent corrections by authors. Not only are these difficulties avoided, but electronic copies also obviate the necessity of any particular artistic skills on the part of the copyist to produce high-quality text copies. Most text copies and drawings in the present publication were produced with this method.

In future, the traditional methods of copying cuneiform texts by hand will doubtless be replaced by similar or even more sophisticated procedures of computer-assisted text copying. For the time being, the method is still restricted by technological limitations. Many of the advantages provided by computer graphics are in this particular case dependent on the apparent physical characteristics of the archaic texts. Large cuneiform accounts from the Ur III period, for example, are too complex to be copied with reasonable efficiency using the methods described here. Even the most powerful graphics programs available for the Macintosh systems used in our project cannot as yet compete with the abilities of an experienced copyist in drawing large cuneiform tablets.

P.D./ R.E./H.N.

List of Figures

The following list includes general information concerning the figures and the objects illustrated. In the case of artifacts, the institution in which the object is housed is cited, in part with reference to the accession numbers assigned the objects by the respective museums; the measurements of the objects, in the case of tablets height×width×thickness; the date of the object; previous or planned publications; finally, copyrights of photos and graphics. For Abbreviations, see p. vii.

Figure 19.   From the Oppenländer collection; Seminar für Vorderasiatische Altertumskunde der Freien Universität Berlin; 31×23 mm (height×diameter); date: Late Uruk/Jemdet Nasr. U. Moortgat-Correns, *BagM* 4, pl. 38, no. 19. Photo: M. Nissen.

Figure 20.   Left: From Uruk (W 9579,by2); VAT 15300; 19×25×11 mm; date: Late Uruk. *ATU* 1, no. 3. Photo: courtesy of the Vorderasiatisches Museum, Berlin. Right: From Uruk (W 15662); VAT 21307; 19×25×15 mm; date: Late Uruk. *UVB* 7, pl. 23b. Photo: courtesy of the Vorderasiatisches Museum, Berlin.

Figure 21.   From Uruk (9579,d); VAT 14674; 41×30×17 mm; date: Late Uruk. *ATU* 1, no. 40. Photo: courtesy of the Vorderasiatisches Museum, Berlin.

Figure 22.   From Uruk (6710,a); VAT 14942; 57×43×23 mm; date: Late Uruk. *ATU* 1, no. 353. Photo: courtesy of the Vorderasiatisches Museum, Berlin.

Figure 23.   Authors' original, based on tablet W 21446, now in HD; 44×47×17 mm; date: archaic script phase Uruk III.

Figure 24.   From Uruk (W 13946,n); VAT 16765; 105×96×29 mm; date: archaic script phase Uruk III. *ATU* 2, pl. 48. Photo: courtesy of the Vorderasiatisches Museum, Berlin.

Figure 25.   From Uruk (W 20274,36); HD; 68×43×13 mm; date: archaic script phase Uruk III. *ATU* 2, pl. 30. Photo: courtesy of the Deutsches Archäologisches Institut, Baghdad.

Figure 26.   From Uruk (W 12139); VAT 16773; 76×51×15 mm; date: archaic script phase Uruk III. *UVB* 6, p. 37, pl. 32e. Photo: courtesy of the Vorderasiatisches Museum, Berlin.

Figure 27.   Authors' original.

Figure 28.   Authors' original.

Figure 29.   Authors' originals.
Text a: From Uruk (W 19592,n); HD; 46×35×22 mm; date: archaic script phase Uruk IV.

Text b: From Uruk (W 20368,2); HD; 45×41×20 mm; date: archaic script phase Uruk IV.
Text c: From Uruk (W 20044,58); HD; 90×47×19 mm; date: archaic script phase Uruk IV.
Text d: From Uruk (W 20044,38); HD; 69×40×20 mm; date: archaic script phase Uruk IV.

Figure 30.   Authors' original. From Uruk (W 19726,a); HD; 50×66×17 mm; date: archaic script phase Uruk III. *ATU* 2, pl. 58.

Figure 31.   Upper: From Tell Uqair(?); VAT 5302; 77×66×19 mm; date: archaic script phase Uruk III. *ATU* 1, no. 621.
Lower: From Tell Uqair(?); VAT 5295; 76×46×16 mm; date: archaic script phase Uruk III. *ATU* 1, no. 627. Photos: courtesy of the Vorderasiatisches Museum, Berlin.

Figure 32.   Authors' originals.
Upper: From Uruk (W 5233,b); VAT 15245; 62×40×16; date: archaic script phase Uruk III. *UVB* 2, fig. 15 right; *ATU* 1, no. 605; *ATU* 2, pl. 43.
Lower: From Uruk (W 5233,a); VAT 15246; 64×43×17 mm; date: archaic script phase Uruk III. *UVB* 2, fig. 15 left; *ATU* 1, no 606; *ATU* 2, pl. 43.

Figure 33.   Authors' original. To be published as *MSVO* 3, no. 29. Photo: courtesy of Christie's, London.

Figure 34.   Authors' original. To be published as *MSVO* 3, no. 64.

Figure 35.   Authors' original. To be published as *MSVO* 3, no. 58. Photo: M. Nissen.

Figure 36.   Authors' original. To be published as *MSVO* 3, no. 52. Photo: M. Nissen.

Figure 37.   Authors' original. To be published as *MSVO* 3, no. 51. Photo: courtesy of the Musée du Louvre, Paris.

Figure 38.   Authors' original. To be published as *MSVO* 3, no. 2.

Figure 39.   Authors' original. To be published as *MSVO* 3, no. 11 (text a) and *MSVO* 3, no. 6 (text b). Photo: courtesy of Christie's, London.

Figure 40. From Tello; VAT 4487; 66×66×22 mm; date: Old Sumerian. *VS* 14, no. 90.

Figure 41. Authors' original. BM 123068; 85×44×20 mm; date: Old Akkadian. *CT* 50, no. 55; see M. A. Powell, *RA* 70 (1976): 98–99.

Figure 42. Authors' originals.
Text a: From Tello; Musée du Louvre, Paris; *RTC* no. 57.
Text b: From Tello; VAT 4689; 56×56×26 mm; date: Old Sumerian. *VS* 14, no. 45.
Text c: From Tello; VAT 4915; 47×46×21 mm; date: Old Sumerian. *VS* 14, no. 125.

Figure 43. Authors' original.

Figure 44. From Umma; State of Berlin; 132×73×21 mm; date: Ur III. R. K. Englund, *JNES* 50 (1991): 255–80. Photo: M. Nissen.

Figure 45. Authors' original. Based on the tablet in figure 44.

Figure 46. Authors' original. Based on the tablet in figure 44.

Figure 47. Upper: From Jemdet Nasr; Ashm. 1926,583; 87×56×18 mm; date: archaic script phase Uruk III. *OECT* 7, no. 100; *MSVO* 1, no. 2.
Lower: From Jemdet Nasr; Ashm. 1926,577; 83×56×18 mm; date: archaic script phase Uruk III. *OECT* 7, no 83; *MSVO* 1, no. 3.
Copies courtesy of J.-P. Grégoire.

Figure 48. Authors' originals. Based on the tablets in figure 47.

Figure 49. Authors' original. From Uruk (W 15772,k); VAT 16852; 41×66×14 mm; date: archaic script phase Uruk III. *ATU* 2, pl. 59.

Figure 50. Authors' original. From Uruk (W 19408,76); HD; 89×65×31 mm; date: archaic script phase Uruk IV. *ATU* 2, pl. 59.

Figure 51. Authors' original. From Jemdet Nasr(?); Oriental Institute, Chicago, A 2515; 59×34×16 mm; date: archaic script phase Uruk III. V. Scheil, *RA* 26 (1929): 15, no. 2; *MSVO* 1, no. 10.

Figure 52. From Fara; VAT 12656; 190×190×42 mm; date: Fara. *WF*, no. 53. Photo: courtesy of the Vorderasiatisches Museum, Berlin.

Figure 53. From Fara; VAT 12610; 68×69×21 mm; date: Fara. *WF*, no. 55. Photo: courtesy of the Vorderasiatisches Museum, Berlin.

Figure 54. Authors' original. From Tello; VAT 4731; 86×84×27 mm; date: Old Sumerian. *VS* 14, no. 40.

Figure 55. Authors' original. From Tello; VAT 4630; 74×73×26 mm; date: Old Sumerian. *VS* 14, no. 184.

Figure 56. From Tello; AO 13754; 51×50×24 mm; date: Old Sumerian. *DP* no. 546. Photo: courtesy of the Musée du Louvre, Paris.

Figure 57. Authors' original. From Umma; AO 6060; 75×52×21 mm; date: Ur III. *TCL* 5, no. 6060.

Figure 58. From the Wengler collection; Seminar für Altorientalische Philologie, Freie Universität Berlin; 108×111×29 mm; date: Ur III. *Orientalia* 5 (1922): 60. Copy courtesy of S. Maul.

Figure 59. Same tablet as in figure 58. Photo: M. Nissen.

Figure 60. Authors' original. From Tell Uqair(?); VAT 5307; 30×60×33 mm; date: archaic script phase Uruk III. *ATU* 1, no. 653.

Figure 61. Authors' original. From Uruk (W 9827); VAT 15161; 55×60×28 mm; date: archaic script phase Uruk IV. *ATU* 1, no. 577; A. Vaiman, *BagM* 20 (1989): 124, fig. 3, no. 24.

Figure 62. Text a: From Jemdet Nasr; Ashm. 1926,566; 107×70×20 mm; date: archaic script phase Uruk III. *OECT* 7, no. 22; *MSVO* 1, no. 212.
Text b: From Jemdet Nasr; Ashm. 1926,647; 78×47×16 mm; date: archaic script phase Uruk III. *OECT* 7, no. 73; *MSVO* 1, no. 213.
Text c: From Jemdet Nasr; Ashm. 1926,579; 79×49×16 mm; date: archaic script phase Uruk III. *OECT* 7, no. 140; *MSVO* 1, no. 214.
Copies courtesy of J.-P. Grégoire.

Figure 63. Authors' original. From Susa; AO, Sb 19162; 80×63×20 mm; date: proto-Elamite. *MDP* 17, no. 45.

Figure 64. Authors' original. From Susa; AO, Sb 15228; 91×69×17 mm; date: proto-Elamite. *MDP* 6, no. 4997.

Figure 65. Authors' original based on tablet on figure 64.

Figure 66. Upper: From Fara; VAT 12736; 65×65×18 mm; date: Fara. *WF*, no. 94.
Lower: From Fara; VAT 12454; 72×72×24 mm; date: Fara. *WF*, no. 92. Photos: courtesy of the Vorderasiatisches Museum, Berlin.

Figure 67. From Tello; AO 13322; 140×140×26 mm; date: Old Sumerian. *DP* no. 114. Photo: courtesy of the Musée du Louvre, Paris.

Figure 68. From Tello; VAT 4851; 74×74×24 mm; date: Old Sumerian. *VS* 14, no. 187. Photo: courtesy of the Vorderasiatisches Museum, Berlin.

Figure 69. From Umma; AO 5670; 121×79×28 mm; date: Ur III. *TCL* 5, no. 5670. Photo: courtesy of the Musée du Louvre, Paris.

Figure 70. From Umma; Institut für Außereuropäische Sprachen und Kulturen der Universität Erlangen-Nürnberg; 132×79×22 mm; date: Ur III. Photo: M. Nissen.

Figure 71. Authors' originals.
Text a: From Uruk (W 20274,12); HD; 65×47×20 mm; date: archaic script phase Uruk III. M. W. Green, *JNES* 39 (1980): 32, no. 35; *ATU* 2, pl. 21.
Text b: From Uruk (W, 20274,63); HD; 60×50×17 mm; date: archaic script phase Uruk III. M. W. Green, *JNES* 39 (1980): 32, no. 36.

Figure 72. Authors' originals.
Text a: From Uruk (W 20274,15); HD; 74×51×20 mm; date: archaic script phase Uruk III. M. W. Green, *JNES* 39 (1980): 21, no. 4; *ATU* 2, pl. 22.
Text b: From Uruk (W 20274,55); HD; 53×49×18 mm; date: archaic script phase Uruk III. M. W. Green, *JNES* 39 (1980): 20, no. 1.

Figure 73. Authors' originals.
Text a: From Uruk (W 20274,97); HD; 73×84×16 mm; date: archaic script phase Uruk III. *ATU* 2, pl. 55.
Text b: From Uruk (W 20274,30); HD; 84×78×22 mm; date: archaic script phase III. *ATU* 2, pl. 28.

Figure 74. Authors' original. From Susa; AO, Sb 15083; 66×54×18 mm; date: proto-Elamite. *MDP* 6, no. 212.

Figure 75. From Tello; VAT 4445; 67×67×24 mm; date: Old Sumerian. *VS* 14, no. 89. Photo: courtesy of the Vorderasiatisches Museum, Berlin.

Figure 76. From Drehem (?); AO 5499; 175×117×34 mm; date: Ur III. *TCL* 2, no. 5499. Photo: courtesy of the Musée du Louvre, Paris.

Figure 77. Authors' original; excerpt of figure 76.

Figure 78. Authors' original; excerpt of figure 76.

Figure 79. Authors' original; excerpt of figure 76.

Figure 80. From Drehem; State of Berlin; 69×40×20 mm; date: Ur III. Photo: M. Nissen.

Figure 81. From Tello; VAT 4428; 95×96×27 mm; date: Old Sumerian. *VS* 14, no. 77. Photo: courtesy of the Vorderasiatisches Museum, Berlin.

Figure 82. Authors' original based on copy by M. Sigrist. From Drehem; MMA 11.217,9a–b; 43×40×22 mm; date: Ur III. M. Sigrist, in I. Spar, ed., *Cuneiform Texts in the Metropolitan Museum of Art,* vol. 1 (1980), pp. 19–20, pls. 14–15.

Figure 83. Authors' original. From Ur; BM 128990; 50×50×22 mm; date: Ur Archaic. *UET* 2, no. 275.

Figure 84. Authors' original. From Uruk (W 13982); VAT 16741; 45×52×21 mm; date: archaic script phase Uruk III(?).

Figure 85. From Uruk (W 9656,di); VAT 15293; 57×43×21 mm; date: Late Uruk. Photo: courtesy of the Vorderasiatisches Museum, Berlin.

Figure 86. From Uruk (W 20366,1); HD; 70×106×23 mm; date: archaic script phase Uruk III. Photo: courtesy of the Deutsches Archäologisches Institut, Baghdad.

Figure 87. From Uruk (W 9656,h); VAT 15003; 82×62×19 mm; date: Late Uruk. *ATU* 1, no. 340. Photo: courtesy of the Vorderasiatisches Museum, Berlin.

Figure 88. Authors' original.

Figure 89. From Fara; VAT 9130; 156×161×38 mm; date: Fara. *SF*, no. 75. Photo: courtesy of the Vorderasiatisches Museum, Berlin.

Figure 90. Authors' original.
Text a: To be published as *MSVO* 3, no. 60.
Text b: To be published as *MSVO* 3, no. 64.
Text c: To be published as *MSVO* 3, no. 61.
Photos: (a) courtesy of the British Museum, London; (b) and (c) M. Nissen.

Figure 91. Authors' original.

Figure 92. From Uruk (W 9123,ac); VAT 14807; 50×34×21 mm; date: Late Uruk. *ATU* 1, no. 211. Photo: courtesy of the Vorderasiatisches Museum, Berlin.

Figure 93. Authors' original.

Figure 94. Authors' original.

Figure 95. From Uruk (W 20274,13); HD; 71×51×16 mm; date: archaic script phase Uruk III. *ATU* 2, pl. 21. Photo: M. Nissen.

Figure 96. From Uruk (W 17887,a); VAT 17862; 43×42×18 mm; date: script phase Ur Archaic. M. W. Green, *ZA* 72 (1982): 172, no. 6. Photo: courtesy of the Vorderasiatisches Museum, Berlin.

Figure 97. From Fara; VAT 9122; 95×100×20 mm; date: Fara. *WF*, no. 33. Photo: courtesy of the Vorderasiatisches Museum, Berlin.

Figure 98. Authors' original.

Figure 99. State of Berlin; 74×45×21 mm; date: Old Akkadian. R. K. Englund, *ASJ* 14 (1992): 102, no. 6. Photo: M. Nissen.

Figure 100. State of Berlin; 111×49×23 mm; date: Ur III. R. K. Englund, *ASJ* 14 (1992): 99, no. 1. Photo: M. Nissen.

Figure 101. State of Berlin; 94×51×24 mm; date: Ur III. R. K. Englund, *ASJ* 14 (1992): 101, no. 3. Photo: M. Nissen.

Figure 102. State of Berlin; 113×54×24 mm; date: Ur III. R. K. Englund, *ASJ* 14 (1992): 100, no. 2. Photo: M. Nissen.

Figure 103. State of Berlin; 56×45×18 mm; Date: Old Assyrian. B. Kienast, *Altassyrische Texte* (Berlin, 1960), no. 61. Photo: M. Nissen.

Figure 104. From Assur; State of Berlin; 51×53×21 mm; date: Middle Assyrian. O. Pedersén, *Archives and Libraries in the City of Assur* 1 (1985), M8:32 // 29 = Ass. 11017w. Photo: M. Nissen.

Figure 105. State of Berlin; 30×39×17 mm; date: neo-Babylonian. Photo: M. Nissen.

Figure 106. Authors' original.

Figure 107. From Uruk (W 20987,17); HD; 70 mm diameter; date: probably Late Uruk. Photo: M. Nissen.

Figure 108. From Uruk (W 20987,8); HD; 70 mm diameter; date: probably Late Uruk. Photo: M. Nissen.

Figure 109. From Susa; AO, Sb 1940; 60 mm diameter; date: Late Uruk. Photo: courtesy of the Musée du Louvre, Paris.

Figure 110. Left: From Uruk (W 16139,e); VA 14887; 75×84×20 mm; date: Late Uruk, from the "White Temple." Photo: courtesy of the Vorderasiatisches Museum, Berlin.
Right: From Uruk (W 16139,a); VA 14887; 75×85×20 mm; date: Late Uruk, from the "White Temple." Photo: courtesy of the Vorderasiatisches Museum, Berlin.

Figure 111.   From Susa; AO, Sb 2313; 65×58×31 mm; Date: proto-Elamite. Photo: courtesy of the Musée du Louvre, Paris.

Figure 112.   From Susa; AO, Sb 1932; 63 mm diameter; date: Late Uruk. *MDP* 43, no. 581. Photos: courtesy of the Musée du Louvre, Paris.

Figure 113.   Upper: From Uruk (W 10967,b); VAT 16903; 44×42×17 mm; date: Late Uruk. Photo: courtesy of the Vorderasiatisches Museum, Berlin.
Lower: From Uruk (W 10967,a); VAT 16747; 59×49×24 mm; date: Late Uruk. Photo: courtesy of the Vorderasiatisches Museum, Berlin.

Figure 114.   Authors' original. From Jebel Aruda (Syria).
Upper: 92×77×20 mm; date: Late Uruk. G. van Driel, *Studies Presented to F. R. Kraus,* fig. 1a, no. 6; fig. 5, no. 6.
Lower: 53×43×21 mm; date: Late Uruk. G. van Driel, *Studies Presented to F. R. Kraus,* fig. 1a, no. 2; fig. 4, no. 2.

Figure 115.   From Uruk (W 20274,37); HD; 65×39×17 mm; date: archaic script phase Uruk III. Photo: M. Nissen.

Figure 116.   Authors' original based on copy by J.-P. Grégoire. From Jemdet Nasr; Ashm. 1926,606; 70×40×18 mm; date: archaic script phase Uruk III. *MSVO* 1, no. 216.

Figure 117.   Authors' original. From Uruk (W 21682); HD; 60×40×13 mm; date: archaic script phase Uruk III. *ATU* 2, pl. 54.

Figure 118.   Authors' original. From Uruk (W 20274,96); HD; 65×58×20 mm; date: archaic script phase Uruk III. *ATU* 2, pl. 54.

Figure 119.   From Fara; VAT 12593; 140×140×48 mm; date: Fara. *SF*, no. 82. Photo: courtesy of the Vorderasiatisches Museum, Berlin.

Figure 120.   From Tello; AO 4303; 97×73×25 mm; date: Ur III (Gudea). *NFT* p. 184. Photo: courtesy of the Musée du Louvre, Paris.

Figure 121.   Authors' original.

Figure 122.   From Tello; AO 3448; 67×49×28 mm; date: Ur III. *RTC* no. 407. Photo: courtesy of the Musée du Louvre, Paris.

Figure 123.   Authors' original.

Figure 124.   BM 80150; 170×106×40 mm; date: Old Babylonian. *MKT* I, pls. 49–50; *MKT* II, pl. 61. Photos: courtesy of the British Museum, London.

Figure 125.   BM 17403; 75×37×20 mm; date: Old Babylonian. Photo: courtesy of the British Museum, London.

Figure 126.   BM 17567; 47×45×27 mm; date: Old Babylonian. Photo: courtesy of the British Museum, London.

Figure 127.   Authors' original. State of Berlin; 152×125×36 mm; date: Old Babylonian. Text copy courtesy of J. Friberg.

Figure 128.   Authors' original. BM 22706; 70×103×20 mm; date: Old Babylonian.

Figure 129.   Authors' original.

Figure 130.   Authors' original.

Bibliography

General

Adams, R. McC. *The Heartland of Cities*. Chicago, 1981.

Adams, R. McC., and H. J. Nissen. *The Uruk Countryside*. Chicago, 1972.

Curtis, J., ed. *Early Mesopotamia and Iran*. London, 1993.

Gelb, I. J. *A Study of Writing*. Chicago, 1952.

Kramer, S. N. *The Sumerians*. Chicago, 1963.

Landsberger, B. *Three Essays on the Sumerians*. Trans. Maria deJ. Ellis. Monographs on the Ancient Near East, vol. 1, no. 2. Malibu, 1974.

Nissen, H. J. *The Early History of the Ancient Near East, 9000–2000 B.C.* Chicago, 1988.

Nissen, H. J. *Mesopotamia before 5000 Years*. Dipartimento di scienze storiche, archeologiche e anthropologiche dell'antichità. Sussidi Didattici, vol. 1. Rome, 1988.

Oppenheim, A. L. *Ancient Mesopotamia: Portrait of a Dead Civilization*. Chicago, 1964.

Redman, C. L. *The Rise of Civilization*. San Francisco, 1978.

Roaf, M. *Cultural Atlas of Mesopotamia and the Ancient Near East*. Oxford, 1990.

Strommenger, E. *Habuba Kabira: eine Stadt vor 5000 Jahren*. Mainz, 1980.

Publications of the Berlin Project Archaische Texte aus Uruk

Damerow, P., and R. K. Englund, with an introduction by C. C. Lamberg-Karlovsky. *The Proto-Elamite Texts from Tepe Yahya*. American School of Prehistoric Research Bulletin 39. Cambridge, MA, 1989.

Damerow, P., and R. K. Englund. *The Proto-Cuneiform Texts from the Erlenmeyer Collection*. Materialien zu den frühen Schriftzeugnissen des Vorderen Orients, vol. 3. Berlin, forthcoming.

Englund, R. K. *Archaic Administrative Texts from Uruk: The Early Campaigns*. Archaische Texte aus Uruk, vol. 5. Berlin, forthcoming.

Englund, R. K., and J.-P. Grégoire, with a contribution by R. J. Matthews. *The Proto-Cuneiform Tablets from Jemdet Nasr I: Copies, Translation and Glossary*. Materialien zu den frühen Schriftzeugnissen des Vorderen Orients, vol. 2. Berlin, 1991.

Englund, R. K., and H. J. Nissen. *Die lexikalischen Listen der Archaischen Texte aus Uruk*. Archaische Texte aus Uruk, vol. 3. Berlin, 1993.

Green, M. W., and H. J. Nissen, with a contribution by P. Damerow and R. K. Englund. *Zeichenliste der Archaischen Texte aus Uruk*. Archaische Texte aus Uruk, vol. 2. Berlin, 1987.

Matthews, R. J. *Cities, Seals and Writing: Archaic Seal Impressions from Jemdet Nasr and Ur*. Materialien zu den frühen Schriftzeugnissen des Vorderen Orients, vol. 2. Berlin, 1993.

Chapter 1

Buringh, P. "Living Conditions in the Lower Mesopotamian Plain in Ancient Times." *Sumer* 13 (1957): 30–46.

Jacobsen, Th., and R. McC. Adams. "Salt and Silt in Ancient Mesopotamian Agriculture." *Science* 138 (1958): 1251–58.

Larsen, D., and G. Evans, "The Holocene Geological History of the Tigris-Euphrates-Karun Delta." In W. Brice, ed. *The Environmental History of the Near and Middle East since the Last Ice Age*, pp. 227–44. London, 1978.

Nissen, H. J. "Geographie." In S. Lieberman, ed. *Sumerological Studies in Honor of Th. Jacobsen*. Assyriological Studies 20. Chicago, 1976.

Nützel, W. "The Formation of the Arabian Gulf from 14,000 B.C." *Sumer* 31 (1975): 101–11.

Nützel, W. "The Climatic Changes of Mesopotamia and Bordering Areas." *Sumer* 32 (1976): 11–24.

Wirth, E. *Agrargeographie des Irak*. Hamburg, 1962.

Chapter 2

Aurenche, O., J. Evin, and F. Hours, eds. *Chronologies du Proche Orient 16000–4000 B.P.* BAR International Series, vol. 379. Oxford, 1987.

Carter, E., and M. W. Stolper. *Elam: Surveys of Political History and Archaeology*. Berkeley, 1984.

Finkbeiner, U., and W. Röllig, eds. *Ğamdat Naṣr: Period or Regional Style?* Wiesbaden, 1986.

Le Brun, A., and F. Vallat. "L'origine de l'écriture à Suse." *Cahiers de la Délégation Archéologique Française en Iran* 8 (1978): 11–79.

Nissen, H. J. "The City Wall of Uruk." In P. Ucko et al., eds. *Man, Settlement, and Urbanism*. London, 1972.

Chapter 3

Cassin, E., J. Bottéro, and J. Vercoutter, eds. *Die altorientalischen Reiche*, vol. 1. Fischer Weltgeschichte, vol. 2. Frankfurt, 1965.

Hallo, W. W., and W. Simpson. *The Ancient Near East*. New York, 1971.

Chapter 4

Beale, T. "Bevelled Rim Bowls and their Implications for Change and Economic Organization in the Late Fourth Millennium

B.C." *Journal of Near Eastern Studies* 37 (1978): 289–313.

Brandes, M. *Siegelabrollungen aus den archaischen Bauschichten in Uruk-Warka.* Wiesbaden, 1979.

Collon, D., *First Impressions: Cylinder Seals in the Ancient Near East.* Chicago, 1987.

Gelb, I. J. "The Ancient Mesopotamian Ration System." *Journal of Near Eastern Studies* 24 (1965): 230–43

Gibson, M., and R. D. Biggs, eds. *Seals and Sealing in the Ancient Near East.* Malibu, 1977.

Jasim, S. A., and J. Oates. "Early Tokens and Tablets in Mesopotamia." *World Archaeology* 17 (1986): 348–62.

Nissen, H. J. "Aspects of the Development of Early Cylinder Seals." *Bibliotheca Mesopotamica* 6 (1977): 15–23

Schmandt-Besserat, D. *Before Writing.* 2 volumes. Austin, Texas, 1992.

Schmandt-Besserat, D. "Tokens at Uruk." *Baghdader Mitteilungen* 19 (1988): 1–175 and plates 1–12.

Chapter 5

Falkenstein, A. *Archaische Texte aus Uruk.* Archaische Texte aus Uruk, vol. 1. Berlin, 1936.

Green, M. W., and H. J. Nissen, with a contribution by P. Damerow and R. K. Englund. *Zeichenliste der Archaischen Texte aus Uruk.* Archaische Texte aus Uruk, vol. 2. Berlin, 1987.

Matthews, R. J. *Cities, Seals, and Writing: Archaic Seal Impressions from Jemdet Nasr and Ur.* Materialien zu den frühen Schriftzeugnissen des Vorderen Orients, vol. 2. Berlin, 1993.

Nissen, H. J. "The Emergence of Writing in the Ancient Near East." *Interdisciplinary Science Reviews* 10 (1985): 349–61.

Nissen, H. J. "The Archaic Texts from Uruk." *World Archaeology* 17 (1986): 317–34.

Shendge, M. J. "The Use of Seals and the Invention of Writing." *Journal of the Economic and Social History of the Orient* 26 (1983): 113–36.

Chapter 6

Damerow, P., and R. K. Englund. "Die Zahlzeichensysteme der Archaischen Texte aus Uruk." In M. W. Green and H. J. Nissen, *Zeichenliste der Archaischen Texte aus Uruk*, pp. 117–66. Archaische Texte aus Uruk, vol. 2. Berlin, 1987.

Friberg, J. *The Early Roots of Babylonian Mathematics* I and II. Göteborg, 1978–79.

Friberg, J. "Numbers and Measures in the Earliest Written Records." *Scientific American* 250 (1984): 110–18.

Vaiman, A. "Protosumerische Maß- und Zählsysteme." *Baghdader Mitteilungen* 20 (1989): 114–20.

Chapter 7

Englund, R. K. "Administrative Timekeeping in Ancient Mesopotamia." *Journal of the Economic and Social History of the Orient* 31 (1988): 121–85.

Green, M. W. "The Construction and Implementation of the Cuneiform Writing System." *Visible Language* 15 (1981): 345–72.

Chapter 8

Damerow, P., and R. K. Englund. *The Proto-Cuneiform Texts from the Erlenmeyer Collection.* Materialien zu den frühen Schriftzeugnissen des Vorderen Orients, vol. 3. Berlin, forthcoming.

Chapter 9

Englund, R. K. *Verwaltung und Organisation der Ur III-Fischerei.* Berliner Beiträge zum Vorderen Orient, vol. 10. Berlin, 1990.

Snell, D. C. *Ledgers and Prices: Early Mesopotamian Merchant Accounts.* Yale Near Eastern Researches, vol. 8. New Haven, 1982.

Chapter 10

Powell, M. A. "Sumerian Area Measures and the Alleged Decimal Substratum." *Zeitschrift für Assyriologie* 62 (1972): 165–221.

Thureau-Dangin, F. "Un cadastre chaldéen." *Revue d'assyriologie* 4 (1897): 13–33.

Chapter 11

Englund, R. K. "Hard Work—Where Will It Get You? Labor Management in Ur III Mesopotamia." *Journal of Near Eastern Studies* 50 (1991): 255–80.

Powell, M. A., ed. *Labor in the Ancient Near East.* American Oriental Series, vol. 68. New Haven, 1987.

Struve, V. V. "Some New Data on the Organisation of Labour and on Social Structure in Sumer during the Reign of the IIIrd Dynasty of Ur." In I. M. Diakonoff, ed. *Ancient Mesopotamia*, pp. 127–72. Moscow, 1969.

Vaiman, A. "Die Bezeichnungen von Sklaven und Sklavinnen in der protosumerischen Schrift." *Baghdader Mitteilungen* 20 (1989): 121–33.

Chapter 12

Englund, R. K. "Archaic Dairy Metrology." *Iraq* 53 (1991): 101–4.

Gomi, T. "On Dairy Productivity at Ur in the Late Ur III Period." *Journal of the Economic and Social History of the Orient* 23 (1980): 1–42.

Green, M. W. "Animal Husbandry at Uruk in the Archaic Period." *Journal of Near Eastern Studies* 39 (1980): 1–35.

Chapter 13

Falkenstein, A. "Der 'Sohn des Tafelhauses.'" *Welt des Orients* 1 (1948): 172–86.

Kramer, S. N. *History Begins at Sumer.* New York, 1959.

Kraus, F. R. *Vom mesopotamischen Menschen der altbabylonischen Zeit und seiner Welt.* Amsterdam, 1973.

Naissance de l'écriture: cunéiformes et hiéroglyphes. Exhibition Catalogue. Paris, 1982.

Sack, R. H. "The Temple Scribe in Chaldean Uruk." *Visible Language* 15 (1981): 409–18.

Vanstiphout, H. "How Did They Learn Sumerian?" *Journal of Cuneiform Studies* 31 (1979): 118–26.

Waetzoldt, H. "Der Schreiber als Lehrer in Mesopotamien." In J. G. von Hohenzollern and M. Liedke, eds. *Schreiber, Magister, Lehrer,* pp. 33–50. Bad Heilbrunn, 1989.

Chapter 14

Englund, R. K., and H. J. Nissen. *Die lexikalischen Listen der Archaischen Texte aus Uruk.* Archaischen Texte aus Uruk, vol. 3. Berlin, 1993.

Nissen, H. J. "Zur Frage der Arbeitsorganisation in Babylonien während der Späturuk-Zeit." *Acta Antiqua Academiae Scientiarum Hungaricae* 22 (1974): 5–14

Nissen, H. J. "Bemerkungen zur Listenliteratur Vorderasiens im 3. Jahrtausend." In L. Cagni, ed. *La Lingua di Ebla,* pp. 99–108. Naples, 1981.

Chapter 15

Edzard, D. O. "Die Keilschrift." In U. Hausmann, ed. *Allgemeine Grundlagen der Archäologie,* pp. 214–21. Munich, 1969.

Edzard, D. O. "Keilschrift." In D. O. Edzard, ed. *Reallexikon der Assyriologie,* vol. 5, pp. 544–68. Berlin, 1976–80.

Picchioni, S. A. "The Direction of Cuneiform Writing: Theory and Evidence." *Studi Orientali e Linguistici* 2 (1984–85): 11–26.

Picchioni, S. A. "Die Keilschriftrichtung und ihre archäologischen Implikationen." *Sumer* 42 (1984): 48–54.

Powell, M. A. "Three Problems in the History of Cuneiform Writing: Origins, Direction of Script, Literacy." *Visible Language* 15 (1981): 419–40.

Chapter 16

Damerow, P. "Individual Development and Cultural Evolution of Arithmetical Thinking." In S. Strauss, ed. *Ontogeny, Phylogeny, and Historical Development,* pp. 125–52. Norwood, 1988.

Damerow, P., and W. Lefèvre, eds. *Rechenstein, Experiment, Sprache. Historische Fallstudien zur Entstehung der exakten Wissenschaft.* Stuttgart, 1981.

Friberg, J. "Mathematik." In D. O. Edzard, ed. *Reallexikon der Assyriologie und Vorderasiatischen Archäologie,* vol. 7, pp. 531–85. Berlin, 1990.

Høyrup, J. "Algebra and Naive Geometry." *Altorientalische Forschungen* 17 (1990): 27–69 and 262–354.

Chapter 17

Damerow, P., R. K. Englund, and H. J. Nissen. "Zur rechnergestützten Bearbeitung der archaischen Texte aus Mesopotamien." *Mitteilungen der Deutschen Orient-Gesellschaft* 121 (1989): 139–52.

Index

Deficits, 49, 54, 84, 86, 142, 147; *see also* Balance

Delivery quotas, 92, 95–97

Disbursement, designation of, 14, 74, 117

Discrete units: nature of, 11, 14; symbols for, 97, 125, 131; systems for counting, 27, 138

Drehem, economic center during the Ur III period, 97, 102

Eanna. See Inanna

Eannatum, ruler of Lagash, 123

Ebla, ancient city in Syria, 123

Economy, third millennium, reforms of Shulgi (Ur III ruler), 97, 108

El-Amarna, archive at, 123

Electronic filing techniques, 152

Enentarzi, ruler of Lagash, 49

Enlil, city god of Nippur, 104

Erlenmeyer collection: dating of archaic texts from, 17, 21; inscribed seal from, 17

Eulogy hymns, 108

Euphrates, 1, 8–9

Expected performances, standardization of, 49

Fara period: cities of, 77; field texts from, 58–59, 64

Farmland, leased, 64

Female laborer days, 51, 54, 84, 88

Festivals, 17, 46, 102

Field administration: allotment fields, 58–59, 64; base line, 68; calculations of harvests, 142; circumference calculation, 147; designation of fields, 55, 64; field allocations, 58; field categories, 64; field sections, 64, 68–69; gardens, 64, 68; harvest calculation, 142; in Lagash, 64–68; in the archaic period, 55; in the Fara period, 58–64; in the Ur III period, 68–69; irrigation canals, 64, 68, 82, 83, 107; quadrangles (temen), 68–69; quality specification of soil, 69; scale and preciseness of plans, 55, 68; seed grain, 35, 59, 68; surface calculations, 55, 59, 64, 68–69, 134; surveying, standard terminology, 64; surveyors, 68; Ur III period, 68–69

Flour: as converted into labor, 54, 88; milling, 83; quantities as factors in bread baking, 47, 49

Geometry, early concept of, 55

Girsu, city in Babylonia, 95

Goatherders, user fees, 93

Grand totals, 55, 77

Gudea, ruler of Lagash, 140

Habuba Kabira, site in Syria, 129

Inanna, city goddess of Uruk, 17, 102, 116

Iraq Museum, 43

Jebel Aruda, site in Syria, 130

Jemdet Nasr: site in northern Babylonia, 4; texts, paleography, 21, 105, 119

Karun, river through Khuzestan, 1

Khuzestan, environment, 1, 9

Kish, city in northern Babylonia, 35

Labor: bala service, 54; balancing of work days, 54, 82–84, 88; calculation, 49, 54, 82–83, 88; conversion factors, 51, 86, 88; division of, 8; duties, 54; forced labor, 74; in the Fara period, 77; inspection texts, 54; labor performance, fixing of, 49, 82–83; quotas, 82–83; state controlled, 49; time, 46, 83–84, 86, 88

Laborers: as corvée workers, 49, 77, 81; gangs, 49, 51, 54, 83, 88, 40; rations for, 70, 77, 82; specification of, 70, 74–75, 82

Lagash: capacity system in, 97; city in Babylonia, 77; province of, 64, 142

Language: Akkadian, 109, 111, 117, 123–24, 140; Aramaic, 124; code systems, 117; Elamite, 123; Indo-European, *see* Hittites; phonetic, 30, 106, 117–18, 123, 124; Semitic, consonants, 123; Sumerian, 9, 47, 84, 109, 117, 123; verb, 117

Length units, 55, 64, 68, 69, 139, 143, 147

Lexical lists, 6, 105, 106, 109, 111, 134

Livestock: archaic administration of, 92–93; bulls, 93, 100; calves, 89, 92, 100; categorization, 92, 100; cattle, 89, 92, 97, 100, 102; cow delivery quotas, 95, 97; designation of cattle, 74, 89, 92, 96, 97, 100; economic relevance, 89; equids, 89; fodder, 35, 68, 102, 103; goats, 89, 93, 102, 104; herd growth, 97, 100; in proto-Elamite texts, 93; milk cows, productivity, 92, 97, 100; oxen, 68, 89, 93, 102, 116